Mollie Brumley's Civil War

Mollie Brumley's Civil War

Surviving the Guerrilla War in Arkansas

Theodore Catton

University of Oklahoma Press : Norman

Publication of this book is made possible in part through the generosity of Edith Kinney Gaylord.

Library of Congress Cataloging-in-Publication Data

LCCN 2025038668 ISBN 978-0-8061-9650-3 (hardcover)

The paper in this book meets the guidelines for permanence and durability of the Committee on Production Guidelines for Book Longevity of the Council on Library Resources, Inc. ∞

The manufacturer's authorized representative in the EU for product safety is Mare Nostrum Group B.V., Mauritskade 21D, 1091 GC Amsterdam, The Netherlands, email: gpsr@mare-nostrum.co.uk.

For Diane

Contents

Introduction

Mollie Brumley was thirteen years old at the outbreak of the Civil War. An orphan, she lived with her aunt and uncle and eight cousins on a farm in the mountainous Ozark region of northwest Arkansas. In the course of the war, Mollie betrothed herself to one soldier boy who later disappeared on the battlefield, then she married another who fought with Rebel guerrillas in the hills around her home. She briefly left her mountain home to work as an army laundress. Back in the Ozarks again, she saw her way through numerous close scrapes with guerrilla fighters. A girl of courage and indomitable spirit, Mollie by war's end was hiding out in caves and hunting for edible plants to keep her family from starving.

Mollie's story unfolds in a borderland region that lay along the northern periphery of slavery and on the western edge of white settlement. Her state of Arkansas, which achieved statehood in 1836, would be the second youngest state in the Confederacy after Texas. The state was not far past its pioneer days. In 1860, Arkansas was barely connected to the spreading network of railroads and telegraph lines. Mollie's home in Searcy County in northwest Arkansas lay just three counties away from the border with the Indian Territory. Also nearby were the border slave state of Missouri and the free territory of Kansas. A proxy war around the issue of slavery had begun along the Kansas-Missouri border five years before Mollie arrived in Arkansas in 1859.

During the Civil War, Arkansas suffered terrible destruction, but the death and hardship did not come primarily from fighting between large opposing armies. In the war between the Union and Confederate states, grand strategy relegated the state of Arkansas and all the borderlands lying west of the Mississippi River to a peripheral theater of the war. There, the struggle turned mostly on which government had military control of the Mississippi River. When Federal forces got control of the river all the way to the Gulf of Mexico, it left Arkansas, Texas, and Louisiana cut off from the rest of the Confederacy. After that, Federal forces in Arkansas were pared down to a minimum as troops were sent eastward to crucial battlefronts in Tennessee and Virginia. A Reconstruction government was installed in the Arkansas state capital. From this middle period of the war until the final surrender, Confederate Arkansas was conquered but not pacified; an insurgency went on.

Nowhere was the insurgency so devastating to Arkansas's civilian population as it was in the Ozark Mountains in the northwest corner of the state. Here the population was evenly divided between Union and Confederate sympathizers. Most people were mountain farmers like Mollie's family. They wrested a living from the land by their own toil. As the region had few slaves and even fewer slaveholders, fighting a war to defend slavery held little appeal for them. But neither did fighting on the side of the North against their own Southland. If the people around Mollie had had a choice in this conflict, most of them would have wanted Arkansas to be neutral. Neutrality was never an option. When the war began, Confederates among the populace drove Unionists into hiding. When Federal armies swept into the region, the Unionists came out of hiding and turned the tables on their erstwhile oppressors. Then, halfway through the war when the state was conquered and the Federal army in Arkansas mostly transferred to other fighting fronts east of the Mississippi River, the Ozarks became fertile ground for a guerrilla conflict. All able-bodied men were pressed to take up arms with one guerrilla band or another or risk summary execution if they refused. Mollie's homeland was swallowed up in a devil's cauldron of guerrilla warfare and outlawry, shifting loyalties and seesawing advantage, betrayals real and suspected, and finally, death by starvation. Neighbor was pitted against neighbor. By then

Mollie was going on sixteen: she was no longer a naïve and innocent child, but rather a young woman who had chosen a side in the conflict.

Mollie's coming-of-age story reminds us that this was a savage yet sentimental time. In recounting her adventures many years later, she filled her tale with angels of death and tears of woe. Her short autobiography, published in 1902, had the sort of long, breathless title that drew readers in the Victorian age but would be apt to induce eye-rolling in a prospective reader today. Her book was entitled *A Thrilling Romance of the Civil War: The History of Mrs. Mollie E. Williams Written by Herself; Forty-two Days in Search of a Missing Husband; A Lesson of Woman's Fidelity, Fortitude, and Affection.* The antique title speaks to the strong moral convictions and sentimentality that she wove into her storytelling nearly forty years on from the war. The events and relationships and motivations she described are all true, so it is hoped that in this modern retelling of her story the reader will perceive a genuine and illuminating account of the human experience of the time.

Mollie's moral message in her book was clear: *all* war is epic human tragedy, *civil* war is the cruelest kind of war, and *guerrilla* war is the most horrific for it emboldens the worst in human nature. Only in recent decades has the guerrilla war within the American Civil War received much attention. My first aim in this book dovetails Mollie's; it is to highlight the guerrilla war in Civil War Arkansas through a retelling of Mollie's adventurous tale. I have mostly followed her own narrative and point of view about the guerrilla war, fleshing out the story around a few other personalities in the valley where she lived. These other personalities include not only the two soldier boys whom she loved, but a young, enslaved woman Parthenia Hensley who gained her freedom at the war's end. Parthenia Hensley was a little removed from Mollie's circle of intimates, yet her story helps us perceive the civilization of free and enslaved that Mollie lived in.

The second aim of this book is my own, not Mollie's. I want to understand why Southern whites who were not slaveholders nevertheless fought a war to defend slavery. If they were indifferent or even opposed to slavery, why did they support the Confederacy anyway? The perplexing question has been examined many times before. Indeed, it has echoed down the ages. Now it sounds through the din of our divided politics in red and blue America. We witness yet again an upwelling of so many fears and hatreds that we might have thought were settled in our nation's past. Mollie's story holds new meaning in our time.

This book is not historical fiction; it is a work of history. All historical and biographical writing contains at least a modicum of conjecture. There is more conjecture here in the narrative details than is common, but all my conjecture, true to the canons of the historian's craft, comes from reasonable suppositions grounded in historical research. Where I have had to guess at a person's actions, thoughts, or emotions, I have indicated that to the reader. The sparse amount of recorded dialogue in the story comes from Mollie's autobiography or other sources. Some of my sources may lean a little toward folklore or family traditions—perhaps not wholly reliable. But everything that transpires in my retelling of Mollie's story really did happen to these people to the best of my knowledge.

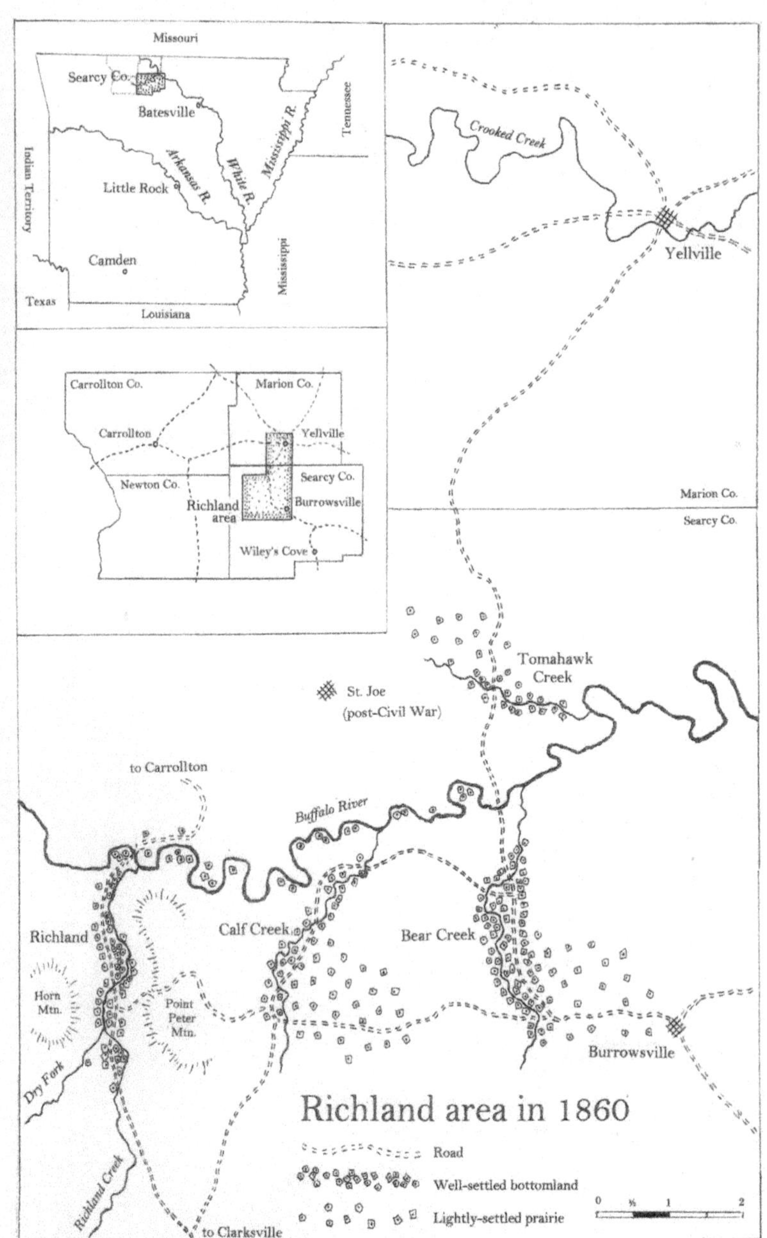
Missouri
Searcy Co.
Batesville
Tennessee
Mississippi R.
White R.
Arkansas R.
Indian Territory
Little Rock
Camden
Mississippi
Texas
Louisiana
Carrollton Co.
Marion Co.
Carrollton
Yellville
Newton Co.
Searcy Co.
Richland area
Burrowsville
Wiley's Cove
Crooked Creek
Yellville
Marion Co.
Searcy Co.
Tomahawk Creek
St. Joe
(post-Civil War)
to Carrollton
Buffalo River
Richland
Calf Creek
Bear Creek
Horn Mtn.
Point Peter Mtn.
Burrowsville
Dry Fork
Richland Creek
to Clarksville
Richland area in 1860
Road
Well-settled bottomland
Lightly-settled prairie
0
½
1
2

Chapter 1

Mollie Brumley

One of Mollie Brumley's earliest memories featured an immense, horse-drawn hearse parked on the street in front of her Memphis, Tennessee, home. In the hearse lay her mother's corpse. In Mollie's recollection of that distant day, the black hearse was so big it seemed to block out the sun. A shadow fell on the house that never went away. Death and mourning would move like cloud shadows across Mollie's whole life, though perhaps never more darkly than on the day her mother died.

Mollie was born September 10, 1847, in Monroe County, Mississippi, the only child of Hiram and Lavicia Brumley. Before Mollie was old enough to remember, the family moved to Memphis where her father became a merchant. After Mollie's mother died, Mollie's father struggled with raising the girl by himself. Six months later, when Mollie was going on ten years old, the father remarried. Mollie's new stepmother did not provide the nurturing love and affection that the girl craved. Hiram Brumley cast about for more help with raising a child and finally got an offer from his sister in Arkansas: Mollie could come live with her. Mollie was informed of their arrangement around the time of her twelfth birthday. The year was 1859.

She and her father made the trip from Memphis to northwest Arkansas in a wagon pulled by oxen, traveling over primitive roads across a hundred miles of swamps and then another hundred miles of hill country. Mollie sat on the seat beside her father with the wagon box behind them loaded up with nearly everything they owned, for Hiram Brumley had decided to leave his second wife in Memphis and move to Texas. After Mollie was deposited with her new family, she said goodbye to her father as he proceeded onward. She never saw him again. He died of yellow fever in Texas not long after.

So, at the pivotal age of twelve—just as she was leaving childhood and starting on the road to becoming an adult—Mollie found herself orphaned and entering upon a new life in the recently settled hill country of northwest Arkansas. A little over a year hence, her adopted homeland would be plunged into four years of war and lawlessness.

Mollie's Aunt Usley and Uncle Jim Greenhaw had emigrated from Tennessee to Arkansas in the mid 1850s. They made their home in a place known as Richland in Searcy County. Richland was then a well-populated valley in the heart of the Boston Mountains. The Boston Mountains are part of a large uplifted and dissected plateau region better known as the Ozarks. The Greenhaw farm occupied the edge of a fertile bottomland that ran north and south along Richland Creek. The bottomland was about five miles long and one mile across, a pocket-size plain in a land of steep hills and narrow, twisting coves. On the west side of Richland rose Horn Mountain, on the east side Point Peter Mountain. The Ozarks contained some of the most rugged country found anywhere between the Appalachians and the Rocky Mountains. Indeed, mountain farmers like Jim and Usley Greenhaw emigrated to the Ozarks precisely because they felt at home in its ruggedness; the farming way of life that they had known in the Southern Appalachians transplanted very well in this rough country farther west. The Ozarks are on the same latitude as the Southern Appalachians, and the mountains are similarly covered with mixed forests of hickory, oak, and pine. The vast majority of settlers in the Arkansas Ozarks were, like the Greenhaws, mountain farmers from Tennessee and western North Carolina. Ozark mountain farmers remarked that the mountains in Arkansas were not as high as the ones back home, but the hollows were mighty deep.

At the north end of the Richland Valley, Richland Creek flows into the Buffalo River. The Buffalo River comes rushing down through highlands, flowing eastward. Where this river passes by Richland, its current moves along at a more languid pace. At the time of the Civil War there was a busy ford at that place where people crossed in wagons or on horseback. From Richland the river flows onward through hill country for another seventy-five miles to its confluence with the White River. Along its path the Buffalo River loops back and forth in countless horseshoe bends, each bend about a half mile across, with sheer bluffs as much as two hundred feet high forming natural amphitheaters around the outside. Today the Buffalo is a lovely, scenic river preserved for recreation and enjoyment, with practically no one residing along its banks. Before the Civil War, farms nestled on the flats inside each riverbend. Only the lower stretch of the Buffalo was navigable to flat boats, and because the river took such a tortuous path through the hill country it did not see much commerce. Instead, the settlers traveled by wagon roads up and over the upland areas—"the barrens" as they called them—to get to the neighboring hollows and places beyond.

Mollie found Richland a strange place, wild and awe-inspiring. Often, while traipsing across the Greenhaw farm, she found herself stopped in her tracks staring up at Point Peter Mountain, enchanted by the natural beauty of her new home. Morning mist would rise from the creek and form a long silver filament along the foot of the mountain. At the end of the day, rays of the setting sun would turn the cliffs along the mountain summit a reddish-purple hue. On clear afternoons she craned her neck to watch dozens of buzzards soaring in circles above the farm. The big black birds with their knotty heads appeared to climb the sky effortlessly as the sun dropped down behind Horn Mountain to the west.

Mollie marveled over the titanic subterranean forces that could raise up such mountain masses as these. In her mind's eye she imagined an underground race of gnomes at work, endlessly hammering on their forges, pushing up the earth from below. Half a century on, a much older Mollie would recall this quiet musing on her part as only "a girlish fancy." And yet, it reveals a lively and sophisticated imagination—one that was stoked by fairytales she had probably heard or read while still a schoolchild in Memphis.

For Mollie, the wild beauty of the place could also be daunting. Being orphaned, she sometimes saw things that would suddenly darken her mood. Looking out across the Richland Valley on a winter day and seeing the mountain's shadow creep across the valley floor, she might see the shadow of death that had come and stolen away her mother and father. At such times, she later wrote, "I was utterly overcome with a sense of my loneliness. . . . a homeless orphan, with seemingly a hopeless career before me."

There were eight children in the Greenhaw family. The oldest Greenhaw child, Elizabeth, was twenty-four. Then there were the older boys, James Jr. and William, and after an interval, two more boys, Green Berry and Calvin. Next came Emily and Mary, two years older and two years younger than Mollie, respectively. And last came little Lucy, age seven. Everyone in the Greenhaw family treated Mollie with kindness. She felt welcome in the Greenhaw family even as her small presence added another body inside what was already a very crowded home.

The Greenhaw farm shared the valley with numerous other farmsteads, and many of them overflowed with children like the Greenhaw place did. This place contained a fertile population. When the census taker went through Richland Township in July 1860, he enumerated 388 people living in 63 households. Children were present in virtually every household. A few households included three generations, a few others combined two families, while the vast majority consisted of one or two parents with a passel of children. People under the age of eighteen outnumbered adults in Richland by nearly two to one.

By the time Mollie came to live with the Greenhaws, she had already received more education than most of her peers in Richland. In Memphis, she had attended school from the age of five. Her first teacher, one Professor Bryant, made a lasting impression on her. He encouraged her to keep a record of her life, as well as to be upstanding and "pure of heart" in all things she did. Being an inquisitive and intelligent little girl, Mollie thrived in her school environment; by the time she left Memphis she had won medals of honor for literary achievement and general good behavior. By then her level of education was already above average for a white female in the antebellum South. About half of Southern white females were never enrolled in school. About three in ten were taught by their parents how to read and write, while the remaining two in ten never learned to read and write at all. Mollie's literacy stood out even more in Richland, where many fewer girls attended school and barely half the adult males could read and write.

Mollie wistfully recalled her school in Memphis and what a far cry it was from her new school in Richland. The Memphis public school occupied a part of the old navy yard along the city's Mississippi River frontage. All the former navy buildings were painted white and kept in trim condition. The well-lit schoolroom had one wall of tall, glazed windows that faced the river. Along the riverfront one could see steamboats tied up to the city's broad cobblestone landing taking on board great bales of cotton, while boats under sail skimmed over the water as elegantly as birds in flight.

In that place she had been surrounded by friends. The crowning glory of her school career came when she was chosen by her schoolmates to be the Queen of May in the school's May Day parade. Seated on a float beneath a canopy strewn with flowers, she had enjoyed the esteem of all her schoolmates as well as the city crowds as the procession wended its way from the old navy yard through the city center to the agricultural fairground. On that glorious day, she was still fair-skinned and dressed up like a doll; now her skin was as brown as a chestnut, and she dressed each day in homespun.

At the foot of Point Peter Mountain, at a central point in the Richland Valley, there was a one-room schoolhouse and a post office. Richland's school looked a good deal different from the one Mollie had known in Memphis. The walls were of rough-hewn logs; the floor was dirt. A single small window in one end of the building—a mere opening in the log wall—let in the only light unless the door stood open. The place was heated in winter by a fireplace with a stone chimney. The single room contained no desks and chairs, only bench seats made of split logs. The school was known as a "subscription school," meaning that a number of settler families subscribed to pay a teacher's salary and maintain the building; there was little state support of schools as yet. The young schoolmaster, John Jones, was a part-time teacher and farmhand. He lived with old John and Sarah Albritton, the Albrittons' daughter and son-in-law, and their five children.

The cost of tuition at a subscription school ran to a dollar per month per child, which was no light expense for Mollie's uncle and aunt. Nevertheless, they enrolled Mollie along with five of their own children for the 1860 school year, for they knew Mollie was a bright girl and would be happy to meet other pupils. When twelve-year-old Mollie went off to school that year it signaled the start of her last year of formal education.

It was a short school year in Richland in any case. School terms were folded into the seasonal rhythms of farm work. A summer term began when the corn crop was "laid by" around mid-July, and it lasted until "fodder pulling and wood hauling time" in early September. A winter term started around the end of January when the days began to lengthen, and it ran about six weeks. The two terms together made up an academic year of about three months' duration. For Mollie, the summer school term came as a welcome break from farm work, which could seem relentless. More and more, she looked back on the years in Memphis as a time of boundless leisure compared to her new life on the farm.

Like other mountain farmers in northwest Arkansas, Jim Greenhaw had around twenty acres in cultivation and that area was called a patch. As each settler family arrived in the country, it began with the first step of making a "deadening" in the forest. This was done by girdling the trees—notching the bark all the way around the base of the trunk to stop the flow of sap so as to kill the tree—and when the trees were dead, felling and burning them in order to let in sunlight. As soon as the farmer had his patch, or clearing in the forest, he would plant the "new ground" with rows of corn. It would take many more years to fell every dead tree and root out every stump in the patch; in the meantime, the rows of corn would just snake around all the stumps and the dead trees that remained standing. In fact, the dead trees were useful to the farmer as long as they let in sunlight because they could be chopped down for firewood later. Ten to twenty acres in cultivation at a time was about what a family needed for its subsistence. After getting a few good corn crops from the soil, it was necessary to clear more "new ground" and let the old field "rest" for a good stretch, maybe ten years or more. So, the laborious effort of clearing the land went on even as the settler family turned most of its efforts to growing and harvesting crops. Richland in 1860 was a patchwork of small clearings, some planted in crops, some resting, some deadening, with a little bit of the valley still shaded by hardwood forest that remained to be cleared.

The Greenhaw farm consisted of one large cornfield together with smaller fields of cotton, tobacco, and cereals. All crops were raised for home use. Each field was surrounded by a rail fence to keep out free-ranging livestock. The Greenhaws owned a number of cattle and hogs as well as a few horses and milk cows.

While Jim Greenhaw and his grown sons did the men's work of clearing the land, Mollie joined her aunt and female cousins in assisting the men with practically every other kind of farm labor. And her farm labor came on top of doing all the housekeeping tasks of cooking, washing, mending, and cleaning. As a twelve-year-old, Mollie was assigned her own set of chores, too. Twice a day she went out to the pasture to milk the cows and suckle the calves. After the milking was done, she carried the full pails back to the house where she put the frothy milk through a strainer and then poured it into clean, glazed crocks. Then she took the crocks to a stone-lined trough that was built into a gurgling spring under a shady elm tree where the milk was kept cool through the day.

Mollie spent much of her time pitching in with others to plant and tend the crops and gather the harvest. The growing season began with sowing the cornfield. Family members, working in pairs, would proceed across the field, with the older person in front making small holes in the earth with a stick and dropping the seed into them, and the younger person behind carefully covering up each kernel with a scoop of dirt and soft tap of the foot. After the corn was planted, seeding of other crops followed. Again, the children would be given the task of coming behind and burying the precious seed before the birds got it. Once the crops were in, the tedious weeding began, row after row being carefully cleared of invaders, while the loosened soil was gently mounded up around the cornstalks. When the corn crop was knee-high it was laid by, or left to ripen on its own, and there was a reprieve of sorts from all the copious field work. Then in September the work resumed with fodder pulling. This began with cutting the tops off of the cornstalks and leaving them out to dry, then stripping the leaves from the cornstalks and bundling them for livestock feed in the winter. Finally, the ears of corn were harvested either by twisting them off the plant or cutting them off with a knife. This was rough work that made one's hands bleed.

A few weeks after the corn harvest, it was cotton-picking time. The Greenhaws along with every other Richland farmer had a small cotton crop to produce their own supply. Mollie and her cousins picked the snowy bunches from the pods and stowed the whole crop under shelter. Then, as time allowed, they set to work separating the seed and lint with their fingers and thumbs. This was Mollie's least favorite task on the farm. "We had no gins to prepare the raw material for use," she would later explain, "but had to separate the lint from the seed with the hand, and I assure you it was a tedious process and at times taxed our patience sorely." Once the lint was cleaned of seeds, it was carded and spun into thread. Through the dark winter months, the females in the household took turns at the spinning wheel. The spun cotton was reeled off and placed as chain and filling in the loom and woven into a loose fabric known as homespun. Mollie soon learned how to sew dresses, shirts, and trousers. With her aunt and two older female cousins, the four women manufactured homespun clothing for the whole family. In the crowded family quarters the busy hum of the spinning wheel became an almost constant sound, mingling with the sizzle and pop of the wood stove and the occasional clatter of kitchenware.

The cotton grown in Richland in 1860 was not a commercial crop as it was on slave plantations in southern Arkansas and elsewhere throughout the South's Cotton Belt; rather, it was a subsistence crop, forming an important part of the mountain farmers' overall subsistence economy. It was strictly a home industry, grown outside of the South's slave labor system and processed by hand rather than mechanically by a cotton gin, of which there was not a single one in all of Searcy County in 1860.

Even though the farms in Richland were all subsistence farms, they were not economically self-sufficient and independent from one another. These settlers were not frontiersmen of the mythical Daniel Boone type, matching their wits against the wilderness and feeling crowded out as soon as they got neighbors. They prized community as much as independence. Neighbors came together for barn raisings, corn shuckings, and hog killings. In clearing land, settlers downed trees, removed limbs, and then invited the neighbors over to help them roll the logs into big piles to be burned. Such a team effort was called a log rolling. Asking for a neighbor's help for any large effort like this was called "swapping work." Richland's farmers shared food with others in need and bartered for use of farm implements and plow horses. John Goats had the only grist mill in the valley and milled small quantities of wheat and oats for most valley residents. The Goats mill together with a few other mills up and down the Buffalo River produced flour almost solely for home consumption. Just a handful of farmers in the region grew substantial cash crops, transporting the produce out of the area to a commercial market. Most farmers were content with a subsistence farm, producing nearly everything they needed plus just a small surplus to raise cash for such town items as shoes, ammunition, kettles, and chinaware. It was said that a man of large family could live for a year on a store account of just $16 to $20.

The Greenhaw family lived in a log cabin made out of oak logs. The home's simple furnishings consisted of a table and chairs at one end of the cabin and two or three beds at the other. A trundle bed may have been tucked underneath one of the beds to be pulled out at night to sleep the smaller children. Indoor lighting was supplied by the glow of the fire, grease lamps, and candles.

Mollie sometimes helped in the kitchen. Aunt Usley's kitchen would have been furnished with a wood stove, a table, a wash basin, and probably a small dish safe. Aunt Usley might have done all her cooking and baking with just a skillet, a black pot or two, a cast iron Dutch oven, and a teakettle. For much of the year, most of the cooking and washing took place outside.

When Mollie was done with her farm and kitchen work, she might be free to play outside with cousins and friends. The younger kids amused themselves with hide and seek, blindman's bluff, and sundry other games. A favorite game in Richland was fox and hound. One person was chosen to be the fox while all the others were hounds who gave chase. There was a course with designated bases where the fox was safe and everyone got a breather. When the fox lit out again, the hounds had to give the fox "wagon room" before starting in pursuit. If the fox got all the way around the course without being tagged, he or she was the winner.

Mollie and her friends played imagination games of pioneers and Indians, recalling the frontier days of their parents' and grandparents' generations. The older kids took pleasure in hunting rabbits, killing snakes, rolling rocks down mountainsides, and other acts of daredevilry. Boys and girls frolicked together; there was no separation of the sexes in their outdoor play. Mollie missed the indoor play she had had in Memphis—mothering her dolls, playing teacher with her friends—but she discovered that her new friends in Richland never lacked for excitement. Down by the mouth of Richland Creek beside the Buffalo River there was an unusual landform. A long fin of limestone jutted out of the hillside and protruded onto the floodplain. At its narrowest point, the top of the fin was no wider than a bench log and sheer on both sides. On a dare, a child could walk or shimmy across it. To sit on that perilous perch and gaze down at the eddying current of the Buffalo River a hundred feet below could put butterflies in your stomach. The landform was called the Narrows, or colloquially, the "Nars."

Mollie appreciated her new life in Richland, although it was a good bit rougher than what she had had in Memphis. In her old Tennessee home, she had been enfolded in a soft cocoon of dolls in dresses and other playthings. Those things were now but a fading memory as she marked her thirteenth birthday in the fall of 1860.

Chapter 2

Free and Enslaved

The people around Mollie said the girl was "coming of age." People in 1860 did not use the terms "teenager" or "adolescent." Instead, what they saw was that young girls and boys around the age of thirteen entered into a kind of adult apprenticeship on the way to becoming grown-ups. For Mollie, that meant she was now learning how to be a Southern lady. She began to receive instruction from adults on everything from proper manners and comportment to what she ought to expect from life.

For her own part, Mollie began looking at adults in a new way, pondering how it would be to assume the role of helpmate, wife, guardian, or mother. She discovered complex new emotions in herself. Bright and imaginative by nature, she found herself daydreaming a lot.

With a little direction from Aunt Usley, she ceased to dress like a girl and acquired a whole new attire. Away went her little dresses; now she wore a full-length skirt over petticoats and a bodice over a woman's corset. She could loosen the laces of the restrictive corset on most days when she had a lot of physical work to do, but she was as pleased as the next teenage girl to draw the laces tight when the occasion called for it so as to show off her skinny waist and growing breasts. Donning a woman's corset was a rite of passage for most any girl of the time, even an orphan girl on a farm in the Ozarks.

Mollie began to form deeper impressions of her neighbors. Aunt Usley and Uncle Jim were sociable folk, with a network of friends extending the length of the Richland Valley and beyond. Mollie had a sociable nature, too. As a thirteen-year-old acquiring a new outlook on the opposite sex, she took a growing interest in meeting the Greenhaws' far-flung neighbors.

Mountain farmers worked hard and endured long spells of isolation, so when they traveled the necessary distance to see friends or kinfolk, they filled the wagon's grub box, packed bedding, and set out to be gone for a piece. The people had a wry saying for these protracted social calls: your visitors stayed at your home "until they got weak."

One clan known to the Greenhaws was the Cole clan. There were two middle-aged Cole brothers, Samuel and Andrew Jackson, and their families. Sam and "Jack" and their wives had emigrated from Tennessee to Arkansas in the same wagon train in 1844. Now sixteen years later, Jack and his family lived at the upper end of Richland Valley, while Sam and his family had a place five miles away at the lower end. Coincidentally, the two Cole brothers had each sired six children, three sons followed by three daughters in each case. All those second-generation Cole boys were around Mollie's age or older, all the Cole girls a bit younger than her.

Of the two Cole families, Mollie got better acquainted with the Jack Cole family. Mollie took a shine to Jack's wife Saba, who liked to tease and joke and laugh. Mollie's Uncle Jim was a teaser, too, and Mollie saw how all four adults got on well.

Jack knew how to tell a good yarn. These Coles had a pet bear cub that Jack had pulled out of a pine tree up on Horn Mountain one day when he was hunting. The story that Mollie heard was that the hunter shot the mama bear in self-defense, then killed one cub with his knife before noticing a second cub up a tree. The hunter then decided to take the surviving cub home alive. In wrestling the cub out of the tree he sacrificed his hat and coat; both were torn to shreds as the cub put up a fierce resistance. Finally, the hunter got a blindfold on the little fellow and subdued him. He named the bear Bob, and soon Bob became attached to the whole family, trailing each family member around the homestead. As a matter of fact, the Coles' bear cub was not the only pet bruin in Richland; Mollie made her acquaintance with others of its kind in the community as well. Typically, the mountain farmer would maintain a pet bear cub for a year or two and then slaughter the animal when it got to be too big to keep. All these domesticated bear cubs formed a part of Mollie's sense that she now lived in a place that was not far removed from its frontier days.

Jack and Saba's three sons were named John, Henry, and Granville. Granville came closest to Mollie in age, but Mollie liked Henry the best. Henry, who was fifteen years old in 1860, was cheerful, polite, and handsome. John, at seventeen was the oldest of all the Cole cousins, and the only one approaching military age, which perhaps gave him a more serious air compared with the others.

As Mollie's social outlook expanded, so did her sense of geography. Her journey from Memphis to Richland in 1859 had been tedious and disorienting, and then she had been dropped into the semiwilds of northwest Arkansas being completely untutored about the lay of the land and the resident people. Resisting the idea that she had come to stay, at first she did not have much curiosity about who else lived in the area or what features lay beyond the Greenhaw farm. A year on, it was clear to her that this place was her new home. Now she began to perceive the wider world as a series of larger and larger geographic provinces extending out from Richland. Beyond the confines of the valley there was Searcy County, with its county seat of Burrowsville, which could be reached by road over Point Peter Mountain in one day's ride or a very long walk. The next biggest province beyond that was the tier of counties that encompassed the Buffalo River: Searcy County in the middle, Newton County upriver, Marion County downriver. The town of Yellville, in Marion County, was a two-day fetch from Richland. Enveloping that province was the state of Arkansas, with its capital city of Little Rock. Here Mollie's new sense of geography became somewhat more abstract, for Little Rock was a journey of several days from Richland and stood outside of her personal experience. Finally, Arkansas was part of a larger province she now knew as that proud entity, the South. Though Mollie's consciousness of being a Southerner began to grow as she ventured out toward womanhood, the idea of Southern pride or patriotism still struck her as lying a little beyond her level of sophistication.

Yet, as her mind matured, Mollie did take more and more interest in this wider world about her. There was talk in the Richland community of a thing called secession. Adults uttered the word with feeling—*see*-cession—and talked about the coming national presidential election. There was talk about a Northern man named Abraham Lincoln who opposed slavery and was on the ballot only in the Northern states. People spoke excitedly about what Lincoln might do to aggravate their section if the unthinkable should occur and he should win the election. Mollie had been aware for some years that the nation was divided into two great sections, and that the people in each section were estranged over the question of slavery. Indeed, in her child's mind she had once assumed that the tension between North and South was as unchanging as the seasons. Now she began to sense that there was a creeping progression—or deterioration—in relations between the two sections. The long simmering mistrust was turning into bitter animosity.

Around this time in her mental growth, Mollie came to understand that she was a free person living in a society that was composed of two types of people, one free and the other enslaved. Along with her peers, Mollie had long since forged a personal identity around the conspicuous social categories of race, gender, and class. But "free" and "enslaved" were a little more abstract to a child; they were fundamentally legal categories. Like the idea of the South, the institution of slavery lay a little beyond her grasp in her childhood years. It belonged to that adult world that she was only now on the threshold of entering.

Mollie's autobiography gives us very little about her indoctrination on the great matter of slavery. All we have to work with are a few shards of information we know about her prior experience as a very young person in Memphis. But common sense tells us that a young girl who was as observant as Mollie must have picked up things in her surroundings that gave her a certain level of awareness about slavery, as the nation prepared to fight a war over it.

Let's start with the knowledge that her father, Hiram Brumley, owned a slave woman named Nance when the Brumley family lived in Memphis. In her autobiography, Mollie did not mention Nance, who was about sixty years old when Mollie left Memphis. It is not known how long Nance belonged to the Brumley family before that time. When Hiram Brumley prepared to go to Texas and to place Mollie in his sister's charge on his way west, he liquidated most of his property in Memphis with the notable exception of his slave Nance. This is known by the fact that his wife, Maria Mallory Brumley—Mollie's stepmother of two years—felt abandoned by him and petitioned the state for a piece of Hiram Brumley's modest estate after he died of yellow fever in Texas a few months after his departure. In the lawyer's report on this matter, the slave woman Nance was described as "infirm," with her cash value placed at only $75.

What kind of relationship Mollie had with Nance is not known. One imagines that Hiram acquired Nance to help with childrearing since there was not much affection between Hiram's second wife, Maria, and Mollie. We may admit the possibility that Hiram hired Nance out or used her at his work place and that Mollie never personally knew her; but even then the twelve-year-old girl surely would have been aware that her father owned a slave. Hiram Brumley was a merchant in one of the principal centers of the slave trade in the South. A slave gave him not just controlled labor but social status, too. Mollie would have understood that her family, even with just one slave, was privileged to be in the city's slave-owning class.

There is also the fact of Mollie's surroundings in Memphis. The city saw a steady traffic of steamboats and barges transporting slaves down the Mississippi River to New Orleans. The kingpin of slave traders in Memphis on the eve of the Civil War was Nathan Bedford Forrest. By the late 1850s, Forrest was buying and selling upward of a thousand slaves annually. It made him fabulously rich. The human trafficking was an important feature on the city's riverfront, and that was the very same place where Mollie attended school. What she might have thought about the city's commerce in human chattel as she looked out of her classroom windows at the slave barges passing by is anyone's guess. It must have registered on her in some way.

When Mollie came to reside in the Arkansas Ozarks, she joined a community that was made up almost entirely of white families who did not own slaves. Richland had just one black resident in its population of around 388: a teenage girl named Parthenia. In the near absence of enslaved people, Richland presented a mighty contrast to Memphis. And yet, slavery still loomed large for the Richland community in 1860, because Arkansas was a slave state. Many if not most of the farmers in Richland were skeptical about slavery, or at least, they were skeptical about the grip that slavery held on the state's politics and institutions. The farmers in the northwest section of Arkansas distrusted the wealthy planters in the rest of the state, who exercised increasing power over state elections and policymaking. Nonetheless, this farming population regarded slavery as vital to the state's whole economy and fundamental to a "Southern way of life" where whites made up a "master race." If many of them were personally averse to owning slaves themselves and if some even found slavery repugnant, paradoxically, they were largely inclined to defend slavery anyway. Youth have been alert to the moral inconsistencies of their elders throughout the ages. It is impossible for us to know what Mollie thought about slavery in 1860, but we might consider that in her keen and youthful mind she began to see the moral paradox in the Southern farmers' defense of slavery.

Chapter 3

Parthenia Hensley

As a white, freeborn, coming-of-age female, Mollie was taught to cherish her feminine virtue, to cultivate self-control, and to take for granted that she was in charge of her own body. In contrast, the solitary young black woman in her community, being enslaved, never had those essential freedoms.

Parthenia Hensley did not leave an autobiography to posterity as Mollie did. The few facts about her that we have were recorded by others, all white people who remembered her through a veil of racial prejudice. But we do know a lot about her circumstances and about the experiences she very likely went through in her growing-up years and during the war. Specific known details about Parthenia's life are few, but we can trace her life's broad outlines and reconstruct a fair picture of her life experiences. Her story allows us to take a close look at what it was like for a girl who was roughly Mollie's age to be unfree. Her story illuminates slavery's miserable hold on the people, free and enslaved, in Mollie's new homeland.

Parthenia was about four years older than Mollie. In 1859, when Mollie came to Richland at age twelve, Parthenia was about sixteen. Mollie would have become aware of Parthenia, the slave of Billy Wyatt and the only slave girl in the valley. Parthenia, for her part, might well have become informed about Mollie, the orphaned Greenhaw cousin who came to live with that family. Their homes were just a couple of miles from each other. If the two girls never actually passed on the road or talked or associated, they most assuredly had occasion to observe one another on church Sundays. Parthenia's enslavers brought her to church with them, and the young black woman sat with her white family and other church goers until shortly before the Civil War, when the rising national tensions around slavery spurred a change of etiquette and Parthenia no longer took a seat with the whites though she still came to worship with them.

A couple surviving photographs of Parthenia in old age show her as a very petite straight-backed woman, and thin as a rail. We may picture her in her youth as a little wisp of a child, probably dressed in a smock-like shirt until she reached puberty, perhaps joining in play with the white children in her neighborhood from time to time. By 1859 when Mollie arrived, Parthenia would no longer have been playing child's games. She would have been clothed as a woman, with her homespun shirt exchanged for a plain dress. She might have been furnished, too, with a brightly hued calico dress for those church Sundays.

Parthenia was born in 1841 to an enslaved black woman named Nannie and John M. Hensley, a Tennessee white man who was Nannie's enslaver. According to the slave law, the instant that Nannie delivered a child it became her enslaver's property. Hensley publicly acknowledged paternity, but he nonetheless regarded Parthenia as a slave first, a daughter second. She was reared through her first five years by her slave mother in the slave quarters. Most of what we know about Parthenia derives from what we know about her father, and about her second owner in Richland, Billy Wyatt, who was Hensley's son-in-law.

A surviving legal document known to the Hensley family reveals that John Hensley inherited from his father's estate two slaves: Nannie and an older black man named Payton. The year was 1841, and it seems that the inheritance marked the start of John Hensley's slaveholding. That same year, John Hensley and his wife Mary and their three small children moved from Tennessee to Searcy County, Arkansas, taking their two slaves, Nannie and Payton, with them. Hensley's younger brother Marcus and wife Rebecca joined in the move, and the second Hensley couple brought two more enslaved people, a man named Jim and a girl named Eveline. Heading into the rugged Buffalo River country, this party of seven adults and four children turned their wagons up Bear Creek, a tributary stream located a few miles east of Richland. Finding a spot that looked promising to homestead, the Hensley brothers and the two black men cleared some forest, built a cluster of cabins, and started two adjacent farms, one for each white man. It was here on John Hensley's farm that Parthenia was born two years later in 1843.

Enslaved people often lived in the same cabins with their enslavers on mountain farms such as these. By the time Parthenia entered the world, John Hensley had probably erected a separate slave cabin on his property, emulating his father's home in Tennessee. He and his wife needed that degree of separation from the slave Nannie and her infant—Hensley's child—for the sake of their marriage. So, it is likely that Parthenia never lived in her father's house. From a very young age, she was oriented to her mother and to a makeshift family of enslaved persons who were unrelated by blood: the older man Payton; Jim, who was in his mid-twenties; the girl Eveline; and later on, a handful of other blacks as John Hensley bought and enslaved more people.

When Parthenia was just five years old she was taken from her mother. Hensley gave Parthenia to his oldest daughter Louisa as a wedding gift when she married Billy Wyatt, telling her to "be good to Thene," as the little slave girl was her half-sister. Louisa was only fourteen or fifteen years old when she married, but the blood tie to Parthenia would not have been new information to her. "Old Jack," as Hensley was known, made no secret of the fact that he had fathered the slave girl. The half-sisters bore a strong family resemblance to one another. Both had their father's long straight nose, thin mouth, and slender build. Louisa had her white mother's weak chin and brown hair while Parthenia had her African American mother's dark skin and black hair. But despite those differences, it was clear that Parthenia was mulatto or mixed race, or as the mountain farmers cuttingly defined her, a "woods colt"—the issue of a furtive union between master and slave.

One sad thing about master-slave offspring was that they usually engendered jealousy or resentment on the part of the slaveowner's wife, which often led the slaveowner to sell the child or the mother, separating mother and child forever. Southern society frowned on those mother-child separations, insisting that slaveowners should rightly do all in their power to keep slave families intact. But in most states the slave law was silent on the matter, or if the law put up any kind of prohibition it was weakly enforced. All enslaved mothers and fathers had to live in fear of being forcibly separated from their children. Slave mothers in Nannie's position faced an extra measure of threat when a child by the enslaver caused discord between the enslaved person's master and mistress. We may imagine Nannie doing whatever she could to shield her young daughter from that constant fear of separation yet preparing her in some way for the dreaded possibility.

Parthenia's separation from her mother, though harsh, was not total. The girl would reside with the Wyatt family in Richland, which was a full day's journey over the mountain from Bear Creek. Whenever Louisa returned to Bear Creek to visit her family she would bring Parthenia with her, allowing the girl to see her mother. Thus, Parthenia moved to a new settlement where she was the only unfree person of color in the whole valley, but she still had occasional contact with her mother and the small slave community that she left behind in Bear Creek.

Still, no mitigating circumstance—neither Hensley's admonishment to treat the slave girl well nor the fact that she would continue to see her mother from time to time at the Hensley place—could have spared Parthenia from the terrible psychological blow of being separated from her mother at such a young age. The five-year-old girl was deprived of trust in the parent-child relationship at a crucial stage in her development. When the parent-child relationship could not be trusted, no other relationship could be trusted either. No matter how well Louisa and Billy Wyatt treated Parthenia in their home, she knew that she was their property, and that they held the power of sale over her. What had happened to her once could happen again. It was a constant reminder that she was unfree; she was the couple's ward only by force.

Young Parthenia's new master, Billy Wyatt, was twenty years old, earnest, proud, and ambitious. Born in Warren County, Missouri, he had come into the country with his parents in the early 1840s when he was fifteen. Richland at that time was still relatively unsettled. The Wyatts picked an excellent location for their farm on a side creek about a mile above the confluence of Richland Creek and the Buffalo River. Later it was claimed that their acreage had "the richest topsoil to be found west of the Mississippi River bottoms."

When Billy was eighteen, the Mexican American War broke out and Billy volunteered. He served as a young private in Gray's Battalion of Arkansas Volunteers, a unit of about 450 officers and men who were called up to guard the state against a possible Indian uprising when regular troops stationed on the Indian frontier were sent south to fight in Mexico. Billy mustered into service in July 1846 and mustered out in April 1847, splitting his time in the army between Fort Smith in Arkansas and Fort Gibson on Cherokee lands in the Indian Territory.

Billy Wyatt's rise to prominence in Richland began just after that time. Billy's father died, and Billy, as the oldest male in the family, inherited the land and became head of the Wyatt farm and household. How he met Louisa Hensley of Bear Creek is not known, but it is clear that the marriage alliance suited the ambitions of both families to acquire much more land and wealth.

The Wyatts probably demanded little or no work from Parthenia at first, as a slave child generally did not get assigned tasks until age five or six. After a while, Parthenia would have begun doing light chores around the place such as gathering kindling, collecting eggs from the chickens, and cleaning up the grounds. Louisa might have required that the slave girl help around the house, making beds, washing clothes, and doing kitchen chores. After Louisa gave birth to the Wyatts' first child, Emma, in 1850, the labor demands on Parthenia no doubt intensified. Very likely Louisa called on Parthenia's help tending the baby. Four years later, the Wyatts had a second child, Perry, and two years after that, Louisa gave birth to twins, Mary Powhatton and Caroline Pocahontas. By then, at age thirteen, Parthenia was deeply involved with helping Louisa rear four children and keep house. Like Mollie at the Greenhaw place, Parthenia probably worked many hours tending the crops and the livestock too.

Billy Wyatt, as Richland's sole slaveholder, claimed a social status beyond his years. Reminding people of his service in the Mexican American War, he preferred that they address him as Captain Wyatt. With his one slave, he qualified as a member of the state's slaveholder class. If owning a single slave counted for little among the big slaveholders who owned plantations in the south and east sections of the state, it was enough to set Billy Wyatt apart among the farmers in northwest Arkansas. The status of slaveholder afforded him an unofficial civil authority in the farming community of Richland. He was the big man in the valley. But he could not be too proud, for slavery had only a thin purchase in the region. Most mountain farmers in the Ozarks neither owned slaves nor aspired to own any. They believed in the Lord's injunction to work the land by the sweat of their brows. Many mountain farmers looked askance at the big plantation owners in the rest of the state who were too proud to do any physical work themselves. Wyatt knew the farmers' sentiments about the big plantation owners and even shared them, to a point. He worked his land the same as his neighbors did, planting corn and raising hogs and cattle, but he was also glad to put his feet up at the end of the day. Being a slaveowner entitled him to a certain amount of leisure, and he wanted his neighbors to see that he enjoyed that privilege.

With his father-in-law, Wyatt built a racetrack on his property and put on horse races, much to the entertainment of the people of Richland. Hensley, meanwhile, built a second racetrack over in Bear Creek. In fact, of the two men it was the father-in-law, Old Jack Hensley, who took the greater interest in this enterprise. The horse races became big social gatherings where ostentatious displays of wealth, courtly manners, and daring-do went hand in hand. The betting on the horses was high-spirited and wild. Hensley once lost a wager of $300, a sum worth about $10,000 today. He later brought a lawsuit to recover the full amount, alleging unfair dealing and fraud, and got a favorable verdict from the court in neighboring Carroll County. The judgment was appealed to the state supreme court where it was upheld. So, Old Jack eventually got his wager back.

The horse racing symbolized the fact that the Hensley-Wyatt family alliance brought together the two wealthiest families in their respective farming communities. While Wyatt enjoyed his status as the sole slaveowner in Richland, Hensley built up his wealth to become the most prosperous man in Searcy County. Initially, Hensley focused on acquiring land. Some of Hensley's land was in Bear Creek and some of it was over in Richland. While most mountain farmers in the Arkansas Ozarks merely squatted on their land holdings because they lacked the financial resources to buy the land from the government, Hensley had the cash to purchase his land. Periodically he went to the General Land Office in Batesville to prove up on his land claims, paying the government $1.25 per acre and steadily adding acreage to his taxable wealth. From his arrival in Arkansas in 1841 until the start of the Civil War in 1861, Hensley amassed a landed estate of 1,600 acres, about twenty times the acreage of most mountain farms in the Arkansas Ozarks. In 1860, the US Census recorded that Hensley produced 3,500 bushels of corn and 500 bushels of oats. His holdings in livestock included 100 cows, 200 hogs, two dozen sheep and oxen, eleven horses, and four mules. The land, livestock, and crop production, together with his medium-size slaveholding, made him one of the wealthiest farmers in the region.

It was the growth of Hensley's slaveholding that must call our attention. During the decade of the 1850s, Hensley doubled and then tripled his slaveholding. Starting with the two slaves he inherited from his father, he held five slaves in 1850 and fifteen in 1860, which made him the largest slaveholder in Searcy County (though still a relatively small slaveholder compared with plantation owners). As his slaveholding grew and the value of slaves shot up at the end of the 1850s, Hensley's wealth in slaves surpassed his wealth in land and livestock. There was only one possible way Hensley built up his slaveholding so quickly during that decade: by entering the slave trade.

In the decades before the Civil War, abolitionists drew attention to the extreme brutality and cruelty of the domestic slave trade. (The United States terminated the importation of slaves from Africa in

1808, and a large domestic slave trade developed when the African slave trade ended.) Abolitionists in particular showed how the slave trade viciously broke up families and treated enslaved persons virtually as livestock. White southerners, despite their stubborn defense of slavery, grew uncomfortable about the slave trade and generally tried to minimize its extent. But in fact the domestic slave trade permeated the entire South. No region was immune from its operation, not even a hill country like the Ozarks where blacks accounted for only a tiny fraction of the population. The economics of slavery were simply too compelling. There was a great demand for slave labor in the Lower South as the Cotton Kingdom spread westward into Mississippi, Arkansas, Louisiana, and Texas, and there was a surplus of slaves in the Upper South in states like Virginia and Kentucky, so the slave trade facilitated a constant forced migration of slaves from the Upper South to the Lower South to match the labor demand and maximize slave values. Since the labor supply was finite, causing the value of slaves to increase over time, price inflation made slaves an excellent cash investment for enslavers everywhere, even in remote places like the Arkansas Ozarks. Slaves accrued value as they grew from small children into older children of working age and then into young adults. In southern Arkansas in 1860, a slave was worth $100 at birth and $500 or more by the time they were five or six years old. In the slave market in New Orleans, a prime field hand would sell at that time for as much as $1,800. For a mountain farmer like Hensley, there was economic incentive to acquire child slaves for relatively cheap and raise them up for later sale in the Lower South.

The Southern slaveholder class was honor bound to denounce the slave trade, or at least to deny personal involvement with it. The Southern defense of slavery rested on the claim that enslaved blacks were well treated by their masters and, as an inferior race of people, were better off in bondage than if they were free. Consistent with that ideology of benevolent paternalism, slaveholders made a pretense of putting the welfare of their slaves ahead of their own best financial interests. They claimed they would bend over backwards to maintain slave families and would only split them up under rare circumstances. Of course, slave traders had to buy slaves from slaveholders, so the slaveholders' collective insistence that they did not engage in the slave trade was largely a fiction. Slaveholders might have true pangs of conscience about selling their human property, but when faced with financial difficulties or interpersonal problems arising with individual slaves, almost invariably they put their qualms aside and sold their slaves. In reality, many, many slaveholders drove their own slaves to and from local slave markets even if they never themselves engaged in driving large numbers of slaves over long distances the way the big slave traders did.

For Hensley, an interest in buying and selling slaves may have begun with his interest in horse racing. In the 1850s, Hensley started to build up a stable of fine quarter horses. He did so by buying a lot of used-up old plow horses each spring, fattening them up on his land over the summer, and taking them down to New Orleans in late summer or fall to trade for one or two expensive young quarter horses. In making his yearly trips to New Orleans, he quite likely saw a financial opportunity in also taking along a few human chattels to sell in the lucrative New Orleans slave market. The sale of one or two children would cover the cost of his trip; the sale of a few more would bring a handsome return. No paper record of Hensley's slave dealings has been found, but this is the most plausible explanation for how he built up his slaveholding and other property wealth so quickly.

Presuming that this is indeed how it went, then Hensley entered a business that most southerners preferred not to talk or think about very much. The slave market in New Orleans operated from September to May, shutting down through the summer months because the city was so unbearably hot and pestilential. Slave traders who acquired their slaves in northwest Arkansas or Missouri generally started the drive to New Orleans in mid-summer after the crops were laid by, arriving in the city around the beginning of September. The slave drive could take up to eight weeks if the whole distance was covered on foot, less if some of it was accomplished by riverboat or barge. Once in New Orleans, the slave traders put their human chattels in pens to await sale while they checked into temporary quarters with other slave traders. The business of selling slaves in the market might take several days or even longer, with the traders serving as witnesses to one another's sales. Meanwhile, the traders ate meals together and entertained themselves in the evenings by going to saloons and gambling. As Hensley entered into this scene, he probably spent much of his time looking for a fine new quarter horse to purchase with a portion of his earnings.

If Hensley came to see horse trading and slave trading as somewhat akin, he was hardly the first Southern race horse man to think that way. Probably Hensley maintained discretion around his slave trading, keeping others' attention on the horses. Indeed, his slave trading was very nearly expunged from the record. A Searcy County newspaper long ago recorded for posterity that on these yearly trips to New Orleans, Hensley, with the help of slaves (who were called "darkies" in the newspaper story) would drive horses to Batesville, "then load them on a boat, and he would send the darkies home, and he would go down the river into Louisiana." This arrangement sounds quite unrealistic, as there is no evident way he could have provided for the bondsmen's safe, reliable, independent travel back to Bear Creek. The story sounds suspiciously like a whitewash for what Hensley was really doing: driving the slaves all the way to the slave market in New Orleans. Long after Hensley was dead, one old-timer in Richland undermined this absurd image of Hensley's faithful slaves dutifully returning home without him, recalling that Hensley was in fact a "slave driver."

Hensley mingled horse racing and slaving in one other way. At some point he decided to look for a male slave of small build to be his jockey and stableman. He found the person he was looking for in a young black man named Anthony. The story that has been passed down is that Anthony was sold to Hensley at Beller's Stand—Beal Gaither's trading post on Crooked Creek in Carroll County about thirty miles northwest of Hensley's place. Anthony had to stand practically naked on a stump for prospective buyers to inspect his body, and Hensley saw in the young man's light but well-formed physique the makings of a jockey. No one can say how scared or humiliated or benumbed

Anthony felt through that dehumanizing treatment. Hensley bought Anthony, provided him the opportunity to become an excellent jockey and proficient stableman, and gave him unusual privileges in going back and forth between the Hensley and Wyatt places. In the years before the Civil War, Anthony seems to have lived part-time with the Wyatts. He was counted in the US Census's 1860 slave schedule while he was at the Wyatt's place. Because of Anthony's diminutive size, the census taker incorrectly listed him as just fourteen years old and female. Although Anthony was roughly the same age as Parthenia, there is no evidence that the two became friends. Anthony stayed in Searcy County after emancipation and died there in 1914. Late in life, Anthony Hensley was interviewed by a white person to whom he reportedly said that back in slavery days he had been treated "like a member of the family" by Old Jack Hensley. Of course, this was the bromide offered by so many blacks to their white inquisitors in those days, because saying anything unkind about their former enslavers was only asking for trouble. Anthony also said in the interview that in the Civil War he accompanied Hensley into the military as his man servant, and that one time he came to Hensley's aid when Hensley had his horse shot out from under him.

Hensley's slaveholding of fifteen people in 1860 included just three adults together with twelve children. Only one adult female was present, so evidently Hensley acquired most of his child slaves in the same status that he acquired young Anthony: separated from their mothers. The high proportion of children in Hensley's slaveholding was typical of slaveholdings on the mountain farms in northwest Arkansas. To a mountain farmer in the 1850s, child slaves could look like a good, sound, ten- to fifteen-year investment—provided that the institution of slavery would be preserved that long—since they doubled and tripled and quadrupled in value as they grew to adulthood.

On her visits to the Hensley place, Parthenia would have found three or four boys and girls about her own age plus a lot of smaller children, plus one or two adults acting as surrogate parents over this large motherless brood. Hensley's slave quarters likely put individuals of all ages and both sexes in one common area. Enslaved children generally lived in sexually integrated spaces and did not experience separate male and female spheres until they approached their teens. As the children came into their teens, they needed instruction from their parents or surrogate parents about how to manage the changing demands and expectations that the slave system placed on them. They had to be taught how to cope with their master's or mistress's wide-ranging efforts to compel their labor, control their movements, and regiment their time. The children also needed instruction on the rules they must follow to become responsible adult members of the slave community. They had to learn, for example, that whatever they heard in conversation in the slave quarters was not to be shared with the whites.

Outside of Hensley's slaveholding, there were another thirty enslaved persons in Bear Creek distributed across five other slaveholdings. The wider slave population would have made up a larger slave community. Enslaved people met their neighbors through a variety of ways, not just on work assignments. They met in social gatherings such as church meetings, dances, suppers, and slave weddings. Neighboring slaveholders had many reasons to allow and even encourage their enslaved people to mix with other enslaved people on nearby farms. Slaveholders allowed such gatherings to occur mainly to further their own selfish interest in seeing slave marriages develop. Slave marriages were good for slaveholders because they lifted morale, deterred husbands and wives from running away, and most importantly, produced children that became the slaveholder's property. Billy Wyatt would have had those considerations in view whenever he or his wife took Parthenia over to Bear Creek to visit the Hensley place.

At some time when Parthenia was still a minor, she lost her mother, Nannie; however, Nannie's death or departure from the scene is not recorded. We have only a vague knowledge of her presence on the Hensley farm. The US Census enumerated individual slaves in the slave schedules, but it did not record their names. Southern members of Congress insisted that the census leave off the names; they did not want to accord enslaved people that kind of personhood. So, individuals were only counted with a tick mark, together with their sex, race (black or mulatto), and age (usually estimated—with the estimate sometimes quite wide of the mark). For the modern-day researcher, specific individuals such as Nannie and Payton cannot be traced in the 1850 and 1860 census record with any degree of certainty. The US Census did record a forty-five-year-old male in Hensley's slaveholding in 1850, presumably Payton, and a sixty-year-old male in 1860, also presumably Payton. No analogous record exists for Nannie. The oldest female in Hensley's slaveholding in 1860 was just twenty-seven, too young to have been Parthenia's mother. We must conclude that sometime before the census was taken in July 1860 Nannie either died or was sold.

Even absent her mother, the slave community in Bear Creek still gave Parthenia a kind of nurturing in the ways of being a black girl in slavery that her white master and mistress could not possibly provide for her. Perhaps the old man Payton gave Parthenia some special care; he had known her since infancy. Or, perhaps, another surrogate parent in Hensley's slaveholding stepped up. No matter what, Parthenia would have welcomed those opportunities to return to that cramped yet welcoming space at Bear Creek where she could eat, sleep, talk, play games, sing songs, and worship with people of her own race. Nannie, for as long as she was present, would have used those opportunities to give Parthenia a mother's love and advise her on how to cope with her isolation in Richland, avoid punishment, and maintain her self-esteem.

But it was impossible for Parthenia to develop a healthy sense of self in a world so malformed as this. If Billy and Louisa Wyatt tried to be nurturing to the child, ultimately they failed her badly. Parthenia was unprepared for the next dreary turn in her life when Billy Wyatt, her master and caregiver since the age of five, cornered her in a secluded spot one day and demanded to have sex.

Untold numbers of enslaved girls had to endure their master's sexual assaults. A girl as isolated as Parthenia would have had virtually no sex education whatsoever. If she had still had her mother's tutelage, she might at least have had some warning of what could befall her.

Nannie, of course, had once endured the same fate at the hands of her enslaver, Hensley. The kind of sex education that a mother could provide to a daughter in these circumstances was grim, but better than nothing. Against a determined slaveowner there was not much an enslaved female could do to prevent her own rape, no matter how savvy she was. She was a piece of property without rights. If she resisted the master's sexual advances, she could be whipped for it and raped anyway. If she feigned a willingness to have sex to lessen the violence in the act, she could find herself being victimized again and again. If she took the latter course, the misery of unwanted sexual relations might be compounded by another torment: endless abuse from the jealous wife of the master. And the sexually exploited enslaved girl was at risk of yet another horror: getting pregnant with a child who would be the master's progeny and slave. Motherhood in those circumstances was especially fraught. Often the master's wife, the enslaved woman's mistress, would insist on selling off the child of the master-slave conjugation as soon as it grew past infancy.

Parthenia must have gone through her rape experience without support of any kind. Growing up in the Wyatt household without any other slaves present, she did not have support from those quarters. It is hard to imagine that, as Billy's wife, her older half-sister Louisa would have provided her with any.

The only recorded facts about Parthenia's and Billy's sexual relationship are that Parthenia bore a child in the first year of the Civil War and Billy claimed paternity for it. After giving birth to their child, a boy, Parthenia and the boy would remain in the Wyatt household for many more years.

Though Parthenia was just four years older than Mollie and the two teenage girls lived on neighboring farms, their experiences of coming into womanhood were worlds apart.

Chapter 4

Under the Brush Arbor

On many a Sunday, Mollie and the whole Greenhaw family climbed into their wagon and went to church. Their church was not as one thinks of a church today. The families in Richland did not have a regular preacher or a dedicated church building. They did not have regular weekly church services, though at certain times of year the gatherings might have been almost that frequent. Rarely, in inclement weather, a church service might be held in the schoolhouse. Usually, though, it was held outdoors under a brush arbor. In the warm southern climate, the brush arbor made a good, serviceable, spiritual meeting place. Ozark settlers would pick a shady spot, perhaps tucked away in a glen or cooled by a nearby spring, where they would construct their house of worship from woody materials at hand. The brush arbor structure consisted of a skeleton frame of sturdy vertical poles and cross poles, which was covered by a lattice of cut saplings, which was in turn covered by smaller pieces of leafy brush. The last layer could be readily cleaned off and replaced from time to time. The brush arbor thus made a nice shelter from the sweltering sun.

In advance of the church service the dirt floor would be swept clean of debris, and a pulpit would be erected so the preacher would have a hard surface on which to lay his Bible and pound his fist for good effect. Permanent log benches were placed down one side of the arbor while the other side was kept clear. Most families came to church by wagon, bringing chairs with them to seat all the females in their group. As the people arrived, they arranged their chairs in the open space. Then the women and girls took their seats on one side of a center aisle, and the men and boys occupied the bench seats on the other.

Nearly all the settlers along the Buffalo were either Baptists, Methodists, or Campbellites. They did not worry too much about the doctrinal differences between denominations. If a circuit-riding preacher or missionary from any denomination came calling in the neighborhood that was good enough for all.

A church gathering was as much a social event as an occasion for religious worship. It would last all day. Usually, the formalities began with a Bible class for the youngsters. Then the preacher gave a morning service centered on a "fire and brimstone" sermon. The afternoon would stretch out with little claim on it. Finally, there was an evening service that was often conducted by lamplight. Following the benediction, the church assembly broke up. As the people rode or walked away, they sometimes held torches aloft. The effect of so many flickering flames dispersing in the gathering darkness presented an inspiring spectacle for all.

Parthenia attended church gatherings with the Wyatts. The white folks remarked on what a devout Christian the young slave girl was. So "filled with the spirit," they said. Rather than take a seat with the white folks, Parthenia would wander around the outside of the brush arbor as everyone else went in. Then, as the preacher got warmed up and the meeting got rambunctious, Parthenia would begin to clap and dance and shout, the whites of her eyes flashing as her eyeballs rolled back in her head. To the white folks, Parthenia's wild movements and exclamations reflected the spirit of the Lord passing through her. They were unalarmed by what they saw, because some had seen it before in black Christian church gatherings. The "frenzy," as it was known, drew on African traditions of conjuration and mysticism as well as the more familiar strains of revivalistic Christianity. The whites sometimes fell into trances also, but Parthenia seemed singularly touched by the spirit.

For Mollie, the church services were welcome events because they were so social. At thirteen, she did not feel the spirit like Parthenia, but she did have religious convictions. Her own religiosity centered on reading the Bible, following Christianity's moral strictures, and acknowledging her faith in God. Fundamentally, though, church appealed to her because she enjoyed the church fellowship. The sight of so many faces—some familiar, some not; the children's games; the "dinner on the ground" in the lazy afternoon; the singing; the ritual; the rapture that came over the group as the preacher thundered from the pulpit; all of it excited her.

One Sunday at church, Mollie experienced something quite new. While she was singing with the congregation, she suddenly broke off in mid-stanza to hearken to an unfamiliar male voice on the opposite side of the aisle. Leaning forward a little in her chair to hear better, she heard the voice carrying above all the others in the choir. Clear and sweet, it sounded like an angel caroling from heaven. So exquisite was the sound to her ear that she checked her own singing and remained listening. She stole a sideways glance across the aisle, eager to find the source of this sweet masculine voice. She sighted him quickly—a handsome, young fellow with dark, curly hair. He glanced her way and for an instant their eyes met. She saw in his face, as she later wrote, "an expression both firm and kind."

After the service, the congregation slowly spilled out of the arbor. All around Mollie the parishioners broke into idle conversations. Such was the customary scene, but on this occasion, she felt an impulse to burrow through the crowd and apprehend this beautiful young man. Yet she checked herself. As much as she wanted to meet him, she feared that it would be too forward for their first encounter. She could not just step up to him and say howdy-do. She must wait for an introduction.

On the way home to the Greenhaw farm that evening, the rhythmic jostling of the wagon put her in a reverie. She thought she might be falling in love.

Over the following days and weeks, she carried her vision of the young man with her as she went about her chores on the farm. Working herself into a thirteen-year-old's happy delirium, she coaxed her mind to wander off to faraway places. In her imagination he sang to her, and she to him.

In her fantasies, the two of them were courting. In her imaginary dialogues with him, he promised to protect her through darkening times. Indeed, this ideal boy whom she kept in her thoughts did succeed in brightening her days for a while. She hummed to herself when others around her withdrew into silence. She felt blissful in spite of the storm cloud that came and settled over their valley in that winter of 1860–61.

~

The election of Lincoln to the presidency of the United States came as a shock to most Southerners. Southern voters went to the polls in 1860 in numbers never seen before. They cast their votes for the Northern or Southern Democratic Party candidate or the Constitutional Union Party candidate. The Republican Party candidate did not even appear on their ballots. As Northern voters broke for Lincoln while Southern voters split their votes three ways, the Northern vote overwhelmed the Southern vote. The Republican Party candidate won the national election without a single Southern vote. After the election, secessionists sprang into action, arguing that the Republican Party triumph confirmed that Southern states must secede from the Union to preserve the institution of slavery and the Southern way of life. Many Southerners were skeptical of that view. A rigorous political debate over secession immediately ensued in all the Southern states.

Secessionists wanted their states to dissolve the Union; Unionists wanted their states to stay in the Union. But the Unionist position was more complicated. Most Unionists said they were "conditional Unionists," meaning that they would oppose secession up to a point, or on condition that the Lincoln administration would show restraint while Northern and Southern politicians worked out a compromise around slavery. A smaller number declared themselves "unconditional Unionists," meaning that they wanted to preserve the Union even if it would jeopardize the future of slavery.

Most people in northwest Arkansas began the winter of 1860–61 in the Unionist camp. Mountain farmers as a class did not have much stake in slavery; only a tiny fraction of them owned slaves. Already wary of planter control over Arkansas's government, now they worried over how the planter class would dominate a Southern Confederacy.

Mollie's people in Richland engaged in the debate over secession along with the rest of Arkansas's citizens. When someone got hold of a newspaper, it was read aloud in the home and shared with neighbors. Editorials were attacked or defended. Many of the people around Mollie would have agreed with this example from the *Van Buren Press*, counselling the state's citizens to be measured in their response to the crisis:

> From our telegraph reports, which are quite full, it is certain that Abraham Lincoln, "the rail-splitter," is elected President. With both houses of Congress opposed to him, we do not see how he can carry out his Abolitionist doctrines if he is so disposed. Give him a trial, and then if his administration is so obnoxious that we cannot honorably live under it, let us cast off. Let us ponder well before we give up a good government, without the certainty of bettering ourselves. Examine well this subject of a Southern Confederacy, fellow-citizens—carefully and practically, without prejudice, and we are willing to abide your decision.

Though secessionists were definitely in the minority in Arkansas and perhaps across the whole South at the start of the secession winter, they quickly got into the driver's seat to drive the secession bandwagon. The most radical had been honing their message of Southern nationalism for years. Several Southern newspapers with wide circulation had been pushing for disunion for a long time. The secessionist *DeBow's Review*, a monthly commercial paper in New Orleans, was one such organ that enjoyed a wide readership among the cotton planters of Arkansas. Now, in the wake of the 1860 election, the secessionists in the southern and eastern counties of Arkansas mobilized. Their counties sent resolutions to the state legislature requesting that it call a statewide convention to vote on the matter. The Unionist-leaning counties in northwest Arkansas soon responded, sending the legislature antisecession resolutions to prevent a vociferous minority from taking control of the process. The state legislature duly answered all these resolutions; a statewide election was held in February to elect county delegates to a secession convention. The secession convention met in Little Rock on March 4—the day of Lincoln's inauguration in Washington.

While Arkansas's political process was unfolding, Arkansas secessionists' machinations steadily chipped away at Unionist strength in the state. Arkansans paid rapt attention as other Southern states seceded from the Union one by one. They followed developments as the seceded states took preliminary steps to form a Southern Confederacy. Arkansas's secessionist governor, Henry Rector, did not wait for the state convention to meet and decide what course the state should take, but made his own efforts to align the state with the Confederate cause. He demanded that Federal troops withdraw from the Federal arsenal in Little Rock and hand it over to state control. He also had artillery pieces moved into position on the edge of the Mississippi River to control navigation down the river along the state's eastern border. Meanwhile, Arkansas's radical secessionists, emboldened by the governor's actions, said if the state convention would not bring about secession, then maybe the state's southern and eastern counties would secede by themselves, splitting Arkansas in two. Arkansas's Unionists still had a majority of votes when the state's secession convention met in March, but their strength in the assembly began to ebb soon thereafter. The Rebel bombardment of Fort Sumter in Charleston Harbor in April turned the tables. Many of Arkansas's "conditional Unionists" became reluctant secessionists, and votes taken by the convention in early May reflected it. The convention finally passed a secession ordinance by a vote of 65 to 5. After further wrangling, another vote was held in an attempt to attain a unanimous vote. The final vote was 69 to 1.

The Greenhaw family followed these events in newspapers that came to hand in Richland, and in conversations with their friends and neighbors in the Richland community. Jim Greenhaw may have gone over to Burrowsville to take part in the countywide public meeting that was held in December. As the single eligible voter in the Greenhaw household, he probably cast his ballot in the special election in February. Searcy County voters elected a prominent farmer from Calf Creek to represent the county at the state convention. The man was a Unionist. It is a reasonable guess that early in the secession winter Jim Greenhaw stood with the majority of Searcy County men who still wanted Arkansas to remain in the Union. Not only would his Tennessee background predict that he was a Unionist, but he also had two sons of military age and two more sons in their mid to late teens, which was an extraordinary number of sons for one family to place on the altar of sacrifice in the event of war. But if Jim Greenhaw was a Unionist at first, by the early spring he and his family had swung into the secessionist camp. All four Greenhaw boys—James, William, Green Berry, and Calvin—would end up enlisting in the Confederate army in 1861 or 1862. For most nonslaveholding Southerners, and probably for Jim Greenhaw, too, the single event that turned them against the Union was Lincoln's decision after Fort Sumter to call up troops to quell the rebellion. The prospect of a Northern army invading their homeland ignited their feelings of Southern patriotism, weak as their commitment to Confederate nationhood might be.

~

Mollie struggled to make sense of it all. Fort Sumter was a world away from Richland. Yet people talked of a coming war between North and South that could place northern Arkansas directly in the path of an invading army. Unless Arkansas's neighboring state of Missouri were to join the Confederacy, then the Arkansas-Missouri state line would become the new boundary between two warring nations. Some of the leading voices in Searcy County warned darkly of the hardships and horrors that could befall the citizens of the county if opposing armies were to rove through the area. The armies would be foraging for food and requisitioning horses and guns, spawning banditry. Southern women would be vulnerable to acts of barbarism by the invading host, especially if the women were left in a defenseless situation with their men away fighting. The vision of Northern marauders coming to one's very home inflamed the Southern man's sense of honor. At the same time, Southern women cottoned to the idea that they had to be stoic and encourage their men to fight. The ladies were to stand guard and prepare to confront war's fury on their own. Mollie heard the conflicting messages—be afraid, be brave—and tried as best she could to reconcile them.

There was no public celebration in Richland when word came in May that Arkansas had seceded from the Union. The residents of the valley could have gathered at the post office to shout a hurrah, but they did not have their heart in it. By then the people knew most of their neighbors' political convictions, and they knew that the population of Richland cleaved pretty well in two, only about half the people being in support of secession. There seemed to be no point in further roiling the community.

The Greenhaw family, however, soon had something to celebrate. On May 21, 1861, Jim Greenhaw gave his oldest daughter's hand in marriage to a young man who lived on a good farm a little way up Richland Creek from the Greenhaw place. Elizabeth Greenhaw was twenty-five years old. The groom, Americus Robertson, was twenty-two. The two families gathered under a shade tree to witness the couple's wedding vows. Mollie stood with her seven cousins and aunt and uncle on one side, while the Robertsons gathered on the other. After a simple ceremony, the families sat down to a sumptuous wedding banquet on the ground. The joyous occasion provided Mollie and everyone else a respite from all their weighty ruminations over disunion.

The Robertsons mirrored the Greenhaws in many ways. James and Mary Robertson, the parents of the groom, were just a bit older than Jim and Usley. They had nine children, five of whom still lived on the farm, compared with the Greenhaws' seven offspring plus Mollie. Whereas Jim and Usley came from Tennessee, James and Mary Robertson came from Kentucky. The Robertsons and Greenhaws alike belonged to the cultural milieu of the Upper South that historians describe as Southern plain folk—subsistence farmers and herders with a penchant for moving west. Like the Greenhaws, the Robertsons were not slaveholders, and like them they were nonetheless moved by recent events to be "Secesh" and bullish on the Confederacy now.

After the wedding, Elizabeth and Americus Robertson moved to a place in neighboring Carroll County that they had picked out beforehand. There they would make their own farm—beyond the crowded confines of the Richland Valley but near enough that they could stay in contact with their respective families.

Mollie still saw her cousin Elizabeth whenever Elizabeth returned home for a visit. Despite their twelve-year age difference, Mollie looked to her older cousin for her model of Confederate womanhood. Before long, Mollie imagined Elizabeth would be tending the home fire while her husband went off to war.

Chapter 5

To Arms! To Arms!

In July 1861, Governor Rector ordered an enlistment of 10,000 troops to protect Arkansas against the Federal army massing on its northern border. "To Arms! To Arms!" shouted the headline in the *Arkansas True Democrat*, the state's leading newspaper in Little Rock. The newspaper printed the full text of the governor's proclamation, and a stack of the newspapers went in the mail to each post office around the state. Richland farmers rode to the post office to get a copy and, knowing that the stack of papers was not enough for everyone in the valley, they passed their copy to their neighbors as soon as they had read it.

The governor's summons notwithstanding, Richland farmers proved reluctant to volunteer for the army. In 1861, Richland could count eighteen men between the ages of eighteen and twenty-five. Only eight of them, including two pairs of brothers, answered the call to arms in that first summer of the war. The brothers were James and William Greenhaw, both twenty-one, and Maston and Irvin Robertson, twenty and twenty-one respectively. Among Richland's sixty-three farmsteads, the Greenhaw and Robertson farmsteads were two of the first to send their boys to war.

The governor's proclamation explained how the state would induct volunteers into military service and rapidly build an army. First, it sought men of authority and persuasion to step forward and serve as recruiters or mustering officers. It named ten locations around the state where those officers would muster volunteers into service. Volunteers would sign up for a period of twelve months. These recruits would form into companies of sixty-four to ninety-six men, and as soon as a company formed, the men would elect their officers. Newly formed companies would gather at some place as directed and become part of a regiment. Each regiment would contain six to ten companies, and as soon as the regiment formed, the men would elect regimental officers.

Sometime around the first of August a mustering officer rode through Richland looking for volunteers. That officer was James Harrison Love, a man of Searcy County who resided a little way down the Buffalo River on the north side. A yeoman farmer of middling prosperity, Love owned two horses, one milk cow, one beef cow, and fifty hogs, according to the 1860 census. His farm produced that year 400 bushels of corn and 25 bushels of sweet potatoes. James Love was not a slaveowner. Why he believed so strongly in the Confederate cause is not known. A surviving photograph of him from the period shows a man of rare conviction, eyebrows knit together and ramrod straight above piercing eyes, mouth tightly drawn beneath a jutting moustache, and a long, bristly beard falling to the top button of his shirt. His military service record states that he stood six feet two inches tall, a head taller than most men in that era. Forty-four years old in 1861, he had no prior military experience, yet he somehow knew that he could be a leader of men. When he heard the call to arms, he put aside his plow and went looking for fellow volunteers. After scouring his own lightly populated Tomahawk Township in Searcy County, he rode over to Richland Township, and then over to Burrowsville and points beyond. Eventually he got eighty men to accompany him to Yellville in Marion County to enlist. Besides the two Greenhaw brothers and the two Robertson brothers, Mollie's friend John Cole agreed to sign up, as did the Richland schoolmaster John Jones.

The young men made a motley crew as they headed off to the mustering ground together. Some of them shouldered their own squirrel rifles or old flintlock muskets, trusting in the governor's promise that the state would compensate them for whatever weapons they brought from home. Some wore Bowie knives or hatchets in their belts.

Richland's subscription school promptly closed after Jones left. Rather than look for a replacement teacher, the farmers decided to close their school for the duration of the war. Most schools in northern Arkansas closed as well.

Mollie wondered if her ideal boy, the dark-haired fellow who sang like an angel, was old enough to enlist. As a young Confederate woman in training, she preferred that if he was to fight then he would fight for the Confederate cause. But in light of her own romantic designs on him, she rather hoped that he would remain in Richland for a while longer. Perhaps he was still underage for the army. She was relieved to learn that he still lived on his parents' farm. His name, she discovered, was Valentine Williams. She went on waiting to receive a suitable introduction.

~

Political revolution and a farming way of life can form a combustible combination. At the beginning of the French Revolution in July 1789, a wave of fear spread among the French peasantry. They thought that the aristocracy was conspiring with the king to restore the Old Regime. Rumors spread that the king's and aristocrats' henchmen were rampaging from village to village through the countryside, looting granaries and homes. The rumors, coming on the heel of poor grain harvests, with bread shortages looming, ignited a general peasant uprising against the feudal landlords. The wave of violence and unrest was called the Great Fear. There have been other such fears in other revolutions, and Arkansas experienced its in the late fall of 1861.

Like the Great Fear in revolutionary France, Arkansas's Great Fear occurred against a backdrop of revolutionary struggle overlain by food insecurity. Northwest Arkansas farmers suffered a general crop failure in 1861, which came on top of a disappointing harvest the year before. While northwest Arkansas's subsistence farmers faced a winter of scarcity ahead, the state as a whole began to look for food imports from Texas and Louisiana to replace those that had come from Iowa in years past but were now cut off by the Federal armies. In November 1861, a sudden fear spread in northwest Arkansas that counterrevolutionary Unionists were conspiring to rise up and murder their secessionist neighbors. Rumor pointed to a Unionist conspiracy centered in Searcy County, with Unionist cells operating in several other northwestern counties as well.

Arkansas's Great Fear began when a vigilante mob gathered in Locust Grove Township on the east side of Searcy County and descended on the farm of one James Treat, a known Unionist. Treat confessed that he was part of a secret organization called the Arkansas Peace Society and further revealed that members of the society kept their association hidden by means of secret signs and passwords. The mob arrested Treat and then went after other suspected conspirators. Someone alerted the local commander of the state militia, Colonel Sam Leslie. Leslie hastened to Locust Grove where he found about fifty men at Henry Bradshaw's place discussing their next move. Already they had a number of Unionists under arrest. Leslie called up two companies of the Forty-fifth Regiment Arkansas Militia—enough men, he thought, to complete the investigation and allay a widespread panic.

As Colonel Leslie gathered more intelligence about the Peace Society, he found that the sworn members had no aims other than to resist military service, or at worst, to organize a separate peace in northwest Arkansas. But the fear of a conspiracy spread much faster than Leslie could gather intelligence. Vigilante mobs soon formed in nearby Izard and Fulton Counties to round up more suspected conspirators there. Vigilante committees in each county began compiling lists of known Unionists who were suspected of being in the conspiracy. As the name lists grew, word reached Governor Rector that the Peace Society had as many as 1,700 sworn members poised to take up arms against the Confederate regime in Arkansas. Governor Rector wired President Jefferson Davis, warning him that Arkansas could face an insurrection. Not waiting for the president's reply, the governor ordered Leslie to apprehend all of the blacklisted Unionists in Searcy County—to conduct a mass arrest of citizens. To comply with the governor's order,

Leslie called up the remaining companies of the Forty-fifth Regiment Arkansas Militia.

It fell to Captain Billy Wyatt to call up the militia in Richland Township: Company B. Altogether, fifty men in Richland collected at the post office, where Wyatt formed them into a column on the Burrowsville to Carrollton Road. They marched over Point Peter Mountain to the rendezvous point in Burrowsville to muster. Company B's muster roll included Mollie's cousin, Green Berry Greenhaw, as well as Americus Robertson and all the remaining Robertson brothers who were not in the army. The middle-aged Andrew Jackson Cole turned out along with Mollie's young crush, Valentine Williams.

But these men did not present themselves as a valorous group marching off to war. Nor did they come together as an excited vigilante mob. They came for militia duty—a fifteen-day stint as it would prove to be—merely to protect their homes. There was no glory in this militia duty; it was just an unpleasant job that had to be tackled, or what the Richland farmer referred to as "uphill work." Indeed, some of the men in the militia company responded to the muster call mainly to prove their own innocence or to get a better bead on the political situation in their community. On the march to Burrowsville, fifteen of the men in Company B deserted during the night after they learned more precisely what they had been called out to do. When these men returned home, they learned that three of Richland's more ardent Unionists, Ben and Tom Slay and Lewis Brewer, had avoided the call-up altogether and had gone into hiding in neighboring Newton County.

At Burrowsville, Company B—now just thirty-five strong—joined the rest of the militia companies in a field at the edge of the village. By then it was December 5 and some of the over 200 militiamen encamped there had been in the field for two weeks. Joseph Stephenson, a local farmer, had set up a commissary wagon to provision the men with food and equipment.

The first few prisoners who were taken in Locust Grove had been placed in the courthouse jail. By the time the Richland men arrived, the number of prisoners had swelled to around seventy-four and they were being held in a temporary pen outside the courthouse awaiting the time when they would be marched under guard to Little Rock. Over the next few days Colonel Leslie sent parties out from Burrowsville to make more arrests.

On December 8, Leslie ordered the prisoners put in chains for the march to Little Rock. There was a stack of iron collars that a local blacksmith had forged for the purpose in recent days. The prisoners were made to stand in line while three militiamen of Company C fastened an iron collar around each prisoner's neck. In the process, the militiamen came face to face with prisoners who were their former friends and neighbors. Some of the militiamen broke down and cried at what they had to do. When all the prisoners were collared, they were arranged in pairs and put in harnesses with trace chains linking each pair. After that, a log chain was run down the center between each pair and fastened to make a long coffle.

Many of the militiamen had seen coffles or chain gangs like this before. Those chain gangs had been made up of enslaved African Americans being driven to a slave market. Whatever the militiamen might think about slavery, they were ashamed to see their own neighbors treated that way. When the chained prisoners were at last ordered to march, the militiamen could hardly bear to watch. After the prisoners had lurched and stumbled for a few hundred paces they were told to halt, and the log chain, harnesses, and trace chains were all removed, and they were chained together in pairs by the neck instead. The prisoners were marched off under an escort guard of about one hundred men toward an unknown fate in Little Rock.

While the Forty-fifth Regiment Arkansas Militia was performing its unsavory task, the Richland farmers of Company B learned what was happening back in Richland. They found that six good men of Richland had surrendered themselves to a justice of the peace at Carrollton, confessing to membership in the Peace Society. These six men recanted their involvement in the Unionist conspiracy and testified about the secret oaths and signs that bound the Peace Society members together, hoping that their cooperation with authorities would buy them leniency. The six men were John Christy and his sons John Jr. and James, Gilmore Smith, David Baker, and Porter

Hensley. Porter Hensley was a nephew of John Hensley. He had recently gone to work as a farmhand at the Wyatt place. Thus, while Captain Wyatt was on militia duty rounding up members of the Peace Society, he was surprised to learn that his own farmhand and Hensley in-law was part of the conspiracy. By this time, Wyatt had come to the same conclusions about the conspiracy as had Colonel Leslie: the Peace Society was defensive in nature, and its members did not deserve harsh punishment.

Billy Wyatt joined with twenty-nine others in signing a petition to the governor calling for the release of the six Richland men, pleading that they were all citizens in good standing before secession. The petition held that the men had been "gulled and deceived" into joining the Peace Society in the belief that it was "a good thing and for the protection of their homes, property and families against robbers and thieves and that it was a neighborhood society." Wyatt was not the only militiaman to sign the petition; Andrew Jackson Cole and Americus Robertson did as well. Most of the thirty petitioners were Richland men. John Hensley of Bear Creek signed the petition, too, presumably out of concern for his nephew.

While the petition went to the governor, the roundup by the militia continued. The Richland fugitives Ben and Tom Slay and Lewis Brewer were captured on December 8. Peter Tyler, a former Searcy County sheriff, went into hiding in late November. Militiamen on horseback found him on December 18, camped in the woods not far from his home on Tomahawk Creek. After Tyler was arraigned at the Carrollton courthouse, he was clapped in chains and marched to Little Rock with another batch of prisoners.

Colonel Leslie discharged the militia on December 20. There were still many suspected conspirators at large, but the mission of capturing them thankfully was transferred to a Confederate cavalry troop stationed in the area. In practical terms, when the militia disbanded it meant the dragnet was ended.

~

Billy Wyatt returned home feeling depressed after his fifteen-day stint with the militia. If the suppression of the Peace Society accomplished anything, it was to demonstrate that the people of northwest Arkansas could not be neutral in this war. Neither the Democratic governor of Arkansas nor the Confederate government in distant Richmond, Virginia, would abide its citizens pledging to stay peaceful and just sit things out. Sadly, with everyone forced to take sides in the conflict, political divisions emerged in unforeseen places. The fact that Wyatt's own farmhand and kinsman, Porter Hensley, had joined the Peace Society troubled Wyatt very much.

When Wyatt took stock of the political loyalties of the people close around him, it made a confusing picture. His father-in-law John Hensley was Secesh. Most of the mountain farmers who lived in the vicinity of his farm were at least nominally Secesh. Wyatt, too, was a Confederate in the eyes of his comrades. As a captain in the state militia, he was sworn to uphold the government of Arkansas. But in truth, he did not support the Confederate cause. He hated the South's planter class and the way it ruled the state of Arkansas through its control of the Democratic Party. Billy Wyatt came from a line of Whigs on his mother's side. He was deeply skeptical of a Confederate government that would govern through one-party rule. The Confederacy represented the planters' interests, but would it represent the interests of small farmers like himself? He thought not. Privately, he favored the Union.

Wyatt lived in a paternalistic society that bestowed great authority on the senior male of every household, whether the domicile was a small farm, a large plantation, a town residence, or something else. In Southern society, the male's paternalistic or patriarchal authority extended to all the women, children, and other dependents in the household. Wyatt's paternalism extended to his twenty-four-year-old farmhand Porter Hensley, because Porter was part of the household as well as a first cousin to his wife Louisa. Wyatt no doubt felt aggrieved when Porter was put in a chain gang and sent to Little Rock.

Later, Wyatt would learn that Porter was given a harsh choice when he arrived in the state capital: either he could await trial for treason and face execution by firing squad, or he could accept a governor's pardon and immediately enlist in the Confederate army. Porter chose enlistment. The other five Richland men who were named in the petition did the same. The group included two old men, Gilmore Smith who was fifty, and John Christy who was fifty-eight. Most of the Peace Society members who were caught up in the dragnet of November and December 1861 enlisted in the 1st Battalion of Arkansas Infantry, Company K. Their company was nicknamed the "Rector Guards" after their putative savior, Governor Rector. Despite their governor's pardons, they were marked men. Most of them deserted when they got the chance. Porter Hensley and numerous others deserted in the Battle of Shiloh. Twenty-one men in this group made their way back to Searcy County. Wyatt secretly offered one of these fugitives, one John Morris, his horse so that he could ride to Springfield, Missouri, to enlist in the Union army.

Wyatt's paternalism covered not only his farmhand Porter but also his slave Parthenia. In his view, the slave girl whom he had raised from the age of five was part of his household, therefore, she was part of his extended family. He was Parthenia's master, but through his benevolent paternalism he was a kindly and righteous master to her—or so he told himself. How Wyatt used his position of superiority to justify raping Parthenia cannot be understood, but somehow he and his wife worked out their feelings about it afterwards, and Parthenia endured it. Now Wyatt confronted the most profound consequence of his act of rape—now he had charge of Parthenia's first child. He returned from the militia to an even busier domestic life than before. Besides an eleven-year-old daughter, a seven-year-old son, and five-year-old twins, he now had two infant offspring by different mothers in the home. Parthenia had borne him a son, and his wife Louisa had delivered another daughter that year as well.

The modern mind boggles at this tangle of relationships. How did Billy and Louisa Wyatt and the enslaved Parthenia accommodate themselves to the situation? How did Parthenia navigate her way through the twin shoals of her mistress being a blood sibling and her master being the father of her child? How did Wyatt feel about his own son by Parthenia being born into slavery? How did he feel about fighting in a war over slavery with his own family so entangled in it?

Another known fact about the home life of Billy Wyatt adds yet another dimension to this conflicted, complicated man. Around this time, Wyatt was out riding when he came upon a nine-year-old white boy walking the road alone. Not knowing the boy, Wyatt asked who he was and where he came from. The boy answered that his name was George Wells and he came from North Carolina. It turned out the boy's family had all been murdered by brigands in the early months of the war. The boy had managed to elude the brigands, but he could not fend for himself on the farm after everyone else had been killed, so he had set out walking. His remarkable solo trek had brought him some eight hundred miles all the way to Searcy County, Arkansas, and he was looking for a new family to take care of him. Wyatt put the boy on his horse and took him home. George Wells would live with the Wyatts until he was a grown man and would live the rest of his life in Richland, eventually marrying and raising a large family. He would die in 1942 at age eighty-nine or ninety. His grave is in the Love Cemetery across the Buffalo River from Richland.

Chapter 6

Arkansas Invaded

For Confederate Arkansans, the threat of invasion by the Union hinged on what happened in the border state of Missouri. On the map of free states and slave states in 1860, Missouri covered Arkansas like a protective shield. With a white population three times that of Arkansas, it would present a strong line of defense for the Confederacy in the Trans-Mississippi West—*if* that border slave state would stand with the Confederate South. Arkansas secessionists were very disappointed, therefore, when Missouri did not secede from the Union as their state did. They were doubly disappointed when Missouri Unionists, with a vital assist from Federal troops, wrested control of the Missouri state capital from secessionists. After the Union's bold opening move in Missouri, most of that state's militia defected to the Confederate cause. The ragtag army of Missouri militiamen, most of whom were equipped only with old muskets or shotguns, retreated to the southwest corner of Missouri to regroup. There the Rebel force came under the command of Major General Sterling Price, a former Missouri governor. By midsummer 1861, a Federal army under Brigadier General Nathaniel Lyon marched against Price's Rebel army with the aim of driving it completely out of Missouri. However, the badly outnumbered Rebels checked the Federal advance at the Battle of Wilson's Creek on August 10, 1861. After this stunning Rebel victory, it seemed the Confederacy might win control of Missouri after all.

Price tried to retake the initiative, but he needed more men. The Fourteenth Arkansas Infantry Regiment—the unit that took the Greenhaw and Robertson boys—was formed shortly before the Battle of

Wilson's Creek and trained at Camp Adams near Yellville through the remaining summer and fall as it waited to be properly equipped with guns and ammo. Secessionist Missourians hoped to liberate their state with the help of troops raised in Arkansas, but they never got the chance.

In January 1862, Brigadier General Samuel R. Curtis took command of the Federal army in Missouri and with a force of 12,000 men moved against the much smaller Rebel army under Price, aiming once again to secure the state of Missouri for the Union. Price retreated into northwest Arkansas, the Federals pursued, and the opposing armies skirmished at Big Sugar Creek on February 16. Price retreated farther southward, ruthlessly burning stores and warehouses in Fayetteville before leaving the Arkansas town to its Northern occupiers.

When word of the Federal advance into Arkansas reached President Davis in Richmond, Virginia, the Confederate leader formed a new Trans-Mississippi Department and appointed Major General Earl Van Dorn to assume overall command there. Van Dorn hurried west and made his initial headquarters at Jacksonport, Arkansas, a steamboat landing on the White River about one hundred miles east of Richland, where he gathered his forces preparatory to moving against the Federal army now based outside Fayetteville.

While in Jacksonport in February, Van Dorn delivered a message to the people of Arkansas. "The enemy has invaded your State," the general wrote in his proclamation. "His army is powerful, disciplined, flushed with success, and he comes with hatred in his heart. He seeks to subjugate your soil—to desolate your homes and to wrest from you and degrade all you hold dearest in life."

Shortly thereafter, Van Dorn marched his army to northwest Arkansas and engaged the enemy in the biggest battle fought in the Trans-Mississippi West, the Battle of Pea Ridge, March 6–8, 1862. The Union position held, and Van Dorn retreated from the field ignominiously with his Rebel army in tatters. Not only did the Confederate general fail in his mission to drive the invader out of Arkansas, but the defeat also left Arkansas in even greater peril than before the start of the Pea

Ridge campaign. The Confederate leadership ordered Van Dorn to evacuate all his forces from Arkansas to shore up Confederate defenses in west Tennessee.

One might ask how much the Greenhaw family and the rest of the people of Richland knew about troop movements at this crucial juncture of the war in the Trans-Mississippi West. One could answer that they did not know nearly enough. Richland's information about the opposing armies was sparse, untrustworthy, and agonizingly slow to arrive. The people of Richland lived in a fog of war. The Ozark farmers' communications from the outside had not been robust to begin with, and when the communications network broke down in the early stage of the war the lack of information created anxiety and confusion. Over time, the isolation from the outside bred a mistrust of all war news and a cynical view of their new national government in faraway Richmond, Virginia.

Van Dorn's message to the people of Arkansas at the start of the Pea Ridge campaign may be used to illustrate this weak communications system. The general put his remarks on paper and sent them by courier from Jacksonport to Little Rock to be printed in the state's leading newspapers. The courier rode for two days to the state capital. Despite the message's gravity, it did not reach the editor of the *Arkansas True Democrat* in time to be printed in that week's edition of the paper. The general's February 24 message sat for another week and was finally printed in the March 6 newspaper. Then, copies of the *Arkansas True Democrat* went by postal carrier from Little Rock to the post office at Richland, a journey of several more days. By the time the people of Richland read Van Dorn's message in the newspaper it was more than two weeks old. During that period, Van Dorn had gathered an army, marched to northwest Arkansas, and engaged the enemy in the major battle at Pea Ridge. Richland's first news of the Battle of Pea Ridge came not from an official source but by way of wild rumors flying from farm to farm as well as by deserters returning home with their jaded accounts of what had happened. (John Cole was one such deserter; wounded in the battle, he walked out of the hospital at Dover and finally reached Richland around the end of April.) So, by the time the people of Richland read Van Dorn's rallying call in the newspaper, they had learned from returning soldiers and the passing of rumors that Van Dorn's army had already met the enemy and suffered a great defeat.

To be sure, most long-distance communications in Civil War America traveled at much greater speed. News and vital communications could be turned into Morse code and sent by telegraph wire across thousands of miles in minutes. But Arkansas lay at the western edge of the telegraph network. The first telegraph connection in the state was completed from St. Louis to Fayetteville, Van Buren, and Fort Smith only in the summer of 1860. A second line was strung from Memphis to Little Rock just before secession in March 1861, and another was installed from Little Rock southeastward to Pine Bluff shortly after secession. But this would be the maximum extent of the state's telegraph system through the end of the war, and once Federal armies entered the state, both sides engaged in cutting the wires to hinder the enemy's communications.

Besides a dearth of telegraph wires, Arkansas had only a primitive transportation system. It had few good stage roads for transporting mail. The Overland Mail Company had a stage road from St. Louis to California that went through the northwest corner of Arkansas through Fayetteville, Van Buren, and Fort Smith. The same company operated a branch line from Memphis to Little Rock and from Little Rock on up the Arkansas River valley to Fort Smith. The stagecoach routes were established just a couple years before the telegraph lines. Before the establishment of the stagecoach routes, most mail was carried by sternwheeler steamboat up the Arkansas and White rivers. The speed of river communication varied with the strength of the river current. During times of low water, river navigation in central Arkansas would slow up and practically cease.

The other vital components of the state's communication network were newspapers and the postal service. In frontier Arkansas, newspapers struggled to survive. The state had no dailies, just weeklies. Many of those weeklies were practically a one-man show, a single fellow serving as editor, reporter, business manager, and printer. When this person enlisted in the army, the newspaper disappeared. Most of Arkansas's newspapers blinked out in the first year of the war. A critical shortage of newsprint soon stifled the operations of the state's few larger newspapers.

Prior to the Civil War, the United States Postal Service played a vital role in sustaining the newspaper industry by providing free mail delivery of newspapers between editors. Exchange of newspapers between editors was vital because much of what newspapers printed in those days was "copy" from other newspapers. Indeed, newspapers in the antebellum South derived much of their copy from the bigger, better-staffed newspapers in the North. An estimated nine-tenths of newspaper readers in 1860 lived in the North, and the inferior Southern press reflected the disproportionately small Southern readership. Before the Civil War, Richland farmers got most of their news by way of the out-of-state *Memphis Daily Appeal* or *St. Louis Republican*, which in turn printed copy from the *New York Herald* and other Northern papers.

The United States Postal Service aided the newspaper industry by subsidizing the distribution of newspapers to rural post offices. Long before the Civil War, the US government recognized the importance of both a free press and a good postal system for creating an informed public and successful democracy. The Confederacy established its own postal service in February 1861 and systematically took over the handling of mail in Federal post offices four months later. While the Confederate Postal Department was intended to function at lower cost to the public treasury than its US counterpart, in reality it barely functioned at all. Postal routes were put up for bid, and when bidders could not be found the routes were simply abandoned. Even main postal routes suffered stoppages when Federal armies began to occupy big swaths of Confederate territory.

The Confederate Postal Department finally got around to advertising postal routes in northwest Arkansas in January 1862. Route 360, which included the post office in Richland, covered a round-trip distance of eighty-two miles to be run once a week. If a brave soul was found to take on that route, the mail run must have been short-lived for it became too dangerous, and Richland's post office was defunct for the remainder of the war.

Wherever the postal system collapsed, as it did in northwest Arkansas, that left only couriers to carry military dispatches and private messengers to carry personal letters. Even Confederate soldiers' letters home had to travel by private means. Whenever a soldier went home on furlough, he would be burdened with delivering letters for his comrades along the way. Civilian visitors to camp were likewise pressed into service as unpaid couriers. Southerners referred to these irregular mail agencies as the "grapevine telegraph."

When the people of northwest Arkansas learned about the Confederate defeat at the Battle of Pea Ridge and the Confederate army's subsequent evacuation order, they were frightened and desperate to get more information. Mollie would later allude in her autobiography to her people's profound isolation from war news around this time. Early press reports about the battle were misleading, some of them even claiming that the battle had been won by the Confederates. The *Arkansas True Democrat* reported ominously on a "great battle" in which many Rebel officers had been killed, wounded, or taken prisoner. But it noted that the news came from the North and therefore could not be trusted. It added further that the Rebel soldiers, though poorly armed, had fought like demons. As late as March 17, more than a week after the battle, the *Memphis Daily Appeal* printed the false story that Generals Curtis and Sigel, the first and second in command of the Union army, had both been killed. The truth of the matter was that two Confederate generals, McCulloch and McIntosh, had been killed within minutes of each other, both in plain view of their troops, which had led to the collapse of one wing of the Confederate attack.

One newspaper or another must have made its way to Richland and the Greenhaw place in March or April 1862. The newspaper reporting on the Battle of Pea Ridge would have added to Mollie's and Usley's concern about the safety of the two Greenhaw boys, James and William. Mollie later wrote: "We had no way of finding out who was killed and who survived this first engagement between our belligerent forces." It made them "frantic," she recalled. Many more weeks would pass before the family learned that the boys had fought at Pea Ridge and survived.

When Van Dorn marched his army back across Arkansas to redeploy in west Tennessee, many Arkansas men deserted. Some of them declared that if the Confederate government would not defend Arkansas, then they did not see the point in fighting for the Confederacy. They had volunteered to defend their homeland. If their regiment left Arkansas soil, they reasoned, then the army no longer had any claim on them. Some who deserted went back to their farms to help with spring planting. Others went off with the intention to join a home guard and fight the Yankees in Arkansas. The Greenhaw brothers were split over the matter. James Jr. vowed to remain with the Confederate army. His younger brother William aimed to quit, go home, and sign up with another Arkansas unit.

Arkansas's political leaders echoed the dismay of the Arkansas soldiers who were now deserting in droves. They appealed to President Davis, protesting General Lee's order to Van Dorn and Van Dorn's ruthless determination to withdraw every last Confederate soldier from the state. Governor Rector threatened President Davis that if Arkansas did not receive military support from the east then his state might secede from the Confederacy and make a separate peace.

In the first week of May, the Federal army under General Curtis reentered Arkansas in the northeast and, being unopposed, briskly marched south as far as Batesville. From there, Curtis threatened to march on the state capital. The Confederates appointed a new commander in the Trans-Mississippi West, Major General Thomas Hindman, to improvise a defense of Little Rock. Hindman, without a regular army to speak of, called on Arkansans to form small "companies" of "partisan rangers" and harry the Federal army with hit-and-run attacks. The partisan rangers were guerrilla fighters by another name. Both the governor and the Confederate government in Richmond supported this grave development. Several guerrilla bands quickly formed, drawing recruits from the many deserters who had just broken away from Van Dorn's army. The guerrilla bands went after Union stragglers, Union scouts, the enemy's supply train—anyone who could be "bushwhacked" without engaging the enemy's main force. The effort succeeded; General Curtis pulled up short of the capital, wary of outrunning his supply lines or losing more men to the hit-and-run guerrilla attacks. At the end of May, Curtis fell back to Batesville to consolidate his position.

Meanwhile, before the emergency had passed, Hindman initiated a call-up of conscripts and more volunteers. Enrolling officers fanned out into the countryside to sign up young men for the army. The statewide effort to raise fresh recruits reached the Richland Valley on May 25, 1862.

Chapter 7

On the Mustering Ground

MOLLIE RELATED IN HER AUTOBIOGRAPHY THAT SHE WENT TO THE "muster place to do what I could do to encourage our men folks to espouse the cause that seemed sacred to us all." From military enrollment records we know that the muster she referred to occurred in Richland on May 25, 1862—the first of just two times in the war that troops were mustered there. In that remote setting, the mustering ground would have been a humble affair. If it met the simplest standard for a muster, the company of recruiters would have consisted of an enrolling officer and two boys with fife and drum. (Mollie mentioned hearing music.) One may imagine this trio of recruiters in uniform, their horses tethered nearby, maybe a field desk placed in a clearing and a flagpole planted in the ground next to it. In all likelihood, the recruiters placed themselves near Richland's post office and school. The mustering ground would not have presented much of a military display, but it was nonetheless notable as the first Confederate muster at that place, not counting the call-up of the state militia. Previous call-ups for Confederate volunteers had been made at larger centers like Yellville and Burrowsville. When the enrolling officer came to Richland on that day in 1862, a few dozen residents gathered to show support, see who was there to sign up, and cheer the boys as they went off to war. Among the assembled was the young Mollie Brumley.

Mollie went to the mustering ground with a dawning feeling of Southern patriotism. The fourteen-year-old now believed it was her duty, as a Southerner entering upon womanhood, to do her part for the war. Together with other females in the valley, Mollie had absorbed the notion that it was the duty of her sex to encourage the menfolk to sign up and fight.

Southern women wanted to contribute to the war effort in whatever ways they could. Confined for the most part to their domestic roles of homemaker and helpmate, they looked for activities around the home that could provide help to the boys at the fighting fronts. Southern women knitted socks for the army. They carded and spun yards and yards of jean cloth for the manufacture of military uniforms. The *Arkansas True Democrat* reported a "record of industry" on these myriad activities, sometimes highlighting individuals such as Mrs. Margaret Engles, a young widow of Independence County, who produced 288 yards of plaid cotton, plaid linsey, and woolen jeans over a five-month period. Farmer-women like Mollie might aspire to producing extra food for the army. (Soon enough, foraging parties would requisition those surpluses whether the farmer-women liked it or not.) Middle-class townswomen had more diverse opportunities to contribute to the war effort. They organized fundraising musical events, worked in hospitals, and stepped into store clerking jobs vacated by boys who went into the army. Mollie probably read about those women's activities in the newspapers in the early stage of the war.

Mollie's Uncle Jim and Aunt Usley did not accompany their precocious niece to the mustering ground but stayed home. As they had already given their older two sons to the Confederate army nine months earlier, that was enough for one family. They needed their younger two sons, Green Berry and Calvin, to stay on the farm.

Green Berry and Calvin's decision not to enlist that day was significant. The previous month, the Confederate Congress passed the Confederacy's first conscription act. By law, Green Berry and Calvin were supposed to sign up. Their staying home was an act of draft resistance. While Mollie aspired to notions of female sacrifice and Southern patriotism, her two male cousins showed a more ambivalent attitude toward the Confederate cause.

As Mollie found herself at the mustering ground on her own, unchaperoned, she stood toward the back of the small crowd at first, feeling less than a full-fledged woman and momentarily uncertain about her presence at that function. Then the fifer and drummer began to play "Dixie," and everyone around her began to thrill to the music. Swept up by the fife's jubilant notes, Mollie felt her heartbeat quicken. She knew the lyrics to the popular song:

> Well, I wish I was in the land of cotton
> Old times there are not forgotten
> Look away, look away, look away, Dixie land
> In Dixie's Land, where I was born in
> Early on one frosty mornin'
> Look away, look away, look away, Dixie land
>
> And I wish I was in Dixie, hooray! Hooray!
> In Dixie's land I'll take my stand
> To live and die in Dixie
> Away, away, away down south in Dixie
> Away, away, away down south in Dixie

On an impulse, Mollie pushed her way to the front of the crowd, anxious to see if her beau, Valentine Williams, stood among the small group of recruits.

When the song ended, nine men and boys stepped forward and formed a ragged line in front of the enrolling officer. There among the nine stood Valentine. His tousled dark hair and heavy eyebrows were a familiar sight, but he looked small. He was flanked by his brothers Benjamin and Hardin. The oldest among this group of recruits was James Goats, son of the millowner, age thirty-four. The youngest was John Cole—now recovered from his wound at Pea Ridge and reenlisting.

No sooner had these nine formed a line when several of them were joined by their wives or sweethearts. Mollie was swept forward with the other women in a surge of adoration. She greeted Valentine with a show of affection like nothing that had passed between them before. He responded in kind. Before this moment they had scarcely conversed, their eyes having done most of their talking. She knew his eyes. In the penetrating look he gave her, and under the pressure of circumstance, Mollie felt they had an understanding. Now he began to whisper in her ear. In hurried phrases he declared that he loved her, that he wanted to be with her, that it filled him with sorrow and regret to be telling her these things only then as he was about to depart on his state's bidding.

Mollie fought back tears as she pressed herself into his chest. Love and war, how they conspired! Life was rushing on her, sweeping her up. Their moment on the mustering ground, so unexpected and transcendent, carried an "earnestness and sincerity," that gave it "a sanctity of religion," she later wrote.

But even in that exquisite moment, a horrid picture of her lover in death suddenly rose up in her fervid imagination. She saw him, so handsome and vital in her arms right then, lying dead on a battlefield a few months hence. Trying to shoo this phantom from her mind, she became aware of crying and snuffling around her. She must not weep, Mollie told herself sternly. She wanted to show her soldier boy her own strength of heart—at least give him that.

Valentine put his arms firmly around her waist and impressed upon her lips a "genuine lover's kiss."

"Heaven bless you," he said to her as they parted.

After the boys marched away, Mollie was desolated.

In the days following, she performed her various chores around the farm in a stupor. "It seemed," she would later write, "that the light of day had fled and that I was wandering in the mazes of a starless night." The terrible apparition of Valentine in death, or in his dying moments, haunted her in her sleep. She would see him lying on blood-spattered ground covered in wounds and crying out for water. She would awaken from her gory nightmare drenched in sweat.

In desperation, she confided the dear secret of her betrothal to her younger cousin Mary. Mollie regarded Mary as her best friend. Yet the two years of age difference between them now opened up like a chasm. When she relayed to Mary the sacred words that had passed between her and Valentine, Mary seemed unimpressed. Mollie's intimate exchange on the mustering ground did not carry the same weight in the retelling. Now she worried to herself: maybe Valentine's sacred words to her were no seal at all, but only a girlish fantasy.

Feeling a need for an older person's counsel, Mollie told her aunt what had happened between her and Valentine. Aunt Usley assured Mollie that their "understanding" amounted to an engagement. After that, Mollie perceived a change in her status. She felt she had become part of a sisterhood—a somber, adult sisterhood. While Aunt Usley endured unremitting anxiety over her sons, the fourteen-year-old Mollie bore her own heavy burden of anxiety and torment as she began praying every night for her fiancé.

~

Confederate Arkansas faced its moment of extreme crisis in that summer of 1862. Although Confederate guerrilla attacks halted the Federal advance on the state capital, the Federal army remained at Batesville, threatening to renew its offensive at any time. Major General Thomas Hindman, the newly appointed commander of Confederate forces in the Trans-Mississippi West, declared martial law in Arkansas and urged rapid mobilization of new regiments. Hindman established recruiting districts across the whole state and appointed a commander and enrolling officer for each one. He authorized the commanders and enrolling officers to purchase or impress arms, ammunition, and necessary supplies within their district, and to coordinate these actions with the quartermasters and commissaries. He instructed them to report in detail upon agricultural and mineral resources in their area, that they might be levied for military use. The requisitioning of war materiel soon expanded to include wagons, harnesses, leather, and shoes. Farmers in northwest Arkansas bristled as the state laid its hand on their crops, livestock, and personal property.

It is unclear how much Mollie knew about these developments or what she thought about them. In her autobiography, she claimed to be somewhat naïve to the situation. "Being reared in the seclusion and solitudes of the mountain fastnesses remote from the commercial centers of our state and nation, I had no conception of the extent of our national resources or the vast preparations for war being made by the belligerent sections," she would later write. In Richland she saw the foraging parties come and go at the Greenhaw place and other farms, and at least through the spring of 1862 she thought that Richland farmers responded "cheerfully" to each new request by the Rebel army for a share of the farmers' food reserves. But that summer Mollie probably heard a growing chorus of farmers' complaints as the foraging parties got more demanding and surlier.

Foraging parties in the first year of the war were polite and deferential. Acting according to custom, the soldiers offered to swap work for the food they requisitioned. They might chop wood or repair a rail fence by way of compensation. If the farmer pled that he had nothing to spare, then the soldiers would honor the plea and go on to the next farm. By the summer of 1862, those niceties began to disappear. Soldiers and farmers started to treat one another as adversaries.

Mollie may have recognized a change in the character and tone of the soldiers who came to the Greenhaw place as the all-volunteer army of 1861 faded away and an army of conscripts took its place. The volunteer enlistments in 1861 were for twelve months of service. When those twelve-month enlistments expired, the soldiers were required under the conscription act to re-enlist for two more years. Fresh conscripts, meanwhile, enlisted for three years. The conscript army that began to take shape in 1862 did not have the elan of the volunteer army of 1861. Northwest Arkansas's farmers noted the difference.

Chapter 8

A Letter from Valentine

Two months after Valentine Williams joined the Confederate army, he sent Mollie a letter. He wrote to her when his regiment was camped near Burrowsville during one week in July. Being so close to home, he took a chance in sending Mollie a message in the care of a soldier who was going to Richland with a foraging party to gather up supplies for the regiment. Valentine's effort to communicate with Mollie succeeded. This letter was Valentine's first attempt at writing to Mollie. It may have been his last attempt, too, as she only received the one missive from him.

Valentine only had time to write his sweetheart a few lines. He found that he was no bard, but he did manage in a humble way to express tender feelings and to affirm that the words of endearment that had passed between them on the mustering ground meant a great deal.

Over in Richland, the foraging party from Valentine's regiment soon brought a wagon up to the Greenhaw place. Mollie was helping her family load the wagon with corn and other supplies when one of the soldiers stepped up to her and asked if she was Miss Brumley. Mollie nodded, and the man handed her a letter. Mollie looked dumbly at the crinkled, soiled paper in her hand. She felt a rush of emotion. Her throat tightened and she could barely choke out a single word of thanks. She turned and fled, anxious to get away from prying eyes and to have the precious letter all to herself.

In private, she carefully unfolded the paper and read. Much to her relief, the brief message affirmed Valentine's bonds of affection. She reread the few lines, studied her lover's script, kissed the words, and pressed the paper to her chest.

Soon she heard the clanking and creaking of the Confederate wagon moving off. There was no time to send a reply. If Mollie had known that this encounter with the foraging party was to be her last chance to get a letter back to Valentine then she might have hastened to send a reply. But she let the moment pass, unaware that the postal system in the Arkansas Ozarks would soon disappear. She would have no more opportunity to get a letter to her lover even by private messenger, and the movements of Valentine's regiment would become unknown to her. Mollie would receive nothing more from him and would learn almost nothing about his whereabouts or wellbeing or ultimate fate until the war ended.

~

Valentine had to scramble when the opportunity to write a letter to Mollie presented itself. Paper, pen, and ink had all become scarce commodities in the Rebel army by this point in the war. The soldiers scrounged for scraps of paper and hoarded their supply whenever they had any. If they received a letter from home, they might use the same sheets of paper to scribble a reply between the lines or in the margins. If they ever got desperate enough to purchase a quire of paper or a bundle of envelopes from the sutler, the cost of the items would set them back a month's pay almost. Pen and ink were hard to come by as well. Soldiers employed a variety of homemade substitutes. Valentine borrowed a quill and a small quantity of red pokeberry juice to write his short letter. The pokeberry juice made his script blotchy. He had to form each alphabet letter with care and gently blow on it so the juice would not run on the page. As Mollie reread his letter over and over, she came to imagine that he had pricked himself and penned it with his own blood.

There was so much more that Valentine wanted to relate but there was no time to put it in writing. Valentine's Company D had formed three months earlier at Washington Barracks in Carroll County, so most of the men in his company came from there. Their captain, Beal Gaither Jr., came from a farm on Crooked Creek. Gaither was twenty-seven years old and just married. He was a congenial fellow, and the men liked him. The commander of the regiment was a man named Shaler who was not so well liked. Against convention, Colonel Shaler had been appointed by the commanding officer in Arkansas rather than elected by the men of the regiment, and the men of the regiment were unhappy about that. Colonel Shaler came from Missouri and had previously served in the Missouri Home Guard. To Valentine and his fellows, it seemed that this colonel talked too much of taking the fight back to Missouri. They concluded that he cared more about liberating his home state than he did about defending their state of Arkansas. Another mark against him: some of the men reckoned he was a Catholic.

After Valentine left Richland and mustered in Yellville, he and his fellows were assigned to Company D, which trained with a handful of other companies at Yellville for four weeks. They waited for more recruits to come in so the companies could build up to the requisite strength to form a regiment. Through most of June, Valentine's company went through basic training at a big field on the edge of the town. Their camp consisted of long rows of "A"-shaped tents and a parade ground. Valentine shared his tent with a few other privates and cooked most of his meals with them. So far, he could not complain about the food. Their rations included beef, flour, corn meal, peas, sugar, salt, and rye coffee. Each tent group was also given a supply of candles and soap. They learned how to cook their own meals and wash their own clothes. Most of the boys wore homespun they brought from home. Only the officers wore Confederate grey uniforms. Valentine's company drilled on the parade ground several times each day, one section at a time, learning how to march and follow commands. They were still awaiting army-issue rifles from the east, but a few of the boys carried their own squirrel rifles or shotguns from home.

It was a two-day march from Yellville to their present encampment near Burrowsville. Some of the boys had their own horses, so they got to ride while the rest of the men walked. They were a ragtag army. Valentine, on foot, carried a haversack, bedroll, and cook kit, but he had no gun yet. He was never so hot and tired as when they got to Burrowsville.

Their camp was a little way past the town where the Richland-to-Burrowsville Road met Bear Creek. There was a fine spring at that place where cold, clear water came gushing out of the hillside. The spring water was conveyed in troughs to a convenient point where a person could hold up a pail-size vessel and fill it in a few seconds. As soon as they arrived at that place the officers and soldiers formed a line so they could replenish their canteens and water their horses. It was nearly dark when they all got to sleep that night.

Soon after reaching Burrowsville, Valentine's regiment moved out to challenge the Yankees in Batesville. His regiment then had its first bit of excitement. A scouting party of about thirty men ran into a Yankee cavalry detachment and got into a brief skirmish. Shots were fired but no one was hurt. Details of the skirmish passed quickly from man to man through the regiment. The surprise encounter disclosed the fact that more Yankee troops were moving southward out of Missouri to reinforce the Yankee army at Batesville. The Twenty-seventh Arkansas fell back to a place on the White River by the name of Mount Olive. After a short time at that outpost, it pulled back farther to Burrowsville to replenish. It was soon after that when Valentine learned that a foraging party was going over Point Peter Mountain to Richland, which precipitated his hurried missive to Mollie.

Not long after Valentine wrote his letter, he had more news he would have liked to share with Mollie. On August 1, a contingent of new recruits transferred into his company. Among the contingent were none other than Mollie's cousins Calvin and Green Berry Greenhaw. They had responded to a second call for recruits in Richland a few weeks after the first call-up.

In the fall, the Twenty-seventh Arkansas Infantry Regiment was posted to Camp Shaver in the town of Pocahontas to undergo more training with several other new Arkansas regiments. There were several thousand men there. In October, an outbreak of measles ripped through the large encampment. Hundreds of men died and were buried in a crude cemetery at the edge of the camp. Among the victims was nineteen-year-old Calvin Greenhaw. The measles outbreak also took the life of James Goats, the older fellow who had signed up when Valentine did.

~

Valentine befriended a fellow in the Twenty-seventh by the name of Silas Turnbo. The name will be familiar to some readers, as he was an inveterate storyteller who later in life published several books of collected stories about Civil War times and pioneer days in the Ozarks. Turnbo kept a diary during the three years he was in the Twenty-seventh Arkansas Infantry Regiment. The diary was lost in a fire after the war, but the loss did not stop him from writing a history of the regiment from memory, his first published writing. It is only through Turnbo's description of his friend Valentine in the regimental history that we know what ultimately happened to Valentine in the war.

Silas Turnbo and Valentine Williams hit it off during their time in the same regiment, probably in part because they shared a penchant for storytelling. Both young men sprinkled their stories with humor, but they each had their own distinctive style of humor. Whereas Turnbo used a sly, gentle humor to poke fun at human nature, Valentine turned all of his wit on himself, employing a mix of false modesty and braggadocio to create an image of an unserious character who, in spite of himself, had some serious things to say. It was a manner of storytelling that enabled Valentine to reveal a little of himself and conceal much more. One wonders if Valentine used humor to mask fear or disillusionment. There are only hints of either one in the few stories that survive.

Valentine teased his fellows with his oft-repeated claim that he had had a dream that when the war was over he would make himself a fortune. But when his fellows asked for details, Valentine would wag his head, grinning: that was secret. Many times, as the men prepared to fight the enemy, Valentine reminded them, "I want to live to get home and see the fulfillment of my dream." They would press him again to divulge more about this vaunted dream of his, and he would still refuse. "He would shut one eye, laugh, and say, 'watch me make that Yankee yonder turn up his toes.'"

Valentine spoke blithely about his reasons for joining the Confederate army, saying that he thought "it would be quite a lot of fun to be out with a number of brave, jolly boys and have a good time, and of course run everybody off that pretended to oppose us."

Only once did the nonchalant character in Valentine's tales ever admit to being afraid to die. The fearful moment occurred in the heat of battle when his company was ordered to make a third charge on a stubborn Yankee position on a hill. Several of his comrades already lay dead or dying on the slope down which his company had just retreated. With a bullet wound in his left shoulder, Valentine felt the fight running out of him. In that deadliest of moments, he later told his listeners, his fighting spirit briefly faltered; he knew not whether he could obey his officer's command to charge. "I had enough of the experience of war, so I thought I would pray a little." Searching his mind for a suitable verse from the Bible, what came to him was this: *You shall be regenerated and born again.* "If I am to be born again," he thought, "maybe I have just this one last charge left in me after all." And then came an afterthought. . . . He prayed aloud: "Please, Mr. Lord, let me be a girl next time." And so braced up, he got to his feet and charged.

Chapter 9

The War Closes In

WHEN CONFEDERATE AUTHORITIES CALLED FORTH GUERRILLAS TO fight off the invading Union army, they summoned an evil genie that was to loom over northwest Arkansas for the duration of the war. The terrible reality of guerrilla warfare took only a short time to manifest itself. During the summer of 1862, the new guerrilla bands steadily grew more numerous and aggressive in the demands they made on the populace. At first they visited farms to request food, just as the army's foraging parties did. Then they began to demand other kinds of assistance: guns, ammunition, blankets, money. Their military requisitioning degenerated into thievery. All too quickly, the guerrilla war came home to the people.

When the Union army came into northwest Arkansas, it emboldened Unionists to come out of hiding and form their own "home guards" for home defense. Unionist home guards quickly went over to the offensive in a kind of antiguerrilla campaign. In so doing, they became nearly indistinguishable from the pro-Confederate guerrillas they were fighting. By late 1862, the Arkansas Ozarks became a no-man's-land in which both Rebel and Unionist guerrilla bands marauded. On rare occasions, guerrilla bands on opposing sides tangled with one another in a straight-up fight, but that was not their preferred style. Generally, they employed tactics of ambush, hit-and-run attack, or overwhelming force—such as swarming a few enemy stragglers and wiping them out—in order to hurt the enemy while they survived to fight another day.

With both sides engaged in guerrilla warfare, the Ozarks became a lethal environment for everyone. Confederate guerrillas looked to Confederate sympathizers to spy for them and provide intelligence about enemy movements. Unionist guerrillas expected Union sympathizers to do the same for them. When guerrilla units were betrayed to the enemy, reprisals against the civilian population followed.

Rules of war got muddied or cast aside in this kind of conflict. Some Unionist guerrilla fighters wore Union soldiers' uniforms on the pretext that they were Union army auxiliaries. Most Confederate guerrilla units dressed in Union uniforms as well so that they could operate more stealthily in Union occupied areas. To Union officers, that made the Rebel guerrillas no different than spies. They were liable to be shot for wearing the military uniform. Meanwhile, guerrillas' treatment of prisoners varied widely. Some guerrilla fighters disarmed their prisoners and then released them. Others took to executing them.

At first, the pro-Confederate guerrilla bands answered to Confederate military authorities and operated under terms allowed by the Partisan Rangers Act, which the Confederate Congress passed in April 1862. But as time went on, most guerrilla leaders stopped taking direction from Confederate officers and instead acted on their own account. The genie was out of the bottle.

Some historians point out that Confederate authorities did not have to summon guerrillas like a genie in the summer of 1862, because guerrillas were already present in the land. Those historians remind us that guerrilla war had already broken out in the western borderlands a half a decade before the start of the Civil War. It is true that some of the hardened guerrilla leaders who fought in northwest Arkansas from 1862 to 1865 cut their teeth in Bleeding Kansas before the war. But in Mollie's view, the Civil War's descent into barbarism began at this moment, a little over one year into the war. And because we are following the war in northwest Arkansas through Mollie's story, we may say that her view of the guerrilla war's emergence is probably pretty accurate for the area around Richland.

Some historians say that if the Confederate government is held to account for sanctioning guerrilla warfare in the year 1862, then in fairness it must be said that in the same year, Federal authorities took actions that tended to bring the war closer to the civilian population. Federal authorities sought to reassert "rules of war" that would outlaw the pro-Confederate guerrilla bands. When Federal officers declared that pro-Confederate guerrillas would be treated as brigands and given no quarter, it marked a turn toward "hard war." The Federal leaders' embrace of hard war would culminate with the scorched-earth invasion of Georgia in 1864 and other military actions that were ultimately aimed at breaking the will of the pro-Confederate South. But all this lay far beyond the bounds of Mollie's experience. "Hard war" is not a term that Mollie or her contemporaries would have recognized. She barely understood the term "guerrilla," perceiving these new enemy combatants as being more akin to outlaws, robbers, and brigands.

In the Ozarks, Confederate guerrilla bands came to be known as "bushwhackers," a term once applied to highwaymen who literally hid in the bushes and whacked their victims as they rode by. Unionist guerrilla bands came to be called "jayhawkers," a term previously used in Bleeding Kansas in the 1850s to describe abolitionist-led bands who terrorized the proslavery population in Kansas and Missouri. The ultimate origin of the term jayhawkers is not definitively known; some trace it to the California 49ers and others even farther back to the Texas Revolution of 1835–36. In the Ozarks, the terms connoted opposite partisan leanings for guerrilla groups that were otherwise virtually the same.

The worst part of guerrilla warfare was that it provided cover for banditry. If some guerrilla bands acted on genuine motives of home defense, others only made a thin pretense of it while they mostly robbed and killed for plunder or revenge. As guerrilla warfare was inherently barbarous, there was no clear line between guerrillas and outlaws. There was only the widely held view that the numerous bands of bushwhackers and jayhawkers grew more predatory as the war went on.

Guerrilla warfare began to impact the people of Richland around the time that Mollie received her letter from Valentine. Mollie did not record her own first encounter with guerrillas. Nor did she recount the first time the Greenhaw family was victimized. She only recalled that the scourge began around the time she heard from Valentine in July 1862 and that two guerrilla bands quickly gained notoriety, one led by a lowlife known as "Dog-Eyed Bill" and the other by a badman called "Batterhead Sam." She did not indicate whose side they were on; in her recollection it was beside the point because the men were no better than outlaws. Writing of this scourge forty years later, she still had white-hot feelings about it. "The men engaged in this murderous and outrageous wing of the service belonged to both the Union and Confederate factions and were devoid of all honesty and every sense of justice and patriotism," she wrote. "It has been said that the war made thieves, murderers and prostitutes. This I deny. It only afforded such persons an opportunity to show their real characters. They were thieves, murderers and prostitutes before the war and were held within lawful bounds by the restraints of society; the war removed these restraints and enabled them to act out their true natures."

The war on the citizens started with the stealing of chickens, then grew to horse thieving, then robbing of houses. One Richland farmer named Eli Wasson took the precaution to bury $1800 in gold in his back yard, but it did him no good; bandits tortured him until he confessed to its existence and revealed where it was buried.

One day in the early months of 1863, jayhawkers rode into Richland and murdered Jack Cole at his home near the Greenhaw place. As Jack was Jim Greenhaw's friend, his murder struck close to the Greenhaw family and must have shaken Mollie. Jack's eldest son John was away with his regiment when it happened. The middle son Henry had only recently signed up with another Confederate regiment, the Seventh Arkansas Cavalry, so he was absent as well. Granville, the youngest of the Cole brothers, was still at home but hid from the intruders and escaped detection. Jack's violent death at the age of forty-three left his wife Saba alone on her farm with their three young daughters and

Granville. Jack's body was laid to rest in the Nars Cemetery on a knoll above the Buffalo River.

No place was safe from these brigands. A man named John Standridge who lived on the Buffalo River decided to move his family way up Richland Creek to a remote stretch where the creek tumbles out of the hills in Newton County, hoping the guerrilla bands would never find his family in that spot. The family settled into a little cabin tucked away in a hollow where few people ever ventured. Yet, one early morning bushwhackers were riding up Richland Creek when they heard a rooster crow. They turned up the hollow and followed the sound of the rooster to the Standridges' hideaway. Spying Standridge and his teenage son plowing a little field they snuck up and shot Standridge as he tried to throw off the plow traces and shot the boy as he tried to escape over a rail fence at the back of the field. Then, with their two victims lying dead on the ground in plain view of the cabin, they forced Mrs. Standridge to take the rooster and cook it up for them.

Every man in Richland had to reckon with his own and his family's safety under the changing conditions. Billy Wyatt reckoned that if he stuck around Richland any longer he was a dead man, and he calculated that Louisa and Parthenia and the children could likely deal with any intruders on their own. So, he snuck off to Springfield to domicile with a cousin for a spell. As it turned out, he did not return to Richland for a year and a half.

Jim Greenhaw decided to stand his ground against the guerrilla scourge. With all four of his sons in the Rebel army, he was the only male Greenhaw left on the farm. He aimed to protect his wife and three young daughters and niece. If outlaws rode up to their place, he would be ready for them. He hoped it would not come to that. As he saw it, if the outlaws knew he was there they would think twice before trying to rob the place.

In these circumstances men were of two minds about what constituted the best defense of the home. Some saw it the way Jim Greenhaw did, and others figured it like Billy Wyatt. Wyatt's choice to flee struck a few people as yellow, but so many men either fled or hid out that there was not much call for criticism. There was also another side to it. Some reckoned that any male who stayed in his home actually made his home a target for jayhawkers and bushwhackers, putting his loved ones in more peril than if he were to clear out. If a man tried to stand watch over his place he would just get himself killed and make his wife a widow. So, the best plan for the family was for the man to disappear for a while. As more time passed, that is what most men did.

Mollie had begun to think that her world could not get any bleaker. Her last place of refuge was in her lively imagination. Often, she day-dreamed of her dear, dark-haired fiancé. She imagined the two of them getting married when the war was over and making a new home together. She would picture herself living on a farmstead in conjugal bliss, the country at peace. Those pleasant daydreams were sometimes the only thing to brighten her day.

Mollie still experienced occasional flash images of her lover lying dead on the battlefield. The vision of a corpse frozen in agony—the shocking image that first came to her in nightmares when Valentine went off to war—turned into a milder vision of her lover's corpse lying with legs and arms straight, a relaxed expression on the face, the corpse prepared for eternal rest. She carried the latter image with her now in her waking thoughts. It could be a solace to her when she was sunk deep in gloom and had an intuition that her betrothed was already dead.

Today, one might say Mollie had a morbid imagination, or that she dwelt too much on death. But in Mollie's day, impressions of death abounded—in popular songs, pictures, books, and sermons, and in everyday life, and now on the battlefield as well. So, Mollie's morbid thoughts merely reflected the world she inhabited. Most Americans—Northerners and Southerners alike—pondered mortality, death, and the afterlife with endless fascination.

Thus, in a sense, she had already steeled herself for sad tidings when the dreaded army messenger was seen one day approaching the Greenhaw farm. A mounted soldier in grey came cantering up. Slowly dismounting from his horse, bowing his head, removing his cap and clutching it in both hands, his demeanor signaled to everyone gathered outside the cabin that their forebodings were not misplaced. Then came the dreaded words that Mollie desperately hoped would never be uttered: *Is Miss Mollie Brumley here?*

Valentine Williams was missing and presumed dead. He had failed to answer his company's roll call after a large battle, the Battle of Prairie Grove, and his captain had concluded that he should be counted among those who had fallen. As the Rebel army had retreated after the battle, it had been left to the Union side to bury the Confederate dead. Consequently, Williams's regiment had been slow to prepare a list of those killed, wounded, and missing in the battle. The Battle of Prairie Grove took place in early December 1862, and the news about Valentine Williams was finally delivered to Mollie some three months after that.

The news sent Mollie reeling. By turns, she felt dazed, devastated, frightened, depressed, and lonely. Cold fear welled up in her when she contemplated her circumstances. An orphan, fifteen years old, how would she survive on her own in a land so ravaged by civil war? Then for a time, a paralyzing despondency overtook the fear. She felt so drained of energy that she wondered if her heart would fail—and she rather hoped it would. "I was desperate and only tolerated life because I could not die," she would later write.

The days passed drearily by. It was now the spring of 1863. The long, hard work of putting crops in the ground could not be neglected. The necessities of farm living got Mollie back on her feet. Food shortages across the state of Arkansas added urgency to familiar routines. The previous year's corn crop in northwest Arkansas had been another dismal failure. Moreover, the wheat crop had rusted, and the oats had suffered some other kind of blight. All cotton planters in Arkansas were supposed to forgo raising a commercial cotton crop in order to grow corn and cereals for the commonweal instead. Many had failed to do so in 1862. It was hoped they would do better in 1863. In any case, subsistence farmers like the Greenhaws were expected to grow as much corn as they could, notwithstanding the fact that the farmwork now fell mostly upon the women and children.

~

As Mollie began to emerge from her depression, she encountered her prewar childhood friend Henry Cole. He had gone into the Confederate service in February around the time of his eighteenth birthday. Now he appeared back in Richland smartly dressed in a cavalryman's uniform. On seeing Mollie Brumley, he greeted her with a touch more formality than in times past when, as kids, they had gamboled around the neighborhood in company with assorted Cole and Greenhaw siblings and cousins. Mollie saw a look in Henry's eyes—a flash of recognition that the girl of yesteryear standing before him had matured into a pretty young lady.

Mollie experienced much the same jolt as Henry, seeing her old favorite among the Cole boys all of a sudden grown up. When he spoke to her, his sentiments were kind and sympathetic, and the way he formed his sentences sounded strangely adult. Henry told Mollie that he had heard about the death of her fiancé Valentine Williams. He informed her that he had recently lost his own father to the war. Neither Valentine's honor and sacrifice nor his own father's unrighteous killing would ever be forgotten. He pledged to Mollie his friendship and whatever assistance he could render her. Mollie thanked him and allowed that she felt deeply touched by his words.

After they parted company she reconsidered her own words, fearing that in her confused state of mind she had responded to Henry a little too warmly. Sure enough, a courtship ensued. Mollie vacillated in her feelings for Henry, one day providing encouragement and the next day crying out that she could not love another man so soon, or maybe ever, because she still loved Valentine. Henry plowed on. There was no time to wait. After a few more weeks, he asked for her hand in marriage. She admitted to Henry that her attraction was growing stronger, but she told him flatly that she could not give him the "sacred love" that she still cherished for her "sainted" one in heaven. Henry pressed his marriage proposal anyway. Finally, she yielded, telling herself that the marriage was a "necessity under the circumstances."

She still felt rash and ashamed. Having been tutored in the belief that it was the woman's role to exercise restraint, Mollie worried that it was she, not Henry, who had somehow forced the issue between them. She still had guilt pangs about it forty years later when she wrote her story. "Reader, judge me not as unfeeling and forgetful of my lover, now cold in Death's embrace! Remember, I was a thoughtless girl, only fifteen years old, alone and desperate and reaching out for sympathy and companionship." The older Mollie, financially secure and surrounded with family, recalled that the young Mollie of Civil War times worried desperately about her prospects, wondering how she would get by after the war without parents or a husband or any property to her name. She calculated that even if her new husband were to meet the same fate as her onetime fiancé, "better to be an honest, brave soldier's widow than a broken-hearted girl."

We might well imagine Mollie's conflicted feelings under the circumstances, yet there is more to appreciate about her situation if we consider the social conventions of the day. Americans in the Civil War era sentimentalized death and ritualized mourning to a degree that is hard to fathom from our modern perspective. Ideally, a widow in Civil War America would mourn her deceased husband for a period of two and a half years. Indeed, there were three formal stages to a widow's mourning: heavy mourning in the first year, full mourning in the second year, and half mourning in the final half year. A woman who was engaged to be married might be expected to mourn a deceased fiancé for a period of time as well. Although Mollie's betrothal to Valentine lacked that level of formality, the ritualized mourning around the loss of a husband or other loved one still weighed on her.

Even more significant, perhaps, was the era's staunch beliefs around undying romantic love and the afterlife. Women held up faithfulness as a cardinal virtue. People genuinely believed that faithful lovers who were parted by death could be reunited in heaven. People thought of heaven as a recognizable place filled with the familiar objects of one's home on earth. Heaven would contain not only one's familiar earthly surroundings, but it would be peopled by one's family and friends. A central tenet of Americans' thinking about heaven was the concept of "heavenly recognition." Souls were admitted into the kingdom of heaven with their bodies reconstituted. Individuals who had known each other in life would be able to recognize one another in the afterlife. Communities, families, and nuptial unions could all be replicated in heaven.

Mollie believed that she and Valentine would meet again in heaven. Of course, she hoped to live a long, contented life on earth beforehand. His premature death on the battlefield meant that she now faced a lifetime of separation from him. But she would see him again. The pain of long separation was expressed in the song "Weeping, Sad and Lonely," which was perhaps the most popular song of the Civil War.

> When this cruel war is over,
> Pray that we may meet again.

In the three verses of the song, a girl pines for her lover who has gone to war. Like Mollie, the girl pictures her soldier boy lying dead on the battlefield. The lyrics are intentionally ambiguous as to the fate of the soldier, so the line "pray that we may meet again" is laden with two meanings. It could refer to her lover returning to her after the war, or, if he is dead, to their souls meeting in heaven. Her prayer addresses either outcome. If he is dead, her love for him will transcend to the afterlife. That was Mollie's sentiment about Valentine, and it presented her with an agonizing dilemma when she was courted by Henry.

Henry understood her ambivalence, but he was undeterred. He finally convinced her to marry on practical grounds, urging that a conjugal alliance would give them each the strength to get through this cruel war. In the end, Mollie told Henry with painful honesty that her heart yearned for her fallen warrior who was in heaven, but since she had to go on living on this earth, and since she felt so frightened at the prospect of being on her own, then she would marry. If Henry could accept her hand in marriage on those terms, then she would be his bride. He agreed to it.

~

Henry Cole was about to join the guerrilla war. He was not going back to his former regiment. Instead, he was taking the family's horse and joining a troop of about eighty partisan rangers. He would be operating closer to home now, fighting the Federals in the Ozarks. So, he would be able to see Mollie from time to time. But guerrilla fighting would be dangerous, hard duty. Come winter, the men would be sleeping in caves.

His new unit did not have an official designation. It was known simply as Captain Love's Company. As with other guerrilla units, it went by the name of its charismatic leader, James Harrison Love. This was the James Harrison Love of Tomahawk Township, Searcy County, who had raised a company of volunteers in August 1861 that included James Jr. and William Greenhaw.

This man Love, like Henry Cole and many other guerrilla fighters, began his military service in the regular army and moved by stages into the irregular wing of the Confederate military. Indeed, Love's wartime career exemplified how the line between conventional war and guerrilla war became blurred as the war went on.

Captain Love led Company K, Fourteenth Arkansas Infantry Regiment, in the Pea Ridge campaign in February and March 1862. He fought with the Greenhaw brothers at Pea Ridge and afterwards held most of his company together through the bitter experience of General Van Dorn's strategic retreat from Arkansas in April 1862. By the early summer of 1862, Love and his men found themselves encamped in Saltillo, Mississippi, far from their Arkansas homes. That July, Captain Love resigned his commission and returned home, suffering from pulmonary trouble and an old stab wound. About one-fourth of the company, missing their captain and dismayed by the army's abandonment of their state, walked out of camp and followed Love back to Searcy County. Although the men were listed as deserters and a $30 reward was offered for each man's capture, none was caught or ever punished. The following February, Love recovered his health and talked many of his former privates into reenlisting under his command, this time in the Seventh Arkansas Cavalry Regiment. While stationed at Fort Smith, in August 1863,

Love's health again deteriorated, and he went home on sick leave. His departure once again precipitated a mass desertion of the men under his command. Fifty out of sixty-one men in his company—including Private Henry Cole—left the regiment and followed their leader back to Searcy County. Not long thereafter, in the early fall, Love formed most of those followers into a company of irregulars or guerrillas: Captain Love's Company.

Henry Cole and his fellow deserters were officially cited for desertion by the army command at Fort Smith. The Confederate army would sometimes execute deserters by firing squad. But more often it forgave or overlooked the offense if the deserter promptly returned to his unit on his own volition, or joined another unit, or became a guerrilla fighter. Henry's former regimental officer made a strong plea on behalf of all those deserters who had followed Captain Love back to Searcy County. This officer wrote to his superiors: "Theas men hom I reported Diserted is in the north of the Arkansas River with Captain Love fiten the federls Ever chance tha get."

It seems as though Mollie overlooked Henry's status as a deserter as well. One can assume that she knew the facts at the time but decided to put a gloss on them when she wrote about these events many years later. In her autobiography she called Henry Cole a "soldier" and dissembled when she wrote that he returned to his command following their engagement. She never acknowledged that when Henry Cole joined Love's Company he actually entered into the guerrilla war that she herself so strongly condemned.

Meanwhile, the conventional war between regular armies was going badly for Arkansas and the Confederacy. After a long campaign and siege, Vicksburg fell in July 1863. The fortified city on the Mississippi River was the last link between the Trans-Mississippi West and the rest of the Confederacy. After it fell, the North controlled the whole Mississippi River, putting Arkansas in a hopeless position for defense by the Confederates. Union troops occupied Little Rock on September 9. What remained of a Confederate army in the state withdrew south of the Arkansas River and went into winter quarters at Camden.

Chapter 10

Skirmish on Christmas Day

On December 3, 1863, Mollie and Henry were proclaimed husband and wife in a small ceremony attended by the two families. Inevitably, the ceremony focused on the many who were absent as much as it did on the few who were gathered, for the ranks of both families were sadly depleted. Henry's father Andrew Jackson Cole had been murdered by jayhawkers. Mollie's cousin Calvin Greenhaw had died of the measles in the training camp at Pocahontas. Elizabeth Greenhaw's husband Americus had died of illness at home that spring. James Jr., William, and Green Berry Greenhaw had all left their original infantry regiments and were now serving in the Seventh Arkansas Cavalry somewhere in the Arkansas River Valley. John Cole had deserted the Seventh Arkansas Cavalry and gone into Love's Company at the same time as Henry, and he was still with the guerrilla unit.

After Mollie and Henry married, Mollie joined the Cole residence. Henry would go back to the guerrilla unit after a short furlough, and Mollie would live through the remainder of the war with her mother-in-law Saba, her brother-in-law Granville, and the three small Cole sisters. But first, she and Henry would have a brief honeymoon.

The couple loaded a few provisions and a bedroll on the back of Henry's horse and rode off into the mountains for a few days' retreat. Unfortunately, the weather turned cold soon after they started out. Making camp early, they had nothing to do but sit on the ground and shiver as snowflakes sifted down through the bare trees and began to collect on the forest floor. They could not build a fire lest the smoke attract marauders. So, they huddled under their blankets, gazing up through the bare oaks at the leaden sky, wondering what to do with themselves. Sadly, Mollie realized, their honeymoon was not going to afford them the small measure of joy they longed for. No more words of solace could bridge their disappointment. Henry made up their bedroll and strapped it to the back of the saddle, and home to Richland they went.

Mollie felt sure her mother-in-law Saba would be sweet to the two of them when they returned that night crestfallen at being flushed out of the mountains by the unfortunate turn in the weather. But their homecoming was not how Mollie imagined. Saba paced the floor. Jayhawkers were in the neighborhood. If they learned Henry Cole was in Richland, they would most likely kill him. The three of them talked over what to do. Henry and his mother soon agreed that the safest course for all of them would be for Henry to leave before the break of day and return to his unit.

Until then, Mollie had been so downcast over the fact that their honeymoon was spoilt that she gave little thought to anything else. Now, Saba's fear for her son's life and indeed for the safety of the whole family awakened Mollie to a broader view of the situation. Her marriage was not only starting out joylessly, but it was also adding to her peril. The realization could have been crushing, but instead it drew something else out of her. A fierce will to live, to survive the war, was rising in the sixteen-year-old girl. In a rush of clarity—and maturity—Mollie saw that she had to control her emotions and set her heart on a more distant reward.

Yet no sooner had she come to her new point of view when it was time for Henry to go. Henry managed to sound upbeat. Mollie put up a brave front for him. But as she watched her husband climb into his saddle and turn his horse onto the lane, she thought once more her spirit might break. After waving him off, she stood for a long time observing his handsome figure grow smaller and smaller in the distance, fearful that she would never see him again.

~

On December 16, 1863, Captain John I. Worthington, commander of Company H of the First Arkansas Cavalry Regiment (Union), left Fayetteville under orders to scout for Rebels in Searcy, Marion, and Carroll counties. In modern terminology, this was a counterinsurgency operation. Worthington had 112 men and one horse-drawn howitzer in his patrol. In the Boston Mountains, scouting expeditions of this nature did not seek out mountaintops from which to survey the landscape for sighting enemy troops from afar. Rather, they relied on civilians to come forward and tell them where the enemy was hiding; then they would try to ambush the Rebels or chase them down or draw them into a fight. There were plenty of Unionist farmers in the area willing to stick their necks out and provide the Federal scouts with intelligence. There were also lots of Southern sympathizers who would track the Federals' movements and take the first opportunity to alert Rebel guerrillas to the Federals' presence. Once alerted, the Rebel guerrillas might respond by attacking the Federals or by moving farther off, depending on circumstances.

Worthington's patrol was not the first Federal troop movement through the Boston Mountains, but it was part of a strengthening Union initiative to clear the Ozark region of large guerrilla units like Captain Love's Company. As the Federal scouting expedition made its way across Carroll and Marion counties to Yellville, it skirmished almost daily with small groups of bushwhackers. News of those clashes traveled quickly by word of mouth to Richland. Mollie did not know where Captain Love's Company was encamped, but she knew it would soon be getting into action.

Three days before Christmas, Captain Worthington and his men encamped at Stroud's Store where the Carrollton to Yellville Road crossed Crooked Creek. That night, a sizable Rebel guerrilla force positioned itself in the woods on the high ground beyond the crossing to await the Federals' forward march up the Carrollton to Yellville Road the next morning. This group was led by a man named Marshall, and it numbered around 200 to 300 men. When the Federals resumed their march at daybreak, Marshall's guerrillas waited for them from their place of concealment in the woods. When the Federals came into view, the men took aim with their guns at dead level rest against the covering tree trunks. But as the unsuspecting Federals approached, one of the guerrillas fired on the enemy prematurely, and everyone else followed, and the guerrillas' ragged, undisciplined volley fire fell short of the Yankee soldiers, hitting not a one. Captain Worthington then ordered seventy-five of his men to dismount and advance on the Rebel position. Although the guerrillas outnumbered the Federals by more than two-to-one, they had squandered the element of surprise, so they scattered.

Captain Worthington's patrol continued onward. It reached Yellville on December 23, then turned down the Yellville to Burrowsville Road leading into Searcy County. In the meantime, other guerrilla forces learned of the Federal expedition and started gathering. Love's Company joined forces with another guerrilla band led by a Major Gunning, while Marshall's force was reinforced by a unit under a Captain Freeman. Now the converging guerrilla forces numbered perhaps 800 men altogether. The night of Christmas Eve found the Federal patrol encamped on a large flat in a bend of the Buffalo River near the mouth of Richland Creek. Love's and Gunning's guerrilla companies were encamped up the Richland Valley, while Marshall's and Freeman's guerrilla companies were approaching the Buffalo from the northwest. Knowing that the high vertical bluffs along the Buffalo restricted the exits out of the valley, they aimed to trap the Federals in that narrow defile and wipe them out.

On Christmas morning, the sound of rifle fire down along the Buffalo carried up the valley to the Cole farm. Anxious to learn what was happening, Mollie and her new family of in-laws went out into the yard to await news. By and by they saw a Confederate soldier galloping up the road on horseback. Mollie's heart sank as the soldier turned up their lane, shouting her name as he approached. With the other Coles pointing her out, the soldier rode straight up to her and said that she must come immediately because her husband had been gravely wounded. Mollie asked if she could ride on the back of his horse. She and the soldier threw a blanket over the horse behind the saddle, and the soldier lifted her up. There was no time to change her clothes or prepare a kit. In a few minutes they went galloping away toward the skirmish site.

Mollie arrived at the site after the two sides had called a truce to tend to their wounded, bury their dead, and exchange prisoners. She found Henry lying prone in a nearby farmhouse. He had been lifted from the field of combat and carried to that place. He was weltering in his own blood from a bullet wound in his chest. In spite of his heavy loss of blood, he told his new bride to have courage. He would not die he assured her but would recover and resume fighting. And he and Mollie could still look forward to being together when the war was over. She told him to hush and say no more, save his strength, and lie still while she went to work cleaning and bandaging the wound.

Meanwhile, Henry's mother Saba got word to Sam Cole, her brother-in-law and a doctor, that her boy had been wounded. Cole reached the patient at dusk. Working in the dim light of a grease lamp, he and Mollie undressed the wound, and he extracted the bullet.

It seemed that Henry had been among the guerrillas who that morning had run into a Federal foraging party as it went from farm to farm up the Richland Valley, seeking military intelligence as well as food. The guerrillas had surprised the foraging party and driven it back to the Federal encampment. In the ensuing skirmish, Henry was shot along with thirteen others on the Rebel side, nine mortally. On the Federal side, four were killed and four wounded. The truce had been called at three o'clock in the afternoon and it was supposed to hold until dark.

From the farmhouse where Henry lay, Mollie heard the fighting resume at around eight o'clock in the evening. It was the sound of Captain Worthington's patrol attacking Love's and Gunning's encampment. During the truce, Captain Worthington reconnoitered and learned that Captain Freeman had approached from the northwest and was encamped with 500 men just two and a half miles upriver from his camp. Seeing he was hemmed in and badly outnumbered, Worthington took his men and cut his way out before the guerrilla units could fully combine. Under cover of darkness, the Federals were able to get around Love's and Gunning's force without losing another man.

When morning came, Mollie and her uncle weighed their options. They did not have the full picture that Confederate guerrillas had swarmed into the area and very nearly trapped the Federal patrol, nor that the Federal patrol had escaped. All they knew for sure was that Federal troops were in the area still and would likely be returning for another fight. They judged that if Federal troops came back into the area then jayhawkers would likely emerge from their hiding places and scavenge the countryside hungrily and vengefully. The jayhawkers would hunt down a wounded soldier and his defenseless caretakers mercilessly. They would kill Henry if they found him, and they would probably murder Sam Cole, too, if they knew he had treated Henry's wound. Considering the habits of those jackals, Mollie and her uncle concluded that it was far too dangerous to stay where they were; Henry had to be moved to a good hiding place.

Sam thought of a friend who lived a long way up Richland Creek in a cove that was seldom visited. He knew the friend would not refuse them shelter. The problem was how to get there. They could not take Henry in a wagon because soldiers had long since made off with every wagon in the neighborhood. They could not even find the stuff to make a litter; the area all around them had been picked clean. That left just one option: they had to sit Henry on his horse, even with his chest wound. Sam helped Henry mount his horse and got behind him in the saddle to hold him up and brace him. Mollie gave up her blanket shawl to wrap around her husband to keep him from freezing. In this way the three of them set out, Mollie walking beside the horse. It was a slow, painful trip in the cold. Late in the day they reached the home of Sam's friend. They gently lowered Henry from the horse and carried him inside, and Mollie warmed her chilled body in front of a fire.

It being the day after Christmas, the Scripture's declaration of goodwill to all men could not have been far from their thoughts. Sam Cole's friend, acting with Christmas spirit, told them to stay with his family and rest up. His brave invitation gave Mollie and Henry a short reprieve.

After Sam went home, Mollie and Henry still felt hunted. As the days passed, they had to admit their presence put their hosts in too much danger. Word came that the jackals were in the neighborhood again, invading homes and committing depredations. They began to talk over what to do next. Sam Cole's friend said that he was concerned for his family members, not just for himself. As a rule, jayhawkers spared the lives of women and children and murdered only the menfolk, but these guerrillas were rulebreakers by nature. No one's life was safe when jayhawkers came a-calling. Mollie listened and knew what she and Henry must do. They must go farther into the mountains and hide out for a while.

The friend offered that he knew a place way up a mountain glen where there was an overhanging cliff and a spring nearby. He could help Mollie relocate her husband to that spot and then bring them a resupply of food. No one would ever disturb them up there. Mollie agreed. So, up the mountain they went. The campsite was tucked beneath a rock overhang, and the ground was thankfully dry. Mollie fixed up a crude shelter for Henry and herself. When the friend returned with more provisions for the two of them, it seemed they might be set for a while.

But then a new worry arose. Henry's suffering got worse. Mollie took cold water from the spring and washed his wound as often as she might. But the wound grew more irritated and inflamed, and Henry became feverish. Mollie put a cold, damp cloth on his head to break the fever. The more she examined the wound, the more convinced she became that something more had to come out of the wound. She had seen the ball extracted, so she did not know what the additional object could be. But something had to be in there causing the wound to fester. At last, in desperation, she fashioned a crude probe from a stick and used it to reopen the wound and explore the cavity made by the ball and the surgeon's knife. Probing deeper, she found what she was after. The ball, in tearing through his jacket, had carried a piece of the wool lining clear into his chest. She teased the strand of wool back out and bandaged him up again. The wound, once cleared of the foreign object, at last began to heal properly. Much to their relief, Henry's fever went away, and his pain subsided.

The weather cleared, and day by day the winter chill wore off. Henry got back on his feet and steadily regained strength. In two weeks, he was about ready to return to his unit. But Mollie made him rest a few more days for good measure. With blue sky overhead and sunbeams lancing into their little cleft in the mountains, their hideaway became tolerable. To Mollie's way of thinking, it seemed the Almighty had granted them a honeymoon after all.

Chapter 11

The Hensley Sisters

On that Christmas day in 1863 when the skirmish was fought near Richland, Parthenia Hensley was at the Hensley place over in Bear Creek. For many a Christmas past, Parthenia had accompanied her mistress and half-sister Louisa and the Wyatt children when they rode in the wagon over Point Peter Mountain to Bear Creek to spend a few days with extended family. For Parthenia, the Christmas visits to the Hensley place provided a welcome chance to renew old connections with the black community, some of whom had known her mother before she died. On these visits, Parthenia always had to tread the tricky social terrain of being an enslaved mulatto woman in the company of her white father and three half-sisters.

On this, the third Christmas of the war, John Hensley was at home on convalescence. The fifty-six-year-old Hensley, "Old Jack" as his friends knew him, was then officially a first lieutenant in the Seventh Arkansas Cavalry, Company C—James Love's dissolved company. He had enlisted on February 9, 1863, along with thirty-seven other men of Searcy County including Henry Cole. He had deserted from the Seventh Arkansas Cavalry in September along with all those others, opting to go into the irregular guerrilla unit known as Captain Love's Company. Although Hensley was technically a deserter like Henry Cole, his unit's muster roll listed him as "absent on detached service." The unusual notation in the record may have been in deference to his status as a slaveholder.

It seems that Hensley was convalescing at home with a bad case of laryngitis. Today, laryngitis is associated with the common cold, but in the nineteenth century it was more likely to be a result of a serious underlying bacterial infection in the nose, throat, or lungs: usually either diphtheria or tuberculosis. Both of those diseases were highly contagious. Hensley's wife and daughters would have been tending to Hensley's needs carefully to avoid catching whatever illness he had. Probably he lay in a sickbed in a separate room within the large house. (Before the war, Hensley ran a store and hotel at his place so the dwelling must have had several rooms.) Perhaps the three white Hensley sisters left it to their half-sister Parthenia, in her lowly status as Louisa's slave, to attend to the more intimate and hazardous nursing tasks around their sick father.

On Christmas day, the Hensleys remained quite unaware of the clash of arms along the Buffalo. The skirmish occurred about six miles from the Hensley place as the crow flies. But they were situated in a hollow, so the noise of battle did not reach them even across the much quieter soundscape of that era. (Today, a US highway runs right past the former Hensley place, but in the hushed natural world that these people inhabited not a sound came to their ears other than what came from the wind in the trees, the gurgle of the creek, and an occasional animal noise.) So, they went about their Christmas holiday with no knowledge that an enemy force was in the neighborhood, and with no inkling of what would befall them on the following day.

The military record of events at the Hensley place is limited to the day after Christmas, so the scene on Christmas Day itself can only be conjecture. Probably there were no presents in the house that year because the war would have made a gift exchange quite impractical. But there may well have been preparations in the kitchen that morning aimed at putting on a fancier dinner than usual, and perhaps some caroling or other musical entertainment in the afternoon or evening. In the slave quarters, there would have been merriment of some kind. For most enslaved people, Christmas was a rare day of leisure; indeed, typically they enjoyed a longer break of up to a week's duration. Southern slaveholders generally included their slaves in some part of the white family's festivities on Christmas Day to demonstrate their paternalism. So, for Parthenia, Christmas at the Hensley place was likely a special day when her white family and her black community brushed shoulders a tad more than usual. One assumes that the Hensley family experienced Christmas much as the whole divided nation did that year—with greater emotional intensity and more focus on family than ever before.

While the Hensleys celebrated the holiday, a detachment of the Second Arkansas Cavalry that was on scout near Yellville learned of the skirmish along the Buffalo River and went to join the fray. Numbering about forty men, the force arrived at the Buffalo late in the evening on Christmas Day, too late to reinforce Captain Worthington, as he had already escaped with his command into Newton County on his way back to Fayetteville. So, the scout made camp in the dark near the mouth of Bear Creek. The next morning, it proceeded on southward, continuing to make its way along the Yellville to Burrowsville Road where the road led up Bear Creek right past the Hensley place.

Too late, the Hensleys heard the clatter of horses' hooves coming up the road and realized the danger they were in. Distracted by Christmas, the Hensley sisters had failed to prepare to hide their convalescing father. Federal troopers entered their home and found Hensley lying in his sickbed with his cavalryman's pistol, sword, hat, boots, coat, and breaches all in plain evidence.

The troopers lined up the sisters for interrogation. Either the troopers already knew Hensley's identity, or they got it through their interrogation, for his name and rank of first lieutenant went into the official report. They wanted more information on another man named Wright, a Rebel whom they had chased down that morning and eventually shot off his horse. Who was this man Wright? What unit was he in? With whom were they fighting?

The Hensleys knew this unfortunate man. He was Giles M. Wright, a seventeen-year-old "captain" in Love's Company. Wright's kinfolk lived up the road in Burrowsville. Wright had recently married, and his young bride lived with his mother and sister.

Under rough questioning, one of the Hensley sisters gave the troopers the information that they sought about Wright. The record does not identify which Hensley sister it was who talked. Louisa was the oldest. Nancy was a few years younger than Louisa at about twenty-nine, and Mary was the youngest at sixteen. Parthenia, their half-sister, was now about twenty. One might presume that Louisa, as the oldest, was the one who spoke, or one might presume at least that she took charge of the overall situation. The historical record of this incident mentions the involvement later on of a Hensley daughter and "one of Hensley's Negro women." We will hazard a guess that Louisa and Parthenia were the two women referenced.

Once the troopers had the information on Wright, they brutally informed the Hensleys that they had shot Wright eight times, leaving him on the road bleeding to death. Now one of their men would ride back and finish him.

The Federals took John Hensley prisoner. Notwithstanding the fact that he was truly ill and convalescing in a sick bed, the troopers could only assume that his illness was a ruse and if left be, then as soon as they were gone he would jump out of bed and go rejoin his unit. So, they made him dress, bound his hands, and led him out.

The Hensley sisters must have been very dismayed to see their ailing father yanked from his sickbed and hauled off under guard. At that moment, they would have feared that they would never see him again. Indeed, in his weakened condition, imprisonment did prove to be a death sentence for Old Jack Hensley. He was put in the notorious Gratiot Prison in St. Louis, where he succumbed to his illness four months later.

One wonders what mixed emotions Parthenia had about seeing him go. This man was both her father and her original enslaver. Surely her feelings at their parting were different from those of her white half-sisters. Indeed, it is hard to imagine the scene. At this sad farewell, did Hensley treat his three white daughters and one mulatto daughter with equal affection? Probably not.

Parthenia may have looked upon the Federal troopers with conflicted feelings as well. Now, for the first time, she had come face to face with the Southland's invaders. No question, the troopers had struck terror into the Hensley home. But were these very soldiers not the blessed souls who were coming to deliver her own people from slavery?

After the Federals went on their way, Louisa and Parthenia waited for a safe interval and then went to inform Wright's kinfolk of what had happened to their boy. Entering Burrowsville on the heels of these same Federals, they saw several homes had been ransacked. They delivered the sorrowful news to the Wright family. As they consoled the family, another individual brought word that Wright's body had been located. Mrs. Wright requested Louisa's and Parthenia's help to go recover the body.

According to an account of the incident left by Giles Wright's sister, she and her mother, accompanied by a Hensley daughter and an enslaved woman, left on their errand at about midnight. They found Wright's body lying at the edge of the road a little way up Bear Creek where Forest Creek runs in. He had been wounded in multiple places and finally executed with a shot in the head. The four women each took hold of a limb and carried the body about three miles down the road to the Hensley place. The next day, they had a coffin made. A few men of Love's Company came to Burrowsville to bury him in the cemetery there. The modern gravestone reads:

Captain Giles M. Wright
Confederate Partisan Rangers
1846 1863
Son of CSA Capt. J. T. & Mary Wright
Killed after Richland Creek Skirmish

~

Back in Richland again, Louisa and Parthenia resumed their lives on the Wyatt farm. With Billy Wyatt away in Springfield—now a refugee from the fighting—the women were on their own to protect the place and take care of the five children.

A grandson of Saba Cole would recall many decades later that some time before Billy Wyatt fled to Springfield, he took Saba Cole's cattle and guarded them on his land after they were driven off the Cole farm by ruffians. It is unclear from the grandson's hazy account if the Wyatts and the Coles came to this arrangement by mutual agreement or if the Wyatts somehow took advantage of the Coles' misfortune at the hands of ruffians. The Cole grandson did not seem to know the answer (he was not born until twenty years after the war), but he insisted that the Wyatts "treated us awful bad in war times," implying that the grudge had something to do with the cattle. In any case, it seems that at this stage in the war, Louisa and Parthenia and their dependents had cattle on their place and probably did not want for subsistence.

Besides keeping a few livestock, the two women may have worked side by side to get a crop in the ground in the spring of 1864, taking their small children into the field with them or leaving them in the care of Louisa's eldest, Emma, who was now thirteen.

One wonders how these half-sisters, one free and the other enslaved, mothers of children by the same man, pulled together to survive the war. One thing is known: their relationship endured. After Parthenia was emancipated, she would go on living with Louisa for many more years. Again, the facts around Parthenia's life are scant. Neither Parthenia nor Louisa left any written record of how it went between them after Billy Wyatt fled to Springfield to sit out the rest of the war. But historians have looked at other war-torn Southern households where enslaved women and their mistresses worked out new ways to cohabitate and survive. In light of those studies, we can make some informed guesses as to how these two women might have come through their ordeal together.

There was, in the first place, the striking circumstance that both women lived subjugated lives in a patriarchal system. Even if one was free and the other was unfree, they had that subjugation in common. Now, with Billy Wyatt gone, the two women were left to make their own way and experiment with running a household and farm by female labor alone.

With so much work to be done, Parthenia's place in the partnership may have evolved toward something like parity. Louisa, as a yeoman farmer's wife, would have already known hard work. But her newfound circumstances would have forced her to share the burdens with Parthenia more equitably than before. Parthenia, for her part, would have soon recognized how diminished Louisa's hold over her had become. There was little left of the slavery system in Richland to back up Louisa's control of her. She was about the same physical size as her mistress, and she must have seen that she could probably hold her own against her if they ever came to blows.

There is no evidence to suggest that Parthenia ever gave much thought to running away to freedom. Before the war, she had lived with strict controls on her movements. She had needed a pass to go anywhere without the Wyatts. In slavery times any white person could challenge a black person on a public right-of-way and demand to see a travel pass. Arkansas put the force of the state behind the restriction on a black person's movements, handing off law enforcement to a rough class of men who made up the state's numerous local slave patrols. Though not as prevalent in the Ozarks as in other parts of the state, they did exist there. Patrols were empowered by the state to whip any slave they caught without a travel pass. Blacks dreaded harassment or arrest at the hands of the notorious "pattyrollers" or "pateroles." Children came to fear them.

In the war, blacks' movements remained as tightly controlled as ever, and the stakes for getting caught only became higher. The state-sanctioned slave patrols vanished only to be replaced by an even deadlier foe: outlaw bands. No black person—man, woman, or child—wanted to be caught by a gang of ruffians who were armed to the teeth and murderous.

When the Union armies drew closer, more and more enslaved people took their chances and made a bid for freedom in spite of the many dangers. These freedom seekers looked for asylum with Union garrisons in towns or Union armies in the field. If they succeeded in reaching the Union lines, then they were called contraband of war, provided with freedom papers, and absorbed into the Union cause. But Union garrisons in Yellville and Fayetteville were a long way from Richland. Parthenia would have faced enormous risks if she had tried to flee the Wyatt farm and make that trip alone.

Moreover, Parthenia would not have fled the farm alone. She had her beloved son Newt. By the spring of 1864, Newt was a strapping two-year-old. To run away encumbered with Newt would have been virtually impossible. As with many other enslaved women similarly encumbered, the little boy prevented her from running away but also gave her strength to endure. Whenever she beheld the boy's big, bold future as a free man, it was in those moments that she found her own liberation of spirit.

Chapter 12

The Murder of John Cole

At the beginning of 1864, the guerrilla war in northwest Arkansas turned even more savage. On the Confederate side, guerrilla chieftains built up the fighting strength of their units with ever more aggressive recruiting tactics. Small guerrilla bands combed through the Ozarks looking for men to dragoon into service. They went busting into farmhouses, poking into barns, and sniffing out camps in the woods. Whenever they found a male of military age, they presumed the person was a deserter who needed a dose of encouragement to get back into the fight. If the person refused them, he would likely be lynched or blindfolded and shot. The draconian pursuit of recruits gave a cover to outlaw gangs who had no real aim other than to last out the war. They marauded and plundered the country in much the same way that patriotic guerrilla fighters did, gaining strength in numbers as desperate men joined their gangs to avoid being murdered. Meanwhile, on the Union side, Federal commanders saw a need to go into the Ozarks and pulverize the guerrilla units before they got so big that they could combine to make an effective military raid into Missouri. The Federal army sent one cavalry patrol after another into the Ozarks to hunt, kill, and scatter the Rebel guerrillas. Because civilians were the eyes and ears of both the guerrillas and the counterinsurgency forces, the whole civilian population was dragged into the conflict. This new phase in the guerrilla conflict saw an increase in the level of savagery on both sides.

The warfare in the Ozarks had devastating consequences for the civilian population even though the number of fighting men was not large. On the Confederate side, a unit such as Love's Company might swell to about 300 men, or three to four times the size of an ordinary company in the regular army. Early in 1864, Union estimates put the number of "soldiers and bushwhackers" in Searcy, Newton, Carroll, and Izard Counties at 1,200 to 2,000 men, or equal to one or two full-strength regiments. On the Union side, the First and Second Arkansas Cavalry Regiments based in Fayetteville and Bentonville took the lead in the counterinsurgency, drawing support from Missouri cavalry regiments based in Batesville and Springfield, Missouri. Federal scouting expeditions into the Ozarks usually involved just one or two companies of cavalrymen. Sometimes the scouts were reinforced by a howitzer or two. Yet these guerrilla hunters tracked their foes everywhere, making their own roads sometimes. Constant foraging by the opposing forces ravaged the countryside. Dense farm communities like Richland were pillaged again and again.

The Federals found it necessary to fight guerrillas by turning their own tactics back on them. "Night marches, sudden attacks, ambuscades, and untiring pursuit are the only cure for bushwhackers and guerrillaism," wrote one Union general in sizing up the military situation in the Ozarks. To fight Rebel guerrillas required pursuing them into the most perilous terrain. The Federals followed primitive roads into deep hollows and even hacked out their own trails up steep-walled glens. The Federal columns drew fire from an invisible enemy hiding behind rocks and trees or taunting them from clifftops.

Federal officers and men grew to hate individual Confederate guerrillas as much as they hated the dangerous mission of guerrilla hunting. They referred to the guerrillas as assassins, banditti, beasts, and vermin. When they took them prisoner, they might try them as spies and execute them. In one known case of execution, a junior officer condemned three Rebel captives to be shot. He ordered six of his men to take the captives across the road and shoot them. When the captives overheard the order, they broke and ran and were immediately shot down. How often incidents of that kind went unreported is open to question.

Guerrilla captains were even more inclined to shoot prisoners than were Federal officers. When Confederate guerrillas captured Federals, they generally made them undress and hand over their uniforms. One man whose unit captured more than fifty Yankee soldiers in a single attack later recalled, “We ‘swapped’ clothing, shoes, and hats with the prisoners, before sending them back to Batesville for exchange.” Another Rebel stated in his memoir, “We were very poorly armed and were almost naked. It was not long, though, until we captured enough of them to get a good outfit of arms and ammunition, and a full suit of yankee clothes apiece.” In such situations, if the captured Federals were lucky they were given the Confederates’ cast-off clothes and sent packing; if they were unlucky they were lined up in their underwear and shot.

Federal officers reported the final results of their scouts as body counts. Captain Galloway of Company E of the First Arkansas Cavalry (Union) left Fayetteville on January 10 and ended his scout in Yellville five weeks later. Galloway concluded his report by stating that his command killed over 100 of the enemy with the loss of two killed and three wounded. Another Federal officer wrote that he scouted the country for several days, killed twenty-one bushwhackers, and scattered the Rebels into small squads. Another reported on routing Colonel Freeman’s guerrilla company that his command killed over thirty men, captured over fifty, and seized the Rebels’ supply train.

As Federal scouts crisscrossed the Ozarks through the early months of 1864, they confiscated the civilian population’s supplies of grain and fodder. Guerrilla bands did the same. Families needed to be carefully planting their crops in the early spring, but they were so fearful of being molested in their fields that they skimped on tilling and weeding, preferring instead to take their chances with a likely starving time in the following winter instead. Confederate General J. O. Shelby, coming into the country in May, found it utterly denuded of forage and subsistence. The condition of the residents was “pitiable in the extreme.” With hunger across the land, the combatants treated the civilian population even more roughly than before. “Confederate soldiers in nothing save the name, robbers, and jayhawkers have vied with the Federals in plundering, devouring, and wasting the substance of loyal Southerners," Shelby wrote in dismay.

~

Around this time the Cole family suffered an atrocity at the hands of an outlaw band known as the Meek gang. The gang's deed was so unspeakably cruel that Mollie left it out of her autobiography. She related other terrible events, but she totally skipped over the cold-blooded murder of her brother-in-law. Possibly when she wrote her account of the war, she did not want to stir up bad blood with the Meek clan even after the passage of nearly forty years. John Cole's body lies buried next to his father's grave in the Nars Cemetery. His gravestone tells the tale. Even though Mollie omitted it from her autobiography there is no doubt that this incident happened.

While Love's Company encamped near Yellville in the spring of 1864, John Cole found himself ailing from an infection and requested leave to go home and convalesce in his mother's care. As Federal scouts and jayhawkers were active in the area, Captain Love told him to take his brother Henry along with him for protection. John and Henry set out down the Yellville to Burrowsville Road into Searcy County. On the second day, somewhere past Burrowsville, the brothers dismounted to stretch their legs and allow their horses to graze in a forest opening. Unluckily for them, they stopped within earshot of the Meek gang who were concealed in the forest.

In the no-mans-land of the Ozarks, guerrilla fighters could not always distinguish friend from foe. Since Confederate guerrillas generally wore Federal uniforms, they tried to communicate with one another by secret signals, but the system had plenty of room for error. If a signal was given and not returned, or if two groups of guerrillas simply ran into each other, then there was a scramble to find out who was who. When the Meek gang ambushed the Cole brothers, they would have likely burst out of the brush with pistols drawn, yelling at them to drop their guns. What happened for sure—what entered family lore and was passed down from generation to generation—was that the brothers ran for their horses, and while Henry leaped onto his horse and made his escape John could not get the bit into his horse's mouth. John stood helpless as the ambushers swarmed around him. This was the last Henry Cole ever saw of his brother.

The Meek gang were jayhawkers and may have numbered ten to twenty men. They were nominally on the Union side, focusing their depredations on Confederate soldiers and sympathizers. The leader of this band of ruffians was a man named Lewis Meek, who in 1864 was aged twenty-four years and had long, scraggly hair and a blood-curdling scream. He came from a large clan that had come from Tennessee a generation earlier and had settled along upper Richland Creek in Newton County. Lewis's father or uncle, Jeremiah Meek, had a grist mill at a place called Meeks Hollow or Meekstown. Jeremiah was known as a strong Unionist. The outlaw gang comprised kin as well as a few deserters and desperadoes who had attached themselves to the gang. Most of the Meek clan were Unionists but there were Confederates among them, too. With brothers and brothers-in-law in this clan fighting on different sides, and their sisters and sisters-in-law betraying them to the enemy, family feuds began that would wrack the Meek clan for decades. By the third year of the Civil War, members of the clan were fighting an inner civil war of their own. Lewis Meek was both a product and a purveyor of the mayhem in his luckless clan. A decade and a half after the Civil War, Lewis would be murdered by one of his own clan in a long-simmering dispute over the Meekstown mill property.

After the Meek gang captured John Cole, the men interrogated him and determined that he belonged to Love's Company. Satisfied that he was a long way from his unit and that his lone comrade had cleared out, the jayhawkers bound John's hands and put him on his horse. As they were not too far from Richland, they decided they would take him home and see what his mother might offer them for ransom. With their prisoner in tow, they rode to the Cole place.

The parley with Saba Cole over whether or not they would spare her son's life was a charade these outlaws had performed before. In the guerrilla war's pitiless assault on civilians, such encounters followed a common script. The guerrillas came; they killed or captured the men and boys; they demanded food, livestock, or money; often they tortured one or more of the victims to extort information from them; then they generally plundered or burned the place and departed.

The guerrillas seldom raped or murdered women and girls. Those were taboos in the cultural fabric of the nation that tended to control men's actions when nearly every other civil restraint broke down. The men found other ways to act out aggressions toward the female sex. Time and again Southern women stood by defenselessly while guerrillas sacked their kitchens and bedrooms with a peculiar viciousness reserved for those feminine spaces. The men smashed the women's precious chinaware, tore the cloth out of spinning wheels or broke the cards and wheels, ransacked women's wardrobes, and strewed women's undergarments across the yard. Working out their sexual aggression any way they could, some men put on the women's petticoats and clowned to their fellows in their racy, foolish attire.

When the Meek gang rode up to the Cole cabin, Saba may have accurately appraised these men's intentions and realized there was little hope of saving her son's life. Her husband had been murdered by hellhounds such as these. Nevertheless, following the guerrilla war's miserable script, she begged them not to kill her son. Their captive was just a boy, twenty years old. Take the horse but spare the boy, she pleaded.

It is likely the Meek gang gave no thought to sparing John Cole's life in this encounter. If these jayhawkers had a tactical military reason for going to the Cole place, it was only to terrorize this pro-Confederate family into silence and submission. But what came across to the survivors in the Cole family was that the jayhawkers had a perverse interest in amusing themselves. Robbing and killing year after year cultivated a fine sense of cruelty in men.

Finding nothing in the Cole place worth stealing, and growing tired of the old woman's harangue, the ruffians prepared to leave. As a final insult they taunted Saba with a bald-faced lie, saying they would not harm a single hair on the boy's head even as they held him at gunpoint. John Cole said, "Mother, I know every one of these men. They will not hurt me."

After they departed with their prisoner still on his horse and his hands bound, the Meek gang took the trail that headed up over Horn Mountain to Cave Creek. Near the top of Horn Mountain, they took him off his horse, freed his hands, and directed him to strip off all his clothes except his underwear. They made him sit astride a log while they bound his hands again, this time behind his back. Then they stood back and shot seven holes through him. He pitched off the log as the sound of the gunshots thundered down the mountain.

~

By 1864, Richland had few men and boys of military age left. If the menfolk stayed in their homes, they had to be prepared to hide or flee when the situation demanded. Some men resorted to living in nearby caves so they could steal home and work their crops when it seemed relatively safe to do so. Occasionally one might see a man in his field wearing a brace of pistols or pushing a plow with a rifle slung on his back. Usually, the scene was of women and children working in the fields without their menfolk.

More and more of Richland's womenfolk shared the kind of grief Saba Cole experienced from her son's murder. Mary Robertson, whom Mollie knew by way of her cousin Elizabeth's marriage to Americus Robertson, was one such grieving mother. Mary Robertson had lost two sons in 1863, Americus and Irvin, one to illness and the other murdered by jayhawkers. Now Saba Cole and Mary Robertson grieved together. Mary's husband James had gone into hiding. With her husband away, Mary held down the farm with her daughter-in-law Elizabeth and youngest daughter.

At times when Saba Cole and Mary Robertson came together to console each other, Mollie found comfort talking to her older cousin Elizabeth, who was then twenty-eight. Notwithstanding their twelve years of age difference, they were brought closer by the hard times.

Mollie not only dealt with the shock of her brother-in-law's death; she still grieved the loss of her first love, Valentine Williams. It turned out Americus and Valentine had been in the same regiment.

As the women of Richland lost sons and husbands in the war, they formed a kind of sisterhood around their grieving. But, in fact, it would be more accurate to say they formed two separate sisterhoods in Richland: one Unionist and the other Confederate. The opposing families were interspersed through the valley, and by the fourth year of the war it was clear where everybody stood in the conflict. Since the women frequently acted as eyes and ears for the fighting men, they held women of the opposite camp in suspicion and blamed them for the killings. The blame was not altogether misplaced. The women did sometimes say things to the guerrillas that aimed at bringing misfortune on another family: so-and-so spied for the Federal scouts, or the folks in such-and-such farmhouse were harboring a wounded Confederate soldier.

In such a poisonous atmosphere, the few women who had sons fighting on both sides in the war found themselves on treacherous ground without reliable friends in either camp. One Richland woman tried to make the best of the different allegiances within her divided family by playing to the sympathies of whichever type of guerrillas appeared at her door. When jayhawkers showed up, she told them her ma and pa came from Tennessee and her pa was a Yankee. When Confederate guerrillas came to her door, she stressed that her husband's folks came from Mississippi and her husband was a Rebel. Her strategy did not win her any friends, but it got her through the war. In fact, this woman managed to keep her milk cow, a signal feat as the cow was one of very few in the valley that did not disappear by the war's end.

Mollie struggled with the war's growing fractiousness. Next to the sheer barbarism of guerrilla warfare, it was the war's sowing of hatreds that she found most regrettable. Mary Robertson was Saba's friend, yet she talked about the killing of Federal soldiers as if those men were animals. Mollie recoiled at that level of hatred toward the enemy. No amount of fighting, she told herself, would take away her compassion for suffering humanity. It did not matter whether the dead were Union or Confederate; every soldier's death was equal before God, and every fallen soldier left a grieving parent or sibling or sweetheart somewhere. Soon her nonpartisan convictions would be tested as never before when she came face to face with soldier deaths right in sight of her house in Richland.

Chapter 13

Battle Lines in Richland

Captain Love's guerrillas tangled with Federal troops in the White River valley on the eastern rim of the Ozarks during the first quarter of 1864. They skirmished with Federal scouts near Batesville on March 19. Then they engaged with a force twice their number at a place twenty miles south of Yellville on March 24, losing three men killed in action. A week later, they lost most of a small party who were on a foraging expedition to Richland. This party of eight was ambushed while watering their horses; six members were slain and two escaped. A week after that, Love's Company reentered the Ozarks. By then Love had just sixty men. Henry Cole was among the loyal few who remained in the unit.

Around April 12, Love's Company went through Richland looking for forage for their horses. Henry would have been looking for an opportunity to visit his home and see his mother and his bride, if only briefly, but it is not known whether he succeeded in that endeavor. On April 13, the company was surprised in camp by a superior force belonging to the Sixth Missouri State Militia under one Captain Turner. Love's guerrillas fled under a running fire from the enemy. Five of their men were killed, another was taken prisoner, and they lost eight horses and mules and seven sets of arms in their hasty retreat.

The next day, Captain Love's small command met up with two other guerrilla bands. The first merged with his command while the second, under a Captain Cordelle, agreed to combine with them for the time being as they turned to face Captain Turner's Missourians. Later that day the Missourians caught up with them. Though the Rebel guerrillas fought off the attack, Cordelle was killed in the short engagement. After this skirmish Cordelle's guerrillas threw in their lot with Love's command, raising the strength of the company to about one hundred men. But the new recruits were fickle; over the next few weeks many of them disappeared.

Around the first of May a senior Confederate officer with a small escort rode into their camp and took over command of the company. His name was Colonel Sidney D. Jackman, and he was on a mission for General Shelby to raise recruits in the Ozarks. As Captain Love was of subordinate rank, he accepted the change of command.

Love's men soon learned that Colonel Jackman was a seasoned guerrilla fighter. A farmer and onetime Baptist preacher in civilian life, with a farm in Bates County, Missouri, near the Kansas border, his fighting days had begun before the war when he organized a "border guard" to defend against retaliatory raids into Missouri made by antislavery Kansas jayhawkers. At the outset of the war, he had leaned toward the Unionists, but depredations by Federal troops in Missouri had driven him to embrace the Confederate cause. He had quickly risen in the partisan ranks from lieutenant in command of the border guard to colonel in command of a regimental-size guerrilla force. In the war's second year he had briefly held the command of a regiment in the regular Confederate army but had resigned the commission to resume his involvement in the guerrilla conflict. While Jackman showed himself to be a capable and spirited cavalry officer, his greatest skill was in recruiting guerrilla fighters. He was a powerful orator and knew how to excite men's passions. He had even taken Yankee prisoners and persuaded them to change sides and fight with the Rebels. Now General Shelby wanted Jackman to go through the Ozarks and raise a brigade for a great raid into Missouri. Captain Love and his men were the first to join Jackman's new command, providing him the small force he needed to get started on his quest for recruits.

On May 3, 1864, Jackman, Love, and Love's men, including Henry Cole, were encamped on upper Bear Creek, about ten miles from Richland. A woman on horseback came galloping up and told them a

Federal foraging party was encamped on Richland Creek. She estimated the number of men at eighty, and she said she counted twenty-four wagons in a forage train. Jackman and Love and their lieutenants held a council. As they had just sixty men in their command, they were outnumbered. But Jackman wanted to attack in any case, insisting that sixty Rebels could lick five hundred Yankees. So, they struck out on the road over to Richland, taking a little side trail to the top of Point Peter Mountain to spy on the enemy from above before they descended. From the mountaintop they could see where Richland Creek flowed into the Buffalo River. On the north side of the Buffalo a train of government wagons led down to the ford. Evidently the river was running high, and the wagons were held up waiting for the water level to fall. The advance guard was encamped beside Richland Creek on the south side of the Buffalo, while the main escort and rear guard were with the wagons on the north side of the Buffalo. Jackman and Love consulted some more. The Federal advance guard did indeed look vulnerable if they could hit it in that spot, separated as it was from the rest of the force by the river. Jackman was confirmed in his decision to attack.

The Federals in the advance guard were under the command of Lieutenant James Hester. Hester must have heard the thunder of horses' hooves coming down the mountain road and spotted the Rebels coming. Quickly he gauged that there was no time for his men to fall back with the rest of the foraging party across the river; they would have to fight alone on this ground. He deployed his forty or so men in a line of battle. The soldiers lined up in a field without cover, all in kneeling shooting position, about forty yards back from a rail fence. Hester's idea was that the rail fence would block a Rebel cavalry charge. His men would hold their fire until the Rebels dismounted and came clambering over the fence, then give them a volley.

Jackman examined the hasty Federal deployment as he and his men came down the road to the valley floor. He judged that the horses could leap that rail fence. If they could charge the enemy on horse, they would overwhelm the Federal soldiers. He ordered his men to stay on their mounts as they formed a line of battle at the base of the mountain where they were still a little outside the effective range of the Federals' rifles. Henry Cole took his place in the line, sitting erect in his saddle, reins in hand, rifle at the ready. All became hushed as the Union and Confederate lines faced off across a few hundred yards of open field with only the fence line between them. Everything depended on whether the horses could clear that rail fence.

Jackman yelled "Charge!" All down the line spurs jingled and horses leaped forward. They galloped straight toward the fence, reached it nearly in an even line, and leaped across. Hooves knocked a few top rails off the fence as all the horses and riders hurdled over it without a stumble. The Rebels closed the last bit of distance to the Federal line in just a few more seconds.

If any of Lieutenant Hester's men fired their weapons in those last terrifying moments after the horses came flying over the fence at them, the shots went high and wide. When the two sides clashed, the men on horseback fired on the men kneeling with rifles and pistols and then clubbed them with the butts of their guns. The Federal soldiers had no chance of escape. They barely had time to rise from one knee to their feet. The cavalry charge turned into a bloody, whirling mass of pummeling and pummeled men as one Federal soldier and then another were beaten down under the blows raining down on their heads. Most of them fell so close to each other that their bodies lay nearly in a pile. When it was over not one Federal soldier was left alive; not one of Jackman's men was killed or seriously wounded.

The Federal officer across the river who was in overall command, Lieutenant Andrew J. Garner, looked on with horror. His panicked men fled up a draw, leaving the many mules, which were all still hitched to the wagons, to their own fate. Garner had no choice but to retreat with his men. On reaching headquarters, Garner bitterly informed his superior officer that Hester and his men had been overwhelmed by the Rebel cavalry force, and that many of the soldiers killed had been murdered in cold blood as they lay prostrated on the ground. "It is not possible that they all fell dead," the official report declared. "They were slaughtered."

With the slaughter concluded, Jackman's troops splashed across the Buffalo River to investigate the wagons. The Federals had been gathering fodder and grain from farms in Carroll County; many of the wagons were empty still. Jackman selected a couple well-stocked wagons for their own resupply and ordered the rest to be burned. The mules had to be taken care of first. With six mules attached to each wagon, there were 144 mules. Grimly, Jackman gave the order to shoot them all. They were of no use to the guerrillas. One angry Rebel stepped up to the colonel, shoved his pistol back in its scabbard, and swore that he would not "shoot mules for the State of Arkansas." Jackman coolly answered him that there was no useful military purpose in driving all that stock down south to the Confederate army at Camden, and he had no mind to let the damn Yankees have the mules back, either. Even as the two men had their sharp words, others began to carry out the order, and the mules' dying groans rent the air.

While this scene was playing out down along the Buffalo River, a few women had begun to emerge from their homes and gather at the skirmish site to check for survivors. Mollie was among them. The action had taken place within sight of the Cole house. She did not know that the Confederate force was Henry's unit, nor that her husband was nearby. Her attention was on the mass of bodies. Now the women walked gingerly over the blood-spattered ground, practically speechless, looking for signs of life among the fallen. All the men in blue lay completely still.

Mollie and Saba brought blankets with them from their scanty collection of bedding in case they needed to carry any wounded soldiers back to the house. As they rolled each corpse onto its back and saw the staring expression in the sightless eyes, they resolved to give these enemy dead a respectable burial. They would dig shallow pits and use the blankets to move each body to its grave.

Some of the other women in their group were of a different mind, however. One woman declared that all these boys had gotten what they deserved. She even claimed to recognize one or two, asserting that they had been among a party of jayhawkers who had recently murdered her husband and son. She called them dirty scamps and cursed them for taking the lives of her loved ones. She wanted to leave the corpses right where they lay for the buzzards and hogs to eat. The women argued over what to do, and in the end Mollie and her mother-in-law and most of the women set to work on the task of burying the corpses while the woman who spoke with such bitterness stood back. Five of the bodies lay a little apart from the others and those ones were left untouched because the sharp-tongued woman said they lay on her field and that was how she wanted it done. Mollie was horrified to see hogs feeding on those corpses the following day.

Following the skirmish, Jackman calculated that the Federals would soon be back to avenge the soldiers' deaths. He aimed to give the returning Federals another fight, and he needed to find some good defensive ground where he could lay a trap. He needed a local man to help him reconnoiter the terrain. Henry Cole, being a native of Richland, probably served as Jackman's guide at this juncture. Officers usually turned to locals for such things because they lacked printed maps. If Henry did indeed accompany Jackman on his ride up the valley, it would explain why he did not call on his family till later on that day.

Jackman left Captain Love in charge of the company while he took his chosen man and went in search of the right ground for making a stand. His guide led him to a place that satisfied: a hollow on a tributary stream of Richland Creek at the upper end of the valley. Locals called this stream Dry Fork because it ran dry in the fall. At this time of year, it was a fast-running brook flowing over rocks between high banks of moist clay. The steep sidehills and thicket of trees and brush at the foot of this hollow made a natural redoubt. With the camp placed on the south side of the stream, the little stream gully would break up an infantry charge. Having selected the ground, they rode back down the valley and rejoined the company.

Jackman gave the men a speech. Three other guerrilla companies led by Captain Cecil, Lieutenant Colonel Nichols, and Captain Newton would be joining the command the next day. They would fortify their camp at the upper end of the Richland Valley and await the Federals. He reckoned the Federals would be back in a couple of days. He intended to lure them into this lair and give them a whipping they would never forget.

Jackman led the men up the road through Richland and it was then that Henry Cole took leave to visit his home. In Henry's short meeting with Mollie and Saba, he told them he would be camping with Jackman at Dry Fork for a few days. As the spot was a mere two or three miles from the Cole farm and less than a mile from the Robertson place, Mollie suggested she would visit the Robertsons and call on Henry from there. Henry consented, despite the dangers involved.

The next day, Mollie hiked up the road to see her husband. She hiked on by the Robertson place and found the Rebel camp located as Henry had described. The men were busy digging rifle pits and throwing up breastworks to complete their fortification. Mollie soon located her husband, and Henry obtained permission from Captain Love to spend the afternoon with his wife. He put her on his horse, and they rode back to the Robertson house. They found old Mary Robertson at home with her daughter and daughter-in-law Elizabeth, Mollie's cousin. Mrs. Robertson welcomed Henry and Mollie inside.

The other three guerrilla companies joined Jackman's command as anticipated, and the Rebel camp bustled with preparations. By evening, Jackman thought the Federals might appear at any time. Henry was summoned back to camp, and Mollie was advised to go home. But the two wanted more time together, so Henry ignored the summons. Darkness fell and there was still no sign of the enemy. Henry stayed the night with Mollie at the Robertson place, evidently not much concerned about being away from his post. Such was the give-and-take discipline of a guerrilla unit ensconced with the civilian population.

Early the next morning, when the Federals still had not appeared, Jackman sent the three newly arrived guerrilla captains and a few of their men to scout in different directions, hoping that one of the three scouts would come in contact with the Federals and draw them back to the Rebels' lair. An hour or more passed and still there was no sign of the Federals. Some began to think there would be no further action in Richland after all. But later that morning the Federals approached unseen, somehow having bypassed all three guerrilla scouts.

Mollie and Henry were enjoying a peaceful morning at the Robertson place when the sound of gunshots shattered the stillness. They rushed out the cabin door to see what was happening. A single Rebel on horseback—a man on picket duty—broke into the open and went galloping across the Robertson field toward the Rebels' redoubt with Federal scouts in hot pursuit. Henry leapt on his horse and raced toward the redoubt, putting up a running fire to cover his comrade and slow the Federals' chase.

Mollie retreated into the doorway. She watched the Rebel horseman followed by Henry enter the line of woods at the edge of the Robertson field and disappear. Then she saw another Rebel guerrilla step from behind a tree at the edge of the woods and coolly level his pistol at the pursuing Federals. This man stood stock still while the Union cavalryman who was in the lead bore straight down on him across the open field; then, in the last possible instant, he fired his pistol and knocked the cavalryman out of his saddle. As soon as the shot was fired the shooter turned and ran, disappearing back into the woods.

During the brief span when this cool-headed man took aim and held his fire, Mollie had the strange feeling that she was looking upon her former lover, Valentine Williams. Just as the strange feeling flashed through her, the man abruptly turned and vanished from her view. It was almost like he had been an apparition. She wondered what it was about him that made her think of Valentine. Perhaps it was his dark hair, she thought. Perhaps it was the intensity in his stance.

She did not have long to ponder. The Union cavalryman who had been shot out of his saddle lay on the ground gravely wounded, barely stirring. Though he was a Yankee, Mollie had a sudden urge to render him aid. With the help of her cousin Elizabeth and the young Robertson girl, she went and lifted the Yankee soldier up and carried him back to the house.

The three of them laid the man on an improvised couch and tried to ease his pain. He was bleeding from a hole in his chest. They did what they could to staunch the flow of blood. He opened his eyes, but he did not appear to take in his surroundings. He mumbled some words about "Mary"—an anxious, waiting Mary. His voice turned to a whisper as he uttered something about his angel mother. Her ghost was there in the room with him, Mollie realized, floating up there in the rafters where the man held his gaze. The man tried to form some more words with his trembling lips, but no sound came. Mollie had to look away from him, sure that he was expiring. Yet the young soldier hung on, still clinging to life.

When Mollie recounted her story many years later, she got one piece of this incident wrong. She recalled that the Yankee soldier breathed his last breath "and without a struggle he quietly passed to that mysterious 'bourn,' from which, it is said, 'no traveler ever returns.'" The Federals' official report on the skirmish verifies that this incident happened, but it records that the young man taken to the Robertson house actually survived his severe chest wound. The young soldier's name was Joshua Bishop. He was a nineteen-year-old private in Company G who had volunteered at Fort Smith the previous September.

Neither Mollie's act of mercy toward this enemy soldier nor her sentimental reconstruction of the incident years later should surprise us. Civil War America celebrated death on the battlefield even as it mourned the unimaginable death toll being exacted by the war. Through poetry and popular songs, North and South covered the dying soldier in glory. In fact, there was a veritable explosion of dying-soldier poems written during the war. The culture made death in battle an ennobling death, an attractive death, because the person killed would be long remembered on earth and redeemed in heaven. As Mollie tried to ease the suffering of this severely wounded Yankee soldier and prepare him for death, she felt the presence of angels, and it was a sublime moment for her. Strange as that might seem to us today, it only shows that she was a product of her times. Mollie's account of the incident basically mirrored the romanticized treatment of death on the battlefield in the popular song by Stephen Foster:

For the dear old Flag I die,
Said the wounded drummer boy;
Mother, press your lips to mine;
O, they bring me peace and joy!
'Tis the last time on earth
I shall ever see your face
Mother take me to your heart,
Let me die in your embrace.

Do not mourn, my mother, dear,
Every pang will soon be o'er;
For I hear the angel band
Calling from their starry shore;
Now I see their banners wave
In the light of perfect day,
though 'tis hard to part with you,
Yet I would not wish to stay.

Farewell mother, Death's cold hand
Weighs upon my spirit now,
And I feel his blighting breath
Fan my pallid cheek and brow.
Closer! closer! to your heart,
Let me feel that you are by,
While my sight is growing dim,
For the dear old Flag I die.

As Mollie attended to Private Bishop, the rattle of musket fire carried to the house from the place less than a mile away where the two sides now clashed along the Dry Fork. The Federal attacking force belonged to the Second Arkansas Cavalry Regiment (Union) under the command of Colonel John E. Phelps. Colonel Phelps knew better than to charge straight into Jackman's trap. He called his men to dismount, sent his left wing onto one hillside and his right wing onto the other, and then started a careful advance into the well-wooded hollow with his center.

Jackman saw what Phelps was doing and reassessed the situation. The odds for him were not good. Many of the men who had joined his command the previous day were not to be in this fight after all, as the three scouts he had sent out were all probably five to six miles away by now vainly searching for the Federals when the Federals were right here attacking. Finding himself outnumbered by a determined enemy, Jackman ordered a withdrawal.

Colonel Phelps, for his part, saw his quarry slipping away and hastened his advance. More gunfire erupted. In the pawpaw thicket the gunshots and phantom movements of enemy soldiers were more frightening than lethal. Jackman succeeded in getting the whole Rebel company out of the hollow and up a steep trail to safety without losing a single man. Phelps might have pursued them, but in the aftermath of an all-night march his underfed horses were in no shape to go up the mountainside after the retreating Confederates. Prudently, he broke off the chase. Although his command had not succeeded in killing any of Jackman's men, he believed several were wounded including, he thought, Jackman himself. That proved to be wishful thinking, however, as the wily Rebel colonel escaped without a scratch.

Colonel Phelps, gathering up his own side's casualties, found none killed and seven wounded. The last one recovered was the young man Bishop who had been shot off his horse and carried from the field to the Robertson house. The bullet had torn into the young man's lung, but he was going to survive the wound. Phelps thanked the women profusely for what they had done, telling them that they had probably saved the soldier's life. The Federals brought an ambulance up to the house and carried Private Bishop out of the house on a litter.

A little while after Phelps and his men were gone, a Federal straggler came by the Robertson house. After berating the women for being

Confederates, he boasted that his side had just given their side a licking. He told the women, falsely, that the Federals had killed twenty Rebels who were all lying stiff on the ground in the pawpaw thicket. Now that his side was clearing out, he said, the Confederate women could go up there and plant them. Mollie and her companions waited for the braying soldier to depart, then they hastened to the skirmish site to investigate. They were relieved to find it was a lie; there were no dead to be buried. Mollie reckoned that Henry had likely gotten away unscathed, but she would have to wait several weeks to find out for sure.

Chapter 14

Hunting Down the Meek Gang

Henry Cole thought he knew the rugged topography around his home pretty well, but nothing prepared him for the escape route Colonel Jackman took to get them out of the Dry Creek hollow. When they had gone about a mile up the road from the skirmish site, Jackman looked for a way to get out of the draw and up on the level of the prairie in case the Federals should find another way around and cut them off from above. He decided to leave the road and go straight up the hillside out of the draw. The hillside topped out in a cliff face for as far as they could see except for one little gap where Jackman thought they could get the horses through. Up they went, with no time to reconsider the plan if it got too steep. When they reached the notch in the cliff, Jackman had most of the men scramble to the top ahead of the horses and deploy along the top edge of the cliff. From there they could pour a murderous covering fire down on the Federals if they should pursue. Then the rest of the men worked on bringing the horses up through the notch. In places the men had to lift the horses up by handspikes. It took two hours to climb the last fifty feet. Luckily the Federals had given up the chase.

After evading Colonel Phelps's attack, Colonel Jackman retreated to the southeast with his command. The small force once again consisted of Love's Company of around sixty men. Jackman expected to regroup with the three other guerrilla companies belonging to Captain Cecil, Lieutenant Colonel Nichols, and Captain Newton as soon as all their respective scouts made contact. Then his command would be strong enough to go back and resume recruiting.

The company rode about twenty-five miles on the first day of its retreat and about thirty-five or forty miles on each of the next two days. Their route followed the Little Red River toward the town of Searcy in White County.

Around mid-afternoon on the third day the company went into camp and sent out their pickets in pairs. One pair ran into three men and a boy with bridles and ropes slung over their arms, evidently looking for horses to steal. The pickets took the four horse thieves prisoner and brought them into camp for questioning.

Henry Cole recognized an item of apparel worn by one of the prisoners as his brother's. The wretch had stolen it when his brother was murdered! These bastards belonged to the Meek gang! He informed Captain Love, who informed Colonel Jackman. Jackman had had no personal acquaintance with Private John Cole, but he had heard tell of the Meek gang, perhaps straight from Henry. As far as the colonel was concerned, the Meek gang were a band of outlaws operating under the guise of making war on the South.

Jackman cogitated on it and decided he would lead the company in hunting down the outlaws and wiping them out. The hunt would absorb all of the unit's energies over the next few days, preempting Jackman's mission to raise recruits and combine with the three other Rebel guerrilla companies roaming the area. But Jackman reckoned that the diversion was consistent with the unit's purpose to protect the local civilian population. Moreover, it would avenge the killing of one of Captain Love's men. That was how it went in this guerrilla war: even though Jackman had his orders from the regular army's General Shelby to do one thing, he now took his men to do something else. This eye-for-an-eye between opposing guerrilla forces took precedence over wider military strategies and war aims. Darker passions could rule these men. To some of the guerrilla fighters in Jackman's command, including the pair of pickets who made the capture, Jackman's next series of orders would seem erratic, even maniacal. But most of the men—including Henry—would go along with their commander, apparently finding their company's new course of action necessary and just.

With all his men gathered around in camp, Jackman addressed himself to the four prisoners, telling them he knew they were horse thieves and murderers. All four deserved to die, including the boy. He was going to hang all but one of them. He would spare the life of whichever one among them stepped forward first and agreed to lead him to the rest of the Meek gang. He waited. When none stepped forward, he sent for a long rope. He took the rope, tied one end into a noose, and put it around the neck of the biggest, shaggiest man in the lineup. Then he led the fellow a few steps over to a tree and threw the loose end of the rope over a high limb. He pulled the loose end down until the rope was taut. Gritting his teeth, he pulled on it harder until the big fellow went up on his toes. He held him there awhile and let him back down. He asked the man directly, would he take him to the gang's hideout? The man cursed Jackman. He said he would not; he would die first. Jackman coolly removed the rope from the tree limb and ordered two men to walk the prisoner over to a hanging tree about thirty yards away. The big, old tree was broken off near the base and leaned against another tree, with one long limb jutting out from the slanting trunk like a yardarm. Everyone in the company watched in dumb fascination as the two men led the prisoner to the hanging tree, threw the rope over the limb, and hoisted the big fellow up until he dangled in midair kicking his legs while the life drained out of him.

When this man was good and dead, Jackman swore at the remaining prisoners that they would all three get strung up beside him unless one of them stepped forward. When these three still refused to speak, Jackman took another length of rope, made a noose, and put it around the neck of the man who appeared to be the oldest. Repeating what he had done before, he threw the rope over the limb where they were standing and pulled on it until the man was on his toes, then let him down and gave him a last chance. This man, too, still refused to talk, so he was led to the hanging tree and strung up next to his comrade.

That left one more man and the boy. This man broke down and said he would lead Jackman to the Meek gang if Jackman would swear to God that he would spare his life. Jackman said he would. Jackman told the fellow he was a Baptist preacher before the war, and he meant to stand by his word.

However, the boy would still hang.

Some of the men in the company protested Jackman's insistence on hanging the boy. The two pickets who had brought the prisoners into camp argued the point strenuously. Their names were Maddox and Marchbanks. Maddox declared that the killing of prisoners, especially boys, was not his kind of warfare. Jackman ordered Maddox and Marchbanks to go back out and stand picket again. Once they were out of sight, he went ahead and had the boy hanged. When Maddox and Marchbanks returned from picket duty in the morning and saw the boy hanging lifeless from the tree limb beside the others, they were shocked and sickened. Even though Maddox and Marchbanks were hardened guerrilla fighters, it still brought them to tears. Their weeping unnerved the rest of the company. Jackman didn't like it.

The next day the company struck camp about noon and headed back the way it had come, aiming to find the Meek gang and destroy it. Jackman kept the remaining prisoner, whose name was King, close by him as they rode. King was anxious to cooperate now. Much to the company's disgust when they later learned about it, King volunteered information to Jackman about where he could find three members of the gang who were not currently with the rest. Not only did King's disclosure seem gratuitous, but it was also a betrayal of his own kin, for these three men were his father-in-law and brothers-in-law. Acting on King's information, Jackman pushed the company to ride until late that night. At last, they made camp. But Jackman was not through for the day. After most of the men went to sleep, he sent three men with King to capture King's father-in-law and two brothers-in-law. They were hiding out in a cave. The men were captured and brought back to camp where Jackman had all their throats cut. Then he laid their bodies at the feet of Maddox and Marchbanks where the two lay sleeping. That was Jackman's answer to Maddox's insubordinate remarks about the kind of warfare he waged.

From this camp it was just a short way farther to the Meek place. It was early in the morning when Jackman's men snuck up on the house. Lewis Meek had built a large cabin with such heavy logs that the place looked like a fort. He had cut down all the trees around the place and left them lying on the ground like jackstraw to prevent a cavalry charge. Jackman looked it over and decided they would charge the place on foot.

In the house, no one stirred. At Jackman's signal, the whole company of men let out a Rebel yell and charged, clambering over the fallen timbers as fast as they could. With their superior numbers and fearsome racket, they succeeded in panicking the Meek gang and flushing the men out of their lair. Gang members came pouring out the rear of the building, fleeing for their lives. About a dozen were shot down and perhaps another dozen got away.

Maddox and one Captain Bradley pursued Lewis Meek up a steep hillside and got into a gunfight with him. Maddox and Bradley blasted away from prone positions behind a log while Meek returned fire from a standing position behind a tree about twenty feet upslope from them. Maddox could see from Meek's crooked stance behind the tree trunk that he was wounded but he could not tell how badly. Then Bradley got hit in the shoulder and the wound was grave. While Maddox attended to Bradley, Meek limped off.

Jackman came up with his informer, King, and one other man who remained nameless in the account. He may have been Henry Cole. Considering Henry's personal stake in killing Meek, it is a fair bet that the unidentified man was indeed him. The account comes from Maddox, who wrote *Hard Trials and Tribulations of an Old Confederate Soldier* when he reached old age. It is notable that Maddox did recall the name of Henry Cole in connection with Henry's recognizing this gang as the one that murdered John Cole, and it is possible Maddox just left out Henry's name here. Jackman told Maddox and Henry Cole or whoever the man was to take King and go after Lewis Meek. They went up the hill, following the blood trail of their wounded quarry.

But the blood trail soon petered out. They looked around for about an hour and gave up the search. Lewis Meek got away.

Around the Meek place several of the gang lay crumpled on the ground. Most were in their night shirts. If they were found to be still alive, they were shot dead where they lay. One man surrendered without being shot. But he did not last long as a prisoner. Jackman still showed a fondness for hanging. He had this prisoner strung up from the protruding ridge pole under the cabin's eaves. Then he ordered his men to set fire to the house. When Maddox came back down the hill after his pursuit of Meek, he saw the house aflame with the body hanging from the ridgepole. He thought it was the most hellish sight he had ever laid eyes on.

~

After making war on the Meek gang, Colonel Jackman turned his attention back to the military mission that General Shelby had assigned to him. Jackman had to raise enough recruits to form a brigade. So, with Love's Company, Jackman crisscrossed the Ozarks gathering conscripts.

Unfortunately, Henry Cole left no record of his own, so his thoughts and feelings around this time can only be surmised. It may be assumed that Henry went house to house with the other men in the unit, searching for any able-bodied male who could be found. Henry would have been exposed to Jackman's harangues again and again as they proceeded from one cove and hamlet to the next. He would have had to admit that the colonel was an effective recruiter. He could see the company's ranks swell from day to day as all the men gathered and bedded down each night. Soon they had collected several hundred men. Most of their recruits had no guns; many had no shoes and marched barefoot.

Jackman continued to show a zealotry for the Confederate cause that hovered at the edge of depravity. Any male between the ages of eighteen and forty-five who they found hiding at home or skulking in the woods was presumed to be a deserter. As a deserter, the person was liable to be stood up against a tree and shot if he did not join up. Jackman got right to the point with some of the men whom they scraped out of the hills, and usually the threat of summary execution was all these men needed to get them to join up. Yet, on many occasions there was more to Jackman's harangue than brute intimidation. The preacher rose up in him, and he talked to the men like they were wayward souls. He told them that they were sinners, bummers, and traitors, unworthy of the Confederate service. After berating them thus, he told them President Davis had pardoned them all, every last one, giving every Southern man another chance to fight. Now the time had come for them to grasp the outstretched hand and take the proffered gift, their last blessed chance to fight and die as heroes. They must join their brothers in arms, show their fellows they were real men, and wash out the stain on their honor with the blood of the enemy.

After about a week of recruiting in the Ozarks, the company marched south to meet up with General Shelby who was coming north with a large force from Camden. Jackman and Shelby made contact in the little town of Dover in the Arkansas Valley about the middle of May. Shelby was already famous for leading a cavalry brigade on a 1,500-mile raid into Missouri in the fall of 1863; he would participate in the second great raid into that state in the fall of 1864. He thought he would lead another cavalry brigade but in the end he would have only a division, the Missouri Cavalry Division. According to Shelby's adjutant John N. Edwards, who later wrote an admiring biography of the Confederate leader, when Shelby met with Jackman's reinforcements at Dover it marked the formation of his Missouri Cavalry Division.

The dashing brigadier general was greeted by a colorful display of Confederate patriotism as he entered Dover, according to Edwards. A procession of young women and girls came out to meet the brigade and scatter flowers before the leader. The ladies sang patriotic songs, and a large crowd lined the street and cheered. The hoopla must have made an impression on Henry Cole, weary of soldiering as he was by then. It was evident that people had come from miles around to hail the heroic general. Henry's encounter with Shelby was brief. The general took all of Jackman's new recruits and marched northeast, establishing his new base of operations in northern Arkansas at Batesville on the

White River. Henry remained under Jackman's command in Love's Company and went back into the Ozarks to raise more recruits.

On May 27, Shelby was appointed Confederate commander in Arkansas north of the Arkansas River. By this time, the Federals had a firm hold on the state capital with a strong military garrison under the command of General Steele, and they had a more tenuous hold on the rest of the Arkansas Valley with small garrisons posted in river towns up and down the Arkansas River all the way across the state. The Federal ironclad gunboats provided an armed escort to convoys of flatboats carrying supplies to all the garrison towns. Federal troops also garrisoned river towns along the Mississippi River and up the White River to Batesville. When Shelby slipped across the Arkansas River and marched toward Batesville, the small Federal garrison in Batesville quietly pulled out to avoid a lopsided fight. Shelby reoccupied Batesville as well as Jacksonport farther down the White River and established his primary headquarters at the latter location. General Steele in Little Rock was annoyed to have Shelby in his rear, north of Little Rock, but he did not have the troop strength to confront him. Through the months of June and July, Shelby recruited in northeast Arkansas while Jackman continued to recruit in the northwest counties with Love's Company. Shelby's Missouri Cavalry Division, understrength to begin with, steadily gained more men. Toward the end of July, Shelby claimed he had 5,000 men under his command; at the end of August, he said he had 8,000.

Toward the end of summer, Jackman moved his command to Batesville to focus on troop training. Henry found himself tenting with regular-army troops for the first time in almost a year. He was encamped outside of Batesville in a large field that swarmed with men on drill. When they were not drilling, they were having inspections or going about their camp chores or simply sitting around awaiting action. The hot summer days mostly passed by uneventfully as the men looked ahead uncertainly to the promised great raid into Missouri.

Chapter 15

Army Laundress

THROUGH THE GRAPEVINE TELEGRAPH, MOLLIE AND SABA COLE learned that Henry and Henry's uncle Sam Cole were both stationed at Batesville where a Confederate army was forming. Saba proposed that Mollie go to Batesville to see them. The town was a hundred miles away—a three-day journey by horse—and the country was infested with jayhawkers. Nevertheless, Saba encouraged Mollie to hazard the trip. With the corn crop laid by, Saba and the children could manage the farm. The dangers of the trip notwithstanding, Mollie decided to go. She persuaded another young woman, one Miss Johnston, whose brother was in the same unit with Henry, to accompany her.

Mollie had not traveled so far since the start of the war. Even though she knew generally what to expect, the desolation of the landscape astounded her. The road was empty of other travelers and grown over with weeds. Felled trees lay across the road in many places, and from the shriveled-up condition of the leaves she could see that they had lain there for months without being cleared out of the way. They saw burnt houses and abandoned cornfields. They passed by farms where there was no sign of occupancy whatsoever, not a living person or animal anywhere. Perhaps a fourth of the Ozark population had fled to safer territory—to the north if they were Unionists, to southern Arkansas or Louisiana or Texas if they were Confederates. Seeing the ruination all around, Mollie felt disheartened about the Confederacy's prospects, but she kept her downcast thoughts mostly to herself.

Coming across a farmhouse that did look occupied, they cautiously approached to ask if they could spend a night. Before the war, Arkansas travelers might presume to stop at a farmhouse and barter with the occupant for overnight accommodation. Now, the situation was fraught: every traveler on the road was a potential combatant or enemy spy, and every farmhouse was primed to fend off intruders. Luckily, a woman responded to the young ladies' halloes, and after giving them a curt interview and concluding that they were no threat, she welcomed them into the house. The family's name was Tilley. Besides the woman there were children but no men on the premises. In lieu of stating a room charge for her visitors, Mrs. Tilley offered Mollie some homemade combs of cow horn for fifty cents apiece. Mollie bought four, paying her bill with two greybacks. Once they had settled up, Mollie allowed that it was almost the only time in her life she had ever bought anything. They both knew the Confederate money was almost worthless now—just pennies on the US dollar—but the transaction somehow made everyone feel better.

On the second day of their journey, Mollie and her female companion continued through the rugged Ozark highlands. Becoming somewhat inured to scenes of desolation, Mollie took pleasure in the beauty of nature that day. By turns she admired the deep shade of the forest, the patches of dappled sunlight on the road, and now and then a majestic bluff coming into view. Sometimes she and Miss Johnston had the company of songbirds flitting along their path. Mollie enjoyed the tiny birds' trilling and chirping—so merry and unaffected by the desolation of war.

After riding about fifty miles on the second day, they stopped at a country store at a place called Buck Horn. An immense pair of deer antlers sprung from the gable over the store entrance. The proprietor, Armistead Younger, was about fifty-five years of age. He queried the two young women as to which side they were on and where they were going. When they told him truthfully that they were going to Batesville to visit their husbands in the Confederate army, he seemed satisfied even though he declared himself to be a stalwart Unionist. He put them up for the night free of charge.

On their third and last day of travel they rode down the White River valley to Batesville. For the last few miles, the road was in level bottomland. Batesville was built on a plain beside the river. A bustling riverport town at the start of the war—with three distilleries, three sawmills, a hotel and saloon, a livery stable, a hardware store, three churches (Baptist, Methodist, and Presbyterian), and a small coeducational Methodist college (shuttered since 1860), as well as a dozen lawyers' and doctors' offices—Batesville now showed the ravages of war. Many buildings stood empty. Others showed the abuses of army occupation, with broken windowpanes and marked-up walls. As the town was strategically located near the farthest point of navigation on the White River, where it afforded both a waterborne supply point for Union troops and a ferry crossing for Confederate troops, the place had changed hands four times in the last two years of conflict. The reestablished Confederate encampment was located on the town's outskirts in a big field.

Mollie and Miss Johnston found the encampment mostly deserted. They soon learned that nearly everyone, including Henry and Miss Johnston's brother, had departed that place ten days earlier on an expedition to attack Federal garrisons in the Arkansas Valley. However, just as they were being thus informed, a few members of the expedition returned to camp. These soldiers said that the rest would come in later that day or the next. They confirmed that the Confederate force had indeed engaged the enemy, lost a few men but accomplished what it had set out to do.

Mollie located Henry's uncle, Sam Cole, now a forty-four-year-old private in the Thirty-eighth Arkansas Infantry Regiment. She had not seen him since that Christmas Day eight months earlier when she had helped him extract a bullet from Henry's chest. Now Sam Cole led his niece and Miss Johnston to a house where the two young women could take up quarters. Mollie passed a sleepless night there, dreading what might have befallen her husband on the battlefield this time.

The next morning, Sam Cole met Henry riding into camp. Henry had picked up a small kettle for his kit, tying it to his saddle. Sam, laying a joke on his nephew, said to Henry that he would like to have that kettle for himself. Henry said he declined to part with it, because he found it very useful. To which Sam replied, "Would you not give the kettle to see Mollie?" Realizing that his wife must be in camp and playing along with the joke now, Henry exclaimed: "Yes! I would give a hundred of them to see her!" Sam Cole would keep the old kettle through the remainder of the war. Many years later he would present it to Mollie as a memento of her trip to Batesville. The old kettle, Mollie would later write, "was sacredly preserved as a war relic with both bright and sad memories clustering around it."

Mollie remained in Batesville for one week, pitching in with work in camp by washing and mending soldiers' uniforms. She was inducted into what was probably a seasoned corps of army laundresses, for there was always such a group attached to a troop concentration as large as this. In the regular army in Civil War times the military tried to employ one laundress for every twenty men, or five laundresses for a full-strength company of one hundred men. So, there would have been several dozen laundresses in the camp at Batesville. Most army laundresses drew regular pay and daily rations and were assigned tents or barracks in a certain quarter of the encampment.

Mollie fell in with the laundresses' demanding workload of soaking, scrubbing, rinsing, drying, and mending a mountain of laundry. It was hard, physical work: toting heavy tubs of water; transferring the heavy, wet clothing from tub to tub on a dolly stick; wringing out the wet clothes by hand or rolling them through a hand-cranked wringer; wielding a hot iron to press cuffs and collars; and when hands were about as tired and sore as could be, there was still the precision work of taking up needle and thread to mend tears and reattach loose or missing buttons. Laundresses also put in many hours stocking supplies to keep the operation running: they made their own soap and lye and chopped wood to fuel the fire that heated the giant kettles of wash and rinse water. Mollie had done plenty of wash on the farm using a tub and a rubboard, but not on a scale like this. When one week's wash in the camp was hung out to dry, the row upon row of dun-colored drawers and shirts shimmered in the sunlight like a cornfield in August.

Mollie found the laundresses to be a hard-bitten but enjoyable lot. Some were married to soldiers and some were not. They were all stereotyped as loose women who ran through serial husbands or moonlighted as prostitutes, but the stereotype was true of just a fraction of them. Mollie, as an itinerant laundress, could be described as a "camp follower" rather than a regular army laundress. Nonetheless, she had no problem being integrated into the work program. The Confederate army that Colonel Jackman and General Shelby assembled at Batesville that summer of 1864 was a mix of regular and irregular units, so there may have been more laxity around the corps of laundresses than there was in the regular army itself. The fact that Mollie was able to join in the work for just one week speaks to the irregularity.

After putting in long hours as a laundress, Mollie prized the short amount of time she had with Henry at the end of each day. She was able to report how things were at home. He was able to talk about some of his experiences over the past few months.

Henry must have told Mollie about the expedition he had just come back from. They had marched south about one hundred miles to attack Federal detachments guarding a railroad line and to disrupt Federal use of the railroad. For Henry, surely the most unusual feature of the ten-day campaign was the destruction of the railroad. Working in teams, the men pried up the railroad spikes and laid aside the iron rails. Then they pulled up the wooden ties, piled them in big heaps, and set each heap ablaze. Those piles of burning ties made a long row of bonfires that stretched for a mile or more in both directions. The rails were then picked up and hoisted into the towering flames and braced there until they were red hot in the middle and could be grasped at both ends and bent and twisted beyond use. In this fashion the men systematically destroyed ten miles of track. How ironic it was that this was the first railroad Henry ever saw in his life, and when the Rebels were done with it the rails were mangled beyond repair. The line was the Memphis and Little Rock Railroad, the lone railroad in Arkansas.

Only a segment of line had been completed by the start of the war, but even this segment was used by the Federals to supply their occupation forces stationed up and down the Arkansas Valley. Shelby would later refer to this August 24, 1864, attack on the Federal garrisons as "the railroad fight," while the Federals would call it the skirmish at Ashley's Station.

During the week that Mollie was in Batesville, reports reached camp about a great battle that had taken place the previous month near Atlanta, Georgia. Now that city was under siege. Even though Atlanta was three states away from Arkansas, Mollie knew the geography of the South well enough by now to feel the gravity of that city's siege and imminent fall.

Henry confessed to Mollie how weary he was of fighting. There were indications that the army would be moving again soon. The great raid into Missouri was coming. The officers seemed to anticipate a reprise of Shelby's bold and successful Missouri raid the previous year. But the rank and file took a different view of it; for them the impending great raid had the markings of a last-ditch offensive. Many of the new men in camp had not yet been issued guns, let alone trained on how to use them. Yet they heard talk that they would be setting out soon anyway. Johnny Reb had always been called upon to fight against superior numbers, but now he was being called to the battlefield without even a gun to hand.

Henry had strong reservations about going on this Missouri raid. He had a premonition, he told Mollie, that if he went to Missouri he would never return to Arkansas alive. The thought of dying in another state unsettled him. It would be a lonely death among strangers. There would be no pine box, no homeward journey for his body so it could be planted next to his kin on the knoll alongside the Buffalo. No, for him there would be only a coffin-less grave in muddy ground in some forsaken place far from home.

Henry had heard enough soldier talk about Shiloh and Pea Ridge and other battles to know what was in store if he should ever die on a battlefield. His body might be blown to bits. It might lie in the rain or sun for days, until it became bloated and blackened beyond recognition. When the burial party finally came, his remains might be laid beside hundreds of others before being pitched into a long ditch or a large pit, with one nameless corpse unceremoniously piled on top of another, then sod shoveled on top about the same way a farmer covered up his potatoes and root vegetables to protect them from a frost. Before long, hogs would come by and root the corpses out of the earth, feed on them, and scatter the bones.

It was excruciating for Mollie to hear her husband talk of such things, even obliquely. As much as the culture exalted the soldier's death on the battlefield, the cold reality was appalling. Mollie still held in her mind's eye the nightmare image she had conjured of her first lover, Valentine, lying prone and blood-spattered and begging for water as he breathed his last breath. In a culture that invested so much in preparing one for the "Good Death"—a peaceful death in a sickbed in one's home surrounded by one's family—a battlefield death was truly the antithesis of the ideal.

When Henry confessed his fear of death to Mollie, it upended her ideal world in another way. In the world in which she was raised, she was supposed to be a person of the weaker sex. It had been not quite one year since Henry proposed marriage. Back then, Henry had been so confident, so comforting. Now it was he who trembled in her embrace and it was she who had to be strong.

We need to look closely at how Mollie wrote about this crisis moment in her book forty years on from the war. What happened next was this: Henry deserted the Confederate regular army and went back to being a guerrilla again. Thousands of Confederate soldiers deserted in 1864 at the urging of their wives and mothers and sisters who were suffering so much hardship at home. Many soldiers said they quit in response to tearful letters calling them home. The crushing desertion rate in the Confederate army proved to be an important factor in the Confederacy's ultimate defeat. After the war, many veterans suggested that the Confederate women who urged their men home ought to be held accountable for sapping the soldiers' morale and bringing down the Confederacy. From Mollie's recollection of events, it seems that she did not encourage Henry to desert, but we cannot be too sure for it would have been a hard thing to admit even forty years on when she wrote her book. Mollie's reporting of these events is sketchy and not entirely trustworthy.

If we accept Mollie's account on its face, then we are to believe that she said goodbye to her husband in camp and started for home with no inkling that he would desert and follow her out of camp the next day. Mollie departed camp with three other women—Miss Johnston, a Mrs. Addison, and a Mrs. Marshal—because there was safety in numbers for the trek back to Searcy County. She wrote, "I had no other choice but to go with them." On the very day after they departed, Shelby gave the order for the men to get ready to march to Pocahontas where they would combine with General Price's army for the great raid into Missouri. On hearing the order, Henry went at once to Captain Love. As Captain Love had been wounded in the Ashley Station fight, he would not be going on the raid himself. Henry, Mollie later wrote in her book, "applied to his commanding officer for a short furlough, which was granted." Henry then galloped out of camp in hopes of catching up with the four women.

In writing this account forty years on from the war, Mollie chose not to tell her readers that Henry actually deserted the Confederate army at this crucial juncture. Nor did she admit in her book that Henry fought with a guerrilla unit through the first half of 1864 and returned to guerrilla fighting through the final months of the war. Instead, she made her readers believe that Henry was always a regular soldier in the Confederate army and all was square: *he applied to his commanding officer for a short furlough, which was granted*. Yet we know that other guerrilla units were now embedded with Shelby's and Price's army for the great raid into Missouri, and it stretches credulity to imagine that Captain Love had authority under the present Confederate command structure to grant this one private a short leave at such a crux moment. It is probably closer to the truth to say that Henry went to Love to affirm his allegiance to the guerrilla captain before he rode out of camp not to return. He had been in that same place with Love before. He would rejoin Love's guerrilla command back in Searcy County at the opportune time.

There is more in Mollie's account at this point that bears critical examination. She wrote that as her party made its way back to Searcy County, it stopped to rest at the home of a friend of one of the women. As a result of this layover, Henry got all the way back to Richland before realizing he had passed the women by. When Henry got to Richland and found Mollie not there, he feared she had been waylaid by jayhawkers. He immediately started back in search of her. When Mollie saw Henry on the road ahead of her coming from Richland, she was of course surprised. She did not recognize his small approaching figure until he drew quite close. As she later recalled, "Our meeting and recognition were as unexpected to me as though my husband had fallen from heaven." This detail is important as we tease what we can out of Mollie's account to understand what she might have thought about her husband deserting from the regular army. There is no hint in her account that she questioned his so-called short furlough. But she was not naïve. The reasonable inference would be that she understood full well that Henry had deserted the regular army and that he would be going back to the guerrilla war with Captain Love. Those emotions belonged to the younger Mollie in 1864, whereas the older Mollie who authored the book in 1902 had her reasons to sweep the whole matter of Henry's desertion under the rug. There is more to discuss about the older Mollie's obfuscations, but we will save it for later. Here we want to return our attention to the young Mollie of 1864. What was it like for her when her husband resumed guerrilla fighting with Captain Love? What did she think about the Confederate cause by this time?

Chapter 16

The Last Hideout

THE GUERRILLA WAR FOLLOWED HENRY AND MOLLIE BACK TO RICHland. On their first morning back at the homestead, Henry sat cross-legged in the doorway with the door thrown wide open, enjoying the familiar smells and sounds of the farm, while Mollie sat just inside, watching him clean his revolvers. They were not thinking much about jayhawkers, but Henry had taken the precaution to saddle up his mare and to place her in the fenced backyard in case he had to make a quick exit.

While Henry was thus engaged with his revolvers, an enemy guerrilla snuck up within pistol range and tried to shoot Henry, but his pistol misfired. Henry heard the distinctive clap of the primer striking the firing pin and then the ominous moment of quiet following the pop of the cap. He threw down his own revolvers, which were right then useless to him, and jumped on his horse. Mollie heard the pop, too, and ran out to the backyard fence to knock down the top rail. She heard a lead ball zing past her head as Henry's mare leaped over the fence. But at that moment Mollie was too fearful for her husband to think that she might get shot herself. As Henry dashed away on his mount, there were more shots and Mollie fleetingly caught sight of one of the renegades. Then the shooting ceased, and the shooters fell back mostly unseen into the nearby woods.

Only later did Mollie notice that in the volley of shots four balls had torn through her hoop skirt and petticoat, only just missing her legs.

Saba joined Mollie in the yard. They both feared Henry had been hit while making his escape. They reckoned that the phantom shooters in the woods were only out to kill Henry, not to harm the women, as was usually the case with jayhawkers. Since these devils showed no sign of giving pursuit, nor of hanging around, Mollie and Saba guessed they had probably withdrawn after firing their weapons and were unwilling to engage in a gunfight with other Confederates who might be on the premises or in earshot. Thus, Mollie and Saba told themselves they would not be in great danger if they went to look for Henry.

Following the trail of Henry's mare through their cornfield, they found splatters of blood on the trampled cornstalks. After going a little distance, they found Henry's mare lying dead, shot in the neck. There was a narrower gap in the cornstalks leading away where Henry had continued on foot. As they went on, two little children came running toward them with a message from Henry: he was unhurt, hidden, and wanted them to bring him his revolvers and another horse.

Mollie and Saba returned to the house to retrieve the revolvers. Then they took bridles and ropes and headed up to their secret cove to fetch their last two horses. Back at the house again, Mollie saddled the horses while Saba put some bread in a poke. Mollie had decided she would join Henry in his hideout. Even though the jayhawkers had apparently moved on, it would not be safe for him to return home. Mollie took the two horses and the revolvers and the poke and went out alone this time to join her husband. She knew where to look for him. When she caught up to him she confirmed, thankfully, that he was unhurt.

Mollie and Henry did not know if the jayhawkers had tried to kill him simply because he was a Confederate or if their interest in him was more personal. Was this Lewis Meek and what remained of his gang coming for revenge? No matter who it was, Henry could not return home. After just one night back in Richland, he had to go hide out. Mollie insisted on hiding out with him.

They rode over the mountain to Bear Creek. They could pick from a number of caves and overhangs in the limestone bluffs there. They found a spot to conceal the horses and lie low for a few days.

They felt fairly safe in their hideout. At last, they could rest their jangled nerves. It was a good place to stretch out for as long as their stock of bread lasted. As it was now the middle of September, the days were not too hot, the nights cooler. The leaves were just beginning to turn. The hours passed rapidly by.

They talked a little about the jayhawkers, but mostly they lounged on the ground in silence, adrift in their own thoughts. Henry became restless to get back to his company. They had nothing more to eat. The time for another sad parting was upon them.

They left their hideout and led their horses through tall brush and across Bear Creek to the edge of the road. Henry rode off first to make sure the way was clear. His shoulders seemed to sag a little as he passed under a canopy of trees and around a bend. Mollie watched him through a blur of tears. There was a folk saying in the Ozarks: "Forget-me-nots grow where teardrops fall." If she thought about it, she could count the number of weeks she and Henry had had together on the fingers of one hand.

Chapter 17

Collapse

In the fall of 1864, the Confederacy's last hope for survival was that a war-weary North might vote Abraham Lincoln out of office in the upcoming presidential election. If the North were to elect a Democrat for president, many Southerners believed the Confederacy could parley a peace agreement with the new administration. (That logic overlooked the fact that even a lame duck Lincoln administration would still have four more months following the election to bring the Confederacy to its knees.) Aiming for such an election outcome, the Confederacy planned simultaneous counteroffensives in Virginia, Tennessee, and the Trans-Mississippi West in September and October intended to sow discouragement in the North before voters went to the polls in November. General Price's great raid into Missouri formed a part of that master strategy. But Price's raid, like the other counteroffensives, had too little punch to sway the North's determination. After Lincoln won reelection, most Confederate generals saw the situation as pretty nearly hopeless. About all that was left was the hope of a foreign intervention—perhaps an alliance with Maximilian in Mexico. In some sectors of Southern society, the mounting hopelessness of the Confederacy's position began to transmogrify into the diehard myth of the Lost Cause.

For Mollie, the slow, inexorable collapse of the Confederate nation could only be gleaned from vague rumors reaching Richland that disclosed one military defeat after another in the East. There were no newspapers to be had. At one time the community had gotten news of the outside from the Memphis or St. Louis newspapers or the *Arkansas*

True Democrat, but not anymore. In 1863 the *Arkansas True Democrat* had printed its final issues on wrapping paper, then it shuttered the building. The Confederate postal system had long since ceased to function in Arkansas. A fog of war had settled over the land and the people were groping their way through this catastrophe day by day and week by week with no real hope other than to come out the other end alive.

The immediate need was to survive the winter. The threat of starvation loomed. They wondered how they would eke out a subsistence with so little grain in storage. As winter bore down on them, Mollie and her mother-in-law were reduced to scraping the last remnant of shell corn out of the corn crib and carefully doling it out to themselves and the children a few kernels a day.

The Cole family was more fortunate than some. Union officers began to report numerous cases of women and children in the Ozarks starving to death. Twenty-four-year-old Sarah Baker lived on Tomahawk Creek across the Buffalo River. By 1865, all of Miss Baker's neighbors had been burned out and her home was the last one standing. Food was so scarce that she and her mother and sisters and little brothers would walk all the way to Bear Creek to obtain a few bags of shell corn from kinfolk and carry it back home, wading the Buffalo River with the bags held high to keep them above water.

When the people had no corn to eat, they relied heavily on wild meat instead. Deer were still plentiful if one had a rifle and would dare to venture far from home to hunt them. Hogs were a godsend. Wonderfully independent beasts, they rustled around the woods eating mast. As cows and horses had to be tended and fed, and they could not be easily concealed from marauders and horse thieves, their numbers plummeted. Hogs, on the other hand, just melted into the hills and went feral. As the corn bins emptied, pork became people's last mainstay.

Amidst the destruction of the farmers' subsistence economy the women and children showed amazing resourcefulness. They were desperate for salt to use for a meat preservative. To get salt, they dug up dirt floors in the smoke houses. Since meat had been salted and hung up to dry in these outbuildings, and the salty brine had dripped onto the smoke house floors time after time, the dirt was rich in salt. They put the dirt in hoppers, poured water on it, and boiled down the salty drippings to provide the needed preservative.

People supplemented these morsels by gathering wild greens. Before the war, Mollie had learned from her cousins how to look for edible plants. But now they harvested the wild greens in deadly earnest. Hungry children could be seen following behind the rare cow that still lived in the neighborhood, the children picking whatever plants the cow ate so as to avoid picking poisonous ones. The children brought home a goodly variety: field lettuce, sour dock, poke, lamb's quarter, tongue grass, deer's tongue, dandelion, sheep sorrel, and others. The greens were boiled down into a soup. Poisonous plants sometimes crept into the mix, giving everyone a sore stomach.

When it came time to plant the next year's crops, the Coles had no plow horse; even their plow had been stolen. Mollie began to attack the earth with nothing to hand but an old hoe. As she went at it, the acres of stubble field spread out before her like a vast desert. She felt hungry and weak. But day after day she went back to the tedious work of tilling the earth, knowing that their lives could easily depend on getting a crop in the ground.

The menfolk were still absent from this scene. Virtually every able-bodied adult male resident of Richland had gone into one military unit or another—Union or Confederate, regular or irregular—or else they had gone into hiding. Mollie's uncle Jim Greenhaw finally went into hiding somewhere. Perhaps he was among those men who hid in nearby caves or rock shelters while still maintaining contact with their families who remained at home. There was another Searcy County man by the name of William Kimbrell whose story is suggestive here. Kimbrell made his home away from home in a small cave several feet up the face of a bluff where tall trees hid the cave entrance from below. He had an arrangement with his wife to bring him a fresh supply of food and water about every three days. Kimbrell's wife used the subterfuge of wandering in the woods and calling for her one remaining milk cow so as not to arouse suspicion. She would carry her husband's food and water in vessels secured to her legs beneath her large hoop skirt. She would leave the items at an agreed spot where her husband would retrieve them after nightfall. Mrs. Kimbrell carried on this ruse for months without detection. Perhaps Jim and Usley Greenhaw had some kind of arrangement like that.

In the final months of the war, the lawlessness that had beset northwest Arkansas almost from the war's beginning escalated yet again. The hills were filled with desperate, predatory men who were willing to rob and kill to keep themselves alive. Mollie called these outlaws "human devils." She and her family had already suffered terrible loss at their hands, but these men were still not finished with them. More than anything else in her Civil War experience, it was the mounting lawlessness in the war that seared itself in her memory and would haunt her for the rest of her life. "I could not see why God did not smite these cruel wretches with instant and violent death," she wrote in her autobiography.

A lone drifter came by the Coles' cabin one day looking for food. After Saba had given him a tiny morsel in hopes he would eat it and go on his way, the man laid his .22 pistol on a table and dragged the table out to the middle of the floor. At one time the sight of the pistol would have checked Saba, but no more. She said to him, "What are you going to do?" The man said, "I'm a-gonna see what you've got up in your loft." Saba answered him, "Why, you ain't," and she pulled a hatchet from under her skirt. Holding it up menacingly she said, "Now whenever you reach up there and pull your weight up, I'm a-gonna split you wide open." The man replied, "Yeah, and I'll shoot you with this .22." Saba said, "Well, just shoot when you get ready. If you don't believe I'll cut you open, why give it a try." The man thought about it and left.

By this time in the war, women had taken to concealing food and valuables wherever they could: in walls or under floorboards or outside the home in hollow logs or rock piles. One woman in the valley even buried her porcelain dishes in the garden. The poverty found in the homes only enraged the desperados. They tore up floorboards in search of hidden food caches.

Desperadoes even tortured women to make them say where they had stashed food. In one home, intruders held a woman down in front of her fireplace and seared the flesh off the soles of her feet. In another, a woman was bound to a chair while hot coals were poured down her back.

On March 4, 1865—Mollie never forgot the date—the Meek gang came to renew its acquaintance with the Cole family. Three members of the gang came riding up to the house. Granville, the youngest of the Cole brothers, now about seventeen like Mollie, saw trouble approaching and bolted for the cover of a canebrake. The men fired shots at him as his dog ran into the canebrake after him. Mollie and Saba came out and watched in horror as the three outlaws rode back and forth at the edge of the canebrake, trying to flush the dog so as to locate the boy. Slowly the chase proceeded away from the house. Granville crawled through the dense brush, with the dog now and then giving away his approximate location. From her vantage point, Mollie could see the outlaws were hesitant to plunge their horses into the canebrake. But then their game of cat-and-mouse proceeded around the back of the canebrake and she could no longer observe their movements; she could only hear an occasional pistol shot. After several anxious minutes passed by, the men came to the house and told Saba that they had "killed the damned son-of-a-bitch." In fact, they had shot Granville's dog. Mollie and Saba and the girls all ran out to find Granville wounded or dead. After a desperate search they found the dead dog but no boy, which gave them hope that Granville had escaped.

Meanwhile, the three outlaws began to ransack the cabin for any food or valuables that might be hidden. Saba in a fury charged into the cabin after them with Mollie on her heels. Saba and Mollie begged the men to leave them what little they had left. The men cursed them, threatening to burn them out if they did not shut up. Saba could not be silenced. So, the men forced her and Mollie out of the house at gunpoint and proceeded to fire the house.

Afraid they would be shot if they resisted, Mollie and her mother-in-law stood back and watched flames lick at the cabin walls. Finally, the outlaws mounted up and rode off. The house could not be saved. As Mollie later wrote in her autobiography, it seemed then that "not only peace, but simple justice had fled the confines of our calamity-ridden country."

All through the afternoon they watched the burnt ruin of their cabin smolder. Sitting benumbed in the yard, darkness descended on them, and a cold rain began to fall. After dark, Granville returned from hiding. He was shaken but unscathed. He reported that the outlaws had wantonly shot one of their hogs in the woods. When the next day dawned, they located the dead hog, skinned it, hung the carcass, removed the entrails, and rinsed the meat with buckets of cold spring water. Then they sliced off pieces and roasted them over a fire. They had no salt or bread to accompany the repast, and no plates or cutlery; they all sat on the ground and ate the pork steaks with their hands.

The destruction of their home was so total as to seem biblical. Mollie went deep inside herself searching for her last reserves of strength and sanity. She thought about the trials of old Job in the land of Uz, and she wondered if she, too, could somehow persevere through this world of torment.

~

After spending a few nights out in the cold, the Coles found shelter in an abandoned cabin. They took joint possession of it with another homeless family. They made what repairs they could to turn the place into a tolerable refuge when the nights were too cool and damp to sleep outside.

The other family was Unionist but Saba and Mollie did not care. That family, too, had been burned out of their home by marauders, and their common misfortune drew the two families together. It now seemed absurd to try to sort out who had terrorized whom or for what purpose. Mollie had suspected all along that the so-called jayhawkers and bushwhackers acted with equal depravity toward the civilian population. To say that jayhawkers were Unionist and bushwhackers were Confederate was to draw a distinction without a difference. In fact, she reckoned, those claims to being partisan one way or the other were just bold-faced lies since all those men were simply looking out for themselves.

There was a Confederate woman living in the neighborhood who had given shelter to a Federal drifter, calculating that her magnanimous gesture toward this enemy soldier would give her a pass from jayhawkers. Some Rebel guerrillas had later nabbed this Federal drifter and hanged him from a tree limb. Someone suggested that the Rebel guerrillas' execution of the Federal soldier had brought a gang of jayhawkers into Richland to exact revenge on a Confederate family—any Confederate family—and the jayhawkers had fallen on the Cole place knowing that the Coles were Confederates. At least that was Mollie's interpretation. She may never have learned of her husband Henry's role in the near extermination of the Meek gang the previous May, which may have also had a part in making them victims of the Meek gang's wrath.

Thinking that the Confederate woman's act of sheltering the Federal drifter was in some way responsible for bringing the jayhawkers' revenge down upon them, a youthful rage over the injustice of it all welled up inside Mollie. She wanted to burn down the woman's barn in retaliation. Taking along her young sister-in-law as an accomplice, she climbed into the barn's stable and lit a pile of corn shucks on fire. The proprietor saw the smoke and extinguished the fire before it did much damage to the property. Mollie felt chagrined. Not only had she flubbed what she had set out to do, but she realized too late how senseless it was to target this poor woman.

Indeed, after that episode Mollie found that her fighting spirit was all played out. Sharing a makeshift cabin with a Unionist family gave her a new perspective. Rather than seeing all her Richland neighbors as Unionist or Confederate, she started to see them all as equal victims of the war.

Mollie began harvesting wild plants for needy families besides her own. Some of these families were Unionist. Sometimes her kindnesses were reciprocated. It seems that numerous families started scrabbling around and taking steps toward restoring the mutualism that had existed in the valley before the war. Mollie's own goodwill campaign may have been inspired by Saba, for Saba had a lot of Unionist kinfolk in Richland and elsewhere in Searcy County, and she could see it was time to make peace with them.

~

Saba's overtures to Searcy County Unionists would lead in due course to the Unionist Bratton family of Wiley's Cove. Benjamin and Laura Bratton had four sons in the Union Army in 1864. Mollie did not know the Brattons yet in 1864, but she was to meet them in the following year. The Bratton family's story is worth a short digression here, because it serves to remind us of the trials Unionists in Searcy County had been through to this point in the war.

Benjamin and Laura Bratton had moved to Searcy County, Arkansas, from Hardin County, Tennessee, in 1834. Benjamin Bratton came from a line of North Carolina Quakers. Though not a Quaker himself, he was antislavery. In 1861, the Bratton family strongly opposed secession.

The Bratton sons—James, John, Francis, and Benjamin Jr.—were all except Benjamin Jr. drafted into the Confederate Army in the summer of 1862. Many years later, James Bratton would describe in an affidavit the circumstances of his enlistment. The affidavit was part of his application to receive a veteran's pension for his subsequent service in the Union Army in 1864–65:

> We were not volunteers in the CSA. . . . We were Conscripted in this way. We were notified to meet at Wiley Cove at a certain date and informed if we did not respond to the notice that we would be arrested. . . . Our Co was not a volunteer Co and was known as a Conscript Company. . . . There was no organized body of soldiers in the Community at the time and the force used was in the nature of a threat.

James, John, and Francis Bratton mustered at Burrowsville and trained at Camp Bragg near Batesville. Their regiment, the Thirty-second Arkansas, fought in the bloody Battle of Prairie Grove on December 7, 1862. Their regiment was pummeled in a long artillery bombardment during which their commanding officer was killed. After the battle, the Confederate army withdrew to Van Buren and went into winter quarters at Camp Mazzard. Soon thereafter, the three Bratton brothers deserted. Their service records show that all three failed to report for roll call on December 16, 1862. As James would later explain his desertion in his affidavit, he and his brothers "ran away and came home."

As conscripts who were more sympathetic to the Union than the Confederate cause, the Bratton brothers were part of a large number of soldiers in the Confederate ranks who historians have called "passive Union sympathizers." The Confederate government drafted legions of these men into the army in the vain hope that the men would lose their Unionism as they took up arms and formed new loyalties to company and regiment. But that was a fatal miscalculation; thousands of Unionists like the Bratton brothers were never won over to the Confederate cause. They studied their chances and switched sides when the time came.

Desertion carried the penalty of death. Still, for the Bratton brothers, walking out of camp was relatively easy; getting home was the hard part. They were renegades without food, and they faced a trek of over 150 miles in winter. Arkansas was under martial law, and the provost martial had squads of conscripts out in the countryside looking for deserters. Yet the brothers also knew that hundreds of deserters had done the same thing as they were doing and had gotten home safely. That was only possible because there was so much Unionist sympathy abroad in the Arkansas populace. Arkansas citizens who were themselves eager to resist the Confederacy offered food and shelter to deserters and draft evaders as a way to support the Union cause. Once the brothers came in contact with the right Unionist household, they could be sent from one sanctuary household to the next till they reached home—much the way freedom seeking blacks were sent along the Underground Railroad to reach the North. The resistance network had begun to form during the months that the Arkansas Peace Society was active. By the end of 1862, many of those households harbored deserters as well as men hiding from the draft.

The Bratton family was reunited in Wiley's Cove for a few brief months in the early part of 1863. But that spring, Confederate leaders in Arkansas sought new ways to locate draft dodgers and deserters in order to fill the depleted ranks of the military and address other critical manpower shortages. A force of conscripts who were unfit for service as frontline soldiers was sent to Searcy County to ferret out deserters. In May 1863, this force rode up to the Bratton farm and arrested the three brothers. Along with fifteen other men, they were put in a chain gang, marched to a nearby saltpeter mine above Big Creek, and pressed into labor to help with the production of gunpowder for the Confederacy.

For seven months the Bratton brothers worked in the saltpeter works above Big Creek, until one day in December 1863—almost a year to the day from when they deserted the army at Camp Mazzard—a Union cavalry scout rode up to the works and called on the men to surrender. The few Rebel soldiers on guard duty laid down their weapons without firing a shot. The Federal officer informed the men he was looking for recruits. The Bratton brothers at last had the opportunity they had been waiting for. They went with this Federal officer, enrolled in his volunteer regiment, and remained with that company through the rest of the war.

The rest of the Bratton family could no longer live safely at home in Wiley's Cove. Ben and Laura Bratton took their sixteen-year-old son Benjamin Jr. and young daughter and fled to safer territory. They were among a growing number of families on both sides of the conflict who abandoned their farms and became refugees. For Confederate refugee families of Searcy County, that usually meant fleeing southward to the southwest counties in Arkansas or all the way to Texas or Louisiana. For Unionist families, it sometimes meant fleeing north into Missouri, but by this point in the war it was safer and easier to flee a little south to one of the towns along the Arkansas River that was garrisoned by

Federal troops. The Bratton family fled to Lewisburg on the Arkansas River where the three older boys' regiment, the Third Arkansas Cavalry (Union), had its headquarters.

Ben Bratton Jr. volunteered for the same regiment in August 1864. He was then just seventeen years old, but he told the enrolling officer he was eighteen. The four Bratton brothers were all in the same company. There were over one hundred brothers in the regiment, but there was not another set of four like the Bratton brothers.

The Third Arkansas Cavalry came to have a total of 1,375 men on its muster rolls. Most of the men came from farms in the Arkansas Valley or the Ozarks. What is most notable is that over 40 percent of the men in this all-volunteer regiment had previously served in the Confederate army. These so-called dual enlistments consisted mainly of reluctant conscripts like the Bratton brothers who had entered the Confederate army under threat only to desert and switch sides at the opportune time.

~

A day came around the middle of March when the sun rose above Point Peter Mountain and it seemed a little warmer than before. The morning chill was gone. The birds were singing, and the lizards were crawling out. Someone observed that the people had now come through their fourth winter of the war. Mollie announced that she was going to call on a neighbor woman who had a starving child to see what she could do for them.

The starving child was in an even worse way than Mollie had anticipated; it was so emaciated it seemed to be at death's door. The mother said if her child had some salad it would probably pull through. Mollie said she knew of a turnip patch where she could pick a good supply of turnip greens. It was an eight-mile trek, but Mollie said she could be back by nightfall. Two little girls joined her for the trip. They planned to bring back as much as the three of them could carry.

Mollie successfully located the turnip patch and she and her two helpers collected an ample supply of greens. But as they were on their way back, three jayhawkers rode up and surrounded them. The men looked about as gaunt and desperate as any guerrillas Mollie had ever seen.

The jayhawkers told Mollie she was under arrest. Mollie demanded to know why. Their leader replied, because she was far from home and could be a spy. How could she be a spy, Mollie protested, when she had these two little innocent girls with her? Because, the man said, we know you are the wife of a Rebel soldier. Mollie did not know these men though they claimed to know her.

The three ruffians led them to a nearby cabin and roughly forced them through the door. As Mollie went in and adjusted her sight to the dim interior she saw another woman crouched in a corner. Mollie was seized with fear, but she did not lose her tongue. She proclaimed again that she was not a spy. She explained her errand with the two girls. She appealed to her captors' better angels. When further entreaties for her own release appeared hopeless, she pleaded for the release of the two small girls, so they could take the salad greens to the poor mother with her starving child. The men gruffly showed the girls the door and they scampered out.

What the men wanted to do with the two women was never made clear. The jayhawkers held them captive in the cabin for three long days. Mollie's initial fear of the brutes turned to impatience and contempt. "They were the most depraved and hardened wretches I had ever met—ignorant and vicious to the lowest degree," she later wrote.

On the third day of her captivity there was a rap on the door. When one of the men opened the door a crack Mollie saw an old woman standing outside. Sternly, the old woman demanded entry. Mollie did not recognize her. Once admitted through the door, she launched into a harangue. She said that Mollie's husband was an honorable man even if he fought on the other side in the war. He had proven his honor by enlisting as a soldier. She told the men they were cowards for not signing up for the Union army; instead, they prowled the hills like mangy dogs, scavenging for food wherever they saw defenseless women and children at home or out working in their patch. She warned the men they had better do something quick or the devil would take them. They had better join the Union army, or else go to work on one of these farms and help the women produce food for their starving children. If they did not, their shame would be everlasting. Listening to the woman's tirade, Mollie was awestruck. The men wilted from the force of this woman's oratory. Recollecting the scene many years later, Mollie described her as a "mountain genius" with a natural gift of speech. "Every word she uttered was a sledge-hammer blow."

Finally, these three drifters had had all of the old woman's harangue they could take and skulked out of the cabin. The only thing they could manage by way of a response was to utter some parting remark about "people meddling with other people's business."

Mollie never discovered the identity of her liberator. Looking back on it many years later, she assumed that the woman must have been a Unionist with some kind of influence over the three jayhawkers. But that would not explain why she came to Mollie's rescue. Evidently, the little girls who were released from captivity informed on the jayhawkers, and someone in the community sought this particular woman's help to secure the release of the other two female captives. It all suggests that at least a few Confederate and Unionist families in Richland had begun talking to each other again, and that Mollie's efforts to help Unionist families had not gone unnoticed.

Chapter 18

Jubilee

PARTHENIA HENSLEY MAINTAINED HER FAITH IN GOD EVEN IF SHE missed the religious fervor that used to come over her in the old-style camp revivals. Religious services all but disappeared from Richland when the war came. Itinerant preachers stopped coming to the area because it was too dangerous. Many clergymen who had previously traveled through the South entered the military service as army chaplains in the Union or Confederate armies. For four years, the brush arbor as well as the little schoolhouse at Point Peter stood unused.

When it was no longer possible to hold church services in the valley, the Wyatt household took its religious observances indoors. In the South's patriarchal culture, Billy Wyatt, as the family patriarch, bore responsibility for providing moral instruction to the family. Thus he would have been the one to read from the Bible to his wife and children and Parthenia if he had been able. But Billy Wyatt could not read.

Christian religion acquired a peculiar cast in the slave states as it came to serve both whites and blacks on either side of the master-slave relationship. Many slave masters took it upon themselves to preach Christianity to their slaves or required their slaves to attend church. In this context, slave masters emphasized how the Bible stressed obedience to God's will. They taught that servants must obey their masters in order to be good Christians. They drew on Christian doctrine to urge their slaves to accept their lot in life, work hard, avoid sinning, and look forward to their reward in heaven. They admonished their slaves not to lie or steal. They warned that runaways would be cast out of the church.

Enslaved blacks by and large recognized the master's religious tutoring for what it was: manipulation. They might play along while discreetly rejecting the points that the master thought he successfully conveyed to them. In place of the master's emphasis on obedience, blacks found other meanings in religion that spoke to their longings for freedom. From Old Testament stories about Moses leading the Hebrews out of bondage, they fashioned their own appreciation of Christian doctrine, which they developed through spirituals and ceremonial practices conducted in slave quarters away from the prying eyes of the white master class. Traces of the blacks' African heritage, especially music and dance, made their way into the black church, and ultimately into the Southern white church as well.

There is no record, but one could suppose that the black slave community in Bear Creek had its own black church, as slave communities generally did. And in that case, Parthenia would have had exposure and access to African American religion through her occasional visits to the Hensley place. Enslaved blacks had an extensive religious life outside of the religious instruction they received through their owners. Historians have called the slaves' religion an "invisible institution," because worship was mostly done in secret, or out of white view. Worship ceremonies took place in the woods, or hollows, or the blacks' own brush arbors. Owing to the popularity of brush arbors among the whites, blacks' furtive prayer meetings were called "hush arbor meetings."

African American Christianity around the time of the Civil War focused most intently on God's plan for the African race, and specifically it focused on deliverance from slavery. There were two lines of belief, both tied to the second coming of Christ. One held out hope for an end to race prejudice, the other speculated on a special role for the African race in Christian history. Sometimes the two lines of belief went hand in hand, though there was an inherent tension between them. The first strain of thought found its basis in Acts 17:26: "God hath made of one blood all nations of men for to dwell on the face of the earth." The other strain of thought could point to Psalm 68:31:

"Princes shall come out of Egypt; Ethiopia shall soon stretch forth her hands unto God."

Assuming that Parthenia had access to African American Christianity through her visits to the slave community in Bear Creek, she would have been familiar with jubilees. Jubilees were African American spirituals that referred to a future time of deliverance and freedom. Usually, they were songs of sorrow about African American enslavement that offered a message of solace around the future day of freedom, or jubilee:

See these poor souls from Africa
Transported to America;
We are stolen, and sold in Georgia,
Will you go along with me?
We are stolen, and sold in Georgia,
Come sound the jubilee!

See wives and husbands sold apart,
Their children's screams will break my heart;—
There's a better day a coming,
Will you go along with me?
There's a better day a coming,
Go sound the jubilee!

On their face, jubilees appeared to equate freedom with the kingdom of God and to equate deliverance with a soul's passage into the afterlife. Slaveholders thought it was all benign. However, blacks experienced the jubilees as subversive texts. The songs used codewords, usually biblical terms, for expressing enslaved people's longing for freedom not in the afterlife but in their earthly lives. "O Canaan, sweet Canaan, I am bound for the land of Canaan," was a line in one African American spiritual. Canaan, the Promised Land of the Hebrews in the Old Testament, could also refer to the kingdom of God or heaven. But to be bound for Canaan meant "something more than a hope of reaching heaven," wrote the abolitionist Frederick Douglass. "We meant to reach the *north*—and the north was our Canaan."

Enslaved blacks understood that North and South fought over the issue of slavery. As the war went on, they saw that Northern victory would likely result in their freedom. As much as they wanted to be free, enslaved blacks still had many mixed emotions around the war and the Confederacy. The South was their homeland as much as it was Southern whites' homeland, and the North was the invader. The humiliation of defeat for the South was in some sense a humiliation for them. They shared in the suffering wrought by the war, since rapine, hunger, and the strains on the agricultural economy all impacted their lives as much as their masters' lives. Many enslaved blacks actually hated to see their masters lose their status and wealth, feeling a certain measure of loyalty through long association.

Probably Parthenia took as much interest in the war as most enslaved persons did, sensing that a Northern victory would likely set her people free. Masters tried various stratagems to prevent their slaves from becoming too personally invested in the prospect of Northern victory. They tried to convince them that the "Yankee devils" would bring ruin not just on the South but on the slave population itself. They sought to screen their slaves from the war news or deceive them into thinking that the North could not win. In most slave communities, enslaved persons found ways to circumvent these stratagems and stay abreast of war developments. On the plantations, if enslaved persons worked as servants in the big house they eavesdropped on the whites' conversations and shared what they heard with the fieldhands. If they knew how to read, they stole newspapers and shared information with all those who did not read. Being on a farm, Parthenia did not have access to those information networks and may have had more difficulty following how the war was going. On the other hand, the Wyatts may have simply shared with her whatever war news they heard.

As the end of the war drew near, the whole Southern population sensed that slavery was disintegrating and would soon fall apart altogether. A few slaveholders, recognizing the inevitable, gathered their slaves and told them they were all free; they could stay or go as each one chose. Others took their slaves and fled to Texas or southern Arkansas, still vainly hoping for a settlement of the war that would allow them to keep their valuable property.

Enslaved blacks ran away from their owners and fled to the Union lines in growing numbers. When so many slaves left their masters, it finally revealed Southern white paternalism for the monstrous fraud it was. Masters who professed to treat their slaves kindly found that their slaves ran off as quickly as slaves of cruel masters did. As the myth of white paternalism was exposed, the master class's feelings of disappointment and betrayal caused many in the slaveholder class to put aside white paternalism and invest in bitter racism instead.

As Parthenia moved toward freedom, she had to reconcile her feelings as best she could with three key people in her life who were in the white master class. The first was her father, John Hensley. The second was her present owner and the father of her child, Billy Wyatt. And the third was her mistress and half-sister, Louisa.

She saw her father for the last time when Federal troops took him prisoner on the day after Christmas in 1863. Parthenia learned eventually that he died in Gratiot Prison. It would likely have been months later, perhaps sometime after the war was over, when she was emancipated. She never had a chance to speak to her father as a free woman.

Nor did Parthenia have the opportunity, as the war drew to an end, to address her present owner about her impending freedom. Wyatt was not around for that conversation. This deeply conflicted man had long since decided that he could not support the Confederacy and would not survive the war if he remained in Richland. So, he had fled to Springfield, Missouri. He returned to Richland a few months after the war was over, surely somewhat humbled by his refugee experience and hopefully feeling a debt of gratitude to Louisa and Parthenia for protecting the farm and sheltering the children during his long absence. How it went between Parthenia and Wyatt on the occasion of his homecoming will never be known.

Nor do we know what words passed between Parthenia and her mistress Louisa when Parthenia became a free woman. How did these half-sisters who had lived in the same household for a decade and a half, one free and the other unfree, talk about that revolution of Parthenia's legal status? There is no record. All we know is that Parthenia did not walk off the Wyatt farm. She stayed.

If another woman's recollection of her own emancipation could stand in for Parthenia's, we might listen to the words of a woman named East, a onetime slave who likewise stayed with her former master when she was emancipated. East was interviewed by the Works Progress Administration in the 1930s. (The hundreds of WPA interviews with former slaves are an invaluable historical source. One point of caution, however, is that they were transcribed in a dialectical form that may sound jarring to the modern ear.)

> After de wah, everybody jist went on working same as ever. Than one day a white mens come riding through the county and tole us we was free. Free! Honey, did yo' hear that? Why, we always had been free. He didn't know what he was talking 'bout. He kept telling us we was free and dat we oughtn't to work for no white folks 'less'n we got paid for it. Well Miss Nancy took care of us then. We got our cabin and a piece of ground for a garden and a share of de crops. Daddy worked in de mill. Miss Nancy saw to it that we always had nice clothes too.

Yet there is something essential to Parthenia that is missing from East's account: her religious faith. For most African Americans—and surely this was the case for Parthenia—emancipation came as an answer to their prayers and a confirmation of their faith in God.

There was an enslaved woman in eastern Virginia, who was recorded in history simply as "Mammy." She was observed putting Sunday dinner on the table for her white family as Union forces initiated an attack on Confederate lines within earshot of the house. With each roar of cannon fire, she was heard to whisper under her breath, "Ride on, Massa

Jesus." There was another enslaved woman in Louisiana who heard the rumble of Union guns in the distance and was similarly thankful. When her companion remarked that she thought the sound they were hearing was thunder rather than cannon fire, this woman insisted, "Dat ain't no t'under, dat Yankee come to gib you Freedom."

There was another enslaved woman in Charleston, South Carolina, whose words may come nearer the mark if we try to imagine what emancipation was like for Parthenia. This woman recalled her reaction upon hearing the low boom of Yankee guns sounding in the distance outside her city. "Come, dear Jesus," she remembered saying to herself. And as the sound of cannonading got louder and louder, she came to feel "nearer to Heaben den I ever feel before."

Chapter 19

Requiem

For Henry Cole, as for hundreds of other Rebel guerrillas scattered across northern Arkansas, the last months of the war devolved into a grim struggle to avoid starvation or capture, and to harry the enemy if possible. Henry's movements in the spring of 1865 are not definitely known, but when his guerrilla unit surrendered, he was directed to go to Dardanelle on the Arkansas River to receive his parole. That would suggest that Henry stuck with Love's Company as it resumed independent operations in the Ozarks from the fall of 1864 to the end of the war. Captain Love and his men may have been among the Rebel guerrilla bands that ventured to the north bank of the Arkansas River in the spring to shoot at Union supply boats as they steamed upriver to Fort Smith. The guerrillas' potshots from the riverbank, though they sometimes took out an unlucky Union soldier, were mere pinpricks to the strong Union forces that by 1865 had come to control the whole length of the Arkansas Valley.

Captain Love was in camp with his men somewhere near Yellville near the end of the war, according to information provided nearly one hundred years later to local historian James J. Johnston by J. C. Love, son of the guerrilla captain. Calling his men together, Love said: "Boys, we have lost this war. If you boys want to, you can go over to the other side. It may be best for you, but as for me, I aim to go on to the end."

News of General Robert E. Lee's surrender of the Army of Virginia at Appomattox on April 9, 1865, reached Arkansas in mid-April, but Confederate forces in Arkansas were reluctant to lay down their arms right away in spite of their hopeless position. General Jeff Thompson had command of Rebel forces in the state north of the Arkansas River. He agreed to terms of surrender on May 11, pledging to assemble his regular troops and guerrilla fighters at Wittsburg and Jacksonport for formal surrender a couple of weeks hence. Union forces were on hand to accept the Rebels' surrender at Wittsburg at the end of May and at Jacksonport on June 5. Meanwhile, the commander of the Trans-Mississippi Department, General Edmund Kirby Smith, who had withdrawn his army from southern Arkansas into Texas, negotiated a surrender on May 26 and brought the men in on June 2. Many small guerrilla bands, such as Love's Company, gave themselves up after that.

Rebel guerrillas in Arkansas feared what would happen to them when they laid down their weapons and tried to make their way home unarmed. Years of fighting between Unionist and Rebel guerrillas had left a bloody trail of revenge killings. Now, with so many unsettled scores across the land, many Rebel guerrillas feared they would be bushwhacked and murdered when they walked home alone or went back to work on their farms.

A Confederate colonel by the name of A. R. Witt, commander of the Tenth Arkansas Cavalry Regiment and a former guerrilla captain, pleaded with Union officers to control the Unionist guerrillas whom he knew were out to murder his men as soon as they gave up their weapons. "When we lay down our arms," he wrote, "at the same time we lay down our lives." It galled him that the very worst breed of jayhawkers who had plundered and murdered civilians now had the temerity to claim they were independent companies operating on behalf of Union occupation forces. Of course, he ignored the fact that his own guerrilla company had been doing the same thing for Confederate authorities at an earlier point in the conflict. Now the shoe was on the other foot. But now the war was over, and the fighting was supposed to stop, so Witt made a legitimate point that some former jayhawkers would go on killing simply because they had scores to settle. Once the indiscriminate violence of guerrilla warfare began, the bloodletting could not be ended easily. Colonel Witt saw with perfect clarity that his men still faced a lethal environment even after surrender. As one historian of the guerrilla war has remarked, "Neither surrender nor decree could turn off the spigot of guerrilla violence."

At the time of surrender, each Confederate soldier was to receive a paper parole pass in exchange for his gun. The parole system that was used to return Confederate soldiers to civilian life followed from the parole system that had taken shape in the early stage of the war to process the thousands of soldiers who were taken prisoner on battlefields. The wartime parole system evolved as a way to facilitate regular prisoner exchanges between North and South, so as to avoid the need to detain tens of thousands of men in prisoner-of-war camps. During the conflict, when a man who had been captured in battle was paroled, he swore an oath not to take up arms again until he was regularly exchanged for a person of the same rank on the other side. Then he was issued an official slip of paper stating that he had a pass to return home on his own recognizance. The parole system that was adopted at the end of the war varied from the parole system in wartime only a little: now each surrendered Confederate soldier was required to take an oath of allegiance to the United States; then he received a parole pass stating that he could go home and return to civilian life. Often he received rations for his journey home.

Henry was probably as apprehensive about being paroled as other Rebel guerrillas were, considering all the terror that the Meek gang had brought on his family and knowing as he did that Lewis Meek had gotten away when Henry's own unit had ambushed and decimated the Meek gang. But he had to take his chances with everyone else. He proceeded to the river port town of Dardanelle on the Arkansas River to take his oath of allegiance and obtain his parole pass. There, he found a steamboat tied up at the wharf where a Union officer and soldier guard were administering the paroles on the top deck.

Henry went aboard the steamboat, took the oath, and received his parole pass. He proceeded down to the lower deck to cross back over the gangway. Just before he reached the gangway, a man stepped in front of him, leveled a pistol at his breast, and fired a shot. Henry slumped against the boat's railing. The man grabbed him before he fell to the deck and hove him over the side. Henry went into the river and when his nearly lifeless body rose to the surface the man fired several more shots into it at short range.

A bystander watched the whole thing but was too surprised or intimidated to do anything. If the Federals on the top deck heard the shots, they did not come down to investigate in time to apprehend the killer. The killer got away from the crime scene without being identified. It is possible the Federals never even heard the shots because they did not recover Henry's body but allowed it to float away with the current.

Was Lewis Meek the man who murdered Henry Cole? Most likely it was he, but the truth will never be known for sure. So many murders like this one took place in the months after the Civil War that military and civil authorities could not begin to investigate them all. The best evidence that Meek was the killer comes from Mollie's own account where she states that her husband's murderer was one of the jayhawkers who had burned the Coles out of their house two months earlier. "This wretch," she wrote, "to save himself from the retaliation which he knew he deserved, pulled his revolver and shot my husband down in cold blood and threw him over the guards of the boat into the river." Although Mollie described her husband's murder as personal and fueled by revenge, she did not identify the Meek gang by name in her account, probably because she was determined to let sleeping dogs lie.

Lewis Meek—or whoever the man was—made a point to visit Richland shortly after he committed the deed so he could tell the Coles firsthand that he had killed Henry. Encountering Mollie on the road and recognizing her as Henry's wife, he boasted that he had given Henry Cole "his final parole." To add clarity, he gloated that he had intercepted Henry where he obtained his parole, at Dardanelle, and had thrown his body into the Arkansas River.

Mollie said not a word in reply when the man confronted her. She did not believe him, nor did she want to engage with him and suffer any more of his insults or violence. But after he passed on down the road, his odious words hung in the air. Was it true?

Mollie reported this brute's pronouncement to her mother-in-law, Saba, and they mulled it over together. They decided it had to be investigated. Mollie would go to Dardanelle to make inquiries. She would take her sister-in-law Laura, who was eleven, and the two would share a horse and make a trip over the Boston Mountains to the Arkansas River, about a three-day ride. Saba had a brother and a sister down that way who would surely assist them. Both were staunch Unionists who had relocated to the Arkansas Valley late in the war when Federal troops established a strong presence along the river. Assuming these two siblings of Saba bore no ill will toward their nephew Henry for having fought for the Confederacy—and Saba was confident they would not—they might have connections among the Federals that could prove helpful to Mollie as she looked into the circumstances around her husband's parole.

Until now Mollie had suppressed the thought that her husband Henry might truly be dead, but once she and her sister-in-law started up the mountain road the real possibility of Henry's murder loomed in her thoughts. Death's dark shadows now seemed to confront them on all sides. She saw death in the vacant, burnt-out cabins. She saw it in the abandoned fields overgrown with brush. Death hovered about the immense tangles of fallen pine trees that lay across the road every few miles, each obstruction forcing them to detour off the road into the forest. How long had it been since anyone had cleared this road of deadfall? The countryside that Mollie had once found so beautiful looked like one big graveyard now. When they stopped for the night, they heard the mournful notes of a whippoorwill. As everyone in Mollie's world knew, when a whippoorwill visited you at night it came as a messenger of death. She took it as a bad omen for the fate of her poor Henry. Later that night she heard an owl hooting. In her bleak mental state, the hooting sounded like a requiem for all the destruction and ruin they had seen that day. In the morning, she felt only dread over what they would learn when they got to the Arkansas River.

When they reached Saba's brother's place, their uncle received them kindly just as Saba had anticipated. But the news was not good. After

Mollie stated their business, her uncle said that he had heard that a man's body had been found in the river a few days before about five miles below his place. He offered to go there with Mollie and her sister-in-law to ascertain if the body was Henry's. Early the next morning they went to the place where the body had reportedly washed up and asked the local people what they knew about it. It turned out to be the body of a black man. The finding might have afforded Mollie fresh hope that her husband was still alive, but it only added to the crushing feeling of dread she now had. Returning to her uncle's place, she fell into bed resigned and exhausted, and throughout the night she was racked by horrible dreams. In the morning, she conferred with her uncle and decided she and her sister-in-law must return home post-haste to console Saba, admitting the probability that Henry was dead.

So, home they went, up and over the Boston Mountains on their sore-footed old nag—another three-day ride through wilderness and abandoned farmsteads. As they neared home, Mollie braced for telling her mother-in-law that Henry was missing and presumed dead. She never had to utter the words. For Saba, the sight of seventeen-year-old Mollie and her eleven-year-old daughter coming up the road by themselves was enough. The mother and her daughters greeted each other with wails of grief.

Many years later, when Mollie wrote about this time in her autobiography, she called on familiar biblical phrases to describe her and the family's despair. "For us remained no joy. Life's cup was filled with wormwood and gall and we had no alternative but to drain it to its bitter dregs." The words were from Lamentations in the Old Testament, which expresses the overwhelming grief of the Hebrews after the destruction of Jerusalem by the Babylonians. Mollie's grief over Henry mingled with her desolation over the end of the Confederacy.

Mollie also alluded in her book to having felt deeply depressed and possibly suicidal. She could not eat or sleep. She felt hopeless and restless, and thought "the grave" was her "only chance for peace and rest." Both she and her mother-in-law said they "longed for death."

After some days, Mollie rallied. She speculated that Henry's body might have drifted farther down the river from Dardanelle before washing up, and that if she made inquiries lower on the river then she might be able to learn what had happened, recover Henry's body, and give it a decent Christian burial. She conferred with her oldest sister-in-law Angeline, who was now fifteen, and the two resolved that they would make the trip together.

They borrowed a stronger horse to carry the two of them, packed a little dry bread in a poke, and set out on the desolate road. At about the midpoint of their journey a band of brigands overtook them and forced them at gunpoint to dismount and hand over the reins of their horse. The girls complied with the brigands' demand swiftly and silently, and moments later they were left standing on the road bereft yet again, trying to shut their ears to the awful whooping and hollering as the men rode away with their horse. Resigned to proceed the rest of the way on foot, they did not waste time on lamentation but began at once on the long march, heads down, trying to stay focused on their mission. They took turns carrying an old rolled up quilt, which they slept with each night. Whenever they came to a spring they lay on their bellies and put their lips to the trickling stream to drink. After four solid days of walking, they reached the house of their aunt, Saba's sister. Like the uncle, their aunt had fled Searcy County and relocated to the Arkansas River valley for the protection by Federal troops stationed along the river. The aunt recognized her niece Angeline and told them they must stay with her awhile and rest up after their hard journey.

By and by the aunt recommended that they visit an old man by the name of Ben Bratton. This was, of course, the father of the four Bratton brothers who had all served with the Union army's Third Arkansas Cavalry. The aunt explained to Mollie that Mr. Bratton and his wife Laura were late residents of Searcy County—Unionist refugees like herself. The Brattons' temporary place was just outside Lewisburg, a river port town with about 2,000 people on the road to Little Rock. Because the four sons were in the Union army, Mr. Bratton would be well connected with the local authorities. Mollie and Angeline walked about ten miles to the Brattons' place and received a cordial welcome from the old couple. Ben Bratton listened intently to Mollie's story. Then he told her he thought he had important news for them—sad but important news.

Bratton explained that he had been up to the Stout plantation a few days earlier, fishing from the upper end of a long sandbar with two other men. One of the other men had discovered the body of a man lodged in a driftwood pile. The three of them had joined together in extricating the body from the driftwood. As the body was swollen and decomposed, they had dug a hole in the sand and rolled it into the hole and covered it. But first, the man who found the body had helped himself to a silver ring on one of the dead man's fingers. As Henry had worn a silver wedding ring, this detail convinced Mollie that the dead man was her late husband and her search for the body was nearly at an end.

The next day Mollie and Angeline walked into the town of Lewisburg to seek confirmation of Ben Bratton's story. The people they interviewed had heard generally about the body, but no one offered more information beyond what Bratton had already told them. At the end of the day, they returned to the Bratton place to report their findings and decide what to do next.

Ben Bratton was willing to help them recover the remains, but he said they would need a sturdy coffin first. Mollie and Angeline decided they would return to Richland to make a proper coffin and return with the coffin to the Brattons as soon as possible. Bratton would take them to the gravesite in the sandbar and help them recover the remains, and then they would take Henry home to be buried next to the graves of his father and brother in the small cemetery by the Buffalo River.

The next day, Mollie and Angeline walked back to their aunt's place to ask for her assistance. The aunt had rented a yoke of oxen and a wagon to move her household belongings back to Searcy County. Mollie asked her if she would postpone that effort and loan them the wagon and ox team so they could execute the more urgent and solemn task of fetching

Henry's body home. The aunt agreed, so Mollie and Angeline drove the wagon back over the Boston Mountains to Richland.

Back in the Richland Valley, Mollie took the wagon around to the Williams farmstead—the onetime home of her first lover, Valentine Williams. The Williams family was gone, and the house stood vacant. As Mollie well knew, the Williams family had fled to safer quarters many months earlier. Mollie entered the cabin and looked around. She was looking for boards to use in making a coffin, but in her mind's eye she saw something else. She saw the young man who had so enraptured her at the outset of the war, her old sweetheart with the raven locks. In marriage she had seldom allowed herself to dwell on the memory of her first betrothed, but in her new status of widow she felt differently. She could almost imagine Valentine being in the room—stooping to put a log on the fire, brushing off his hands, placing an elbow on the mantle. It seemed so long ago now. But she broke off the stream of thought and went back to the task at hand: to obtain floorboards with which to make a coffin for Henry. Studying the cabin floor, she selected some planks that looked suitable. She pulled them up and loaded them into the wagon. The coffin would have a special symbolism for her. Since Valentine had not received a decent burial at home any more than Henry had to this point, the coffin would serve in a way as Valentine's, too. In her heart, both men whom she had loved and lost in the war would rest in peace in the same grave.

From the Williams place she drove the wagon two miles down the road to the Wasson place. She had spoken with Eli Wasson already about making her a coffin. She delivered the planks to him and said she would be back in a few days. When she returned, Wasson had a rough and sturdy coffin built for her. The inside was heavily pitched and watertight so that the coffin could be floated across a side channel of the Arkansas River if necessary and so the decomposed remains could be transported all the way back to Richland.

Mollie made her third and final trip over the Boston Mountains in company with Saba and Angeline, the empty coffin rattling in the bed of the wagon all the way over the mountains. Since the three women were destitute as well as weary with grief, they were not too proud to beg for food as they traveled. At night they slept in the wagon box beside the empty coffin.

They went to Ben Bratton and requested that he guide them to where Henry's remains lay buried in sand. When they all got to the edge of the river, they found that the river had risen, and they could not safely reach the sandbar by wading across the intervening channel. Mollie looked around and found an old black man who had a large feed trough that he sometimes used for a boat. He agreed to take Mollie across the channel. Leaving her mother-in-law and sister-in-law on the bank, Mollie crossed to the sandbar in the leaky, makeshift watercraft. Meanwhile, Bratton found a place where he could wade across in water up to his armpits. Joining up again on the sandbar, they commenced their search for the grave. As the river had risen and fallen several times, the driftwood pile had moved off and all visible sign of the gravesite had been obliterated. Bratton probed the sand over a wider and wider area without any success. With night coming on, they had to give up the search.

Dispirited as well as wet, cold, and hungry, they went to Bratton's place to spend the night. Bratton's wife welcomed the three Coles inside and fussed over them, insisting that they must be warmed up and properly fed before turning in. The next morning, the man who had taken the ring from the corpse came to the house to show Mollie the ring. Seeing her initials M. E. C. engraved on it, she knew that she was looking at her husband's wedding ring. With fresh determination to find the grave, they went back to the sandbar.

While they were unloading the coffin, a man rode up on a horse and told them it would be useless to hunt for the body there. As Mollie and her companions looked at him in disbelief, he elaborated. A rumor had gone around Lewisburg that the dead man buried in the sandbar carried a money belt. Some townsmen, acting on the rumor, had dug up the corpse to recover the booty. Finding there was no money belt after all, they had flung the corpse into the river. Afterwards, someone else had reported seeing it downstream a piece floating well out in the channel.

Mollie was crushed. This was the last sad stroke. There was nothing to do now but go back to Ben Bratton's house and weigh their options.

Mollie had spent more than a month in search of her missing husband. She had made three trips over the Boston Mountains—ridden four hundred miles on horse and walked a hundred miles on foot. She had tried as hard as any young woman might to retrieve her husband's remains and give them a Christian burial. She was physically and emotionally exhausted. All agreed that it was time to give up the search.

Bratton told them about an abandoned farmstead where they could stash the unused coffin. They drove the wagon to this farm, inspected the inside of the deserted house, and tucked the coffin into an empty garret. Then they returned the wagon and ox team to Saba's sister and started for home afoot.

Chapter 20

In the Apple Orchard

On September 10, 1865, Mollie marked her eighteenth birthday. It was a trial for her to count her blessings at that sad time, but she did so all the same. Number one, she still lived with her dear mother-in-law Saba Cole; together, they were making another abandoned house habitable again. Number two, their crops were bountiful, and she was proud of all the work she had put in. Three, after a spell of poor health following her exhausting searches for her dead husband, she felt strong again in both mind and body. Fourth—and best of all—the hot and sticky days of August had passed, and the first lovely days of autumn were now gliding by. The buzz of the cicadas had faded away a few weeks back, and now she heard crickets chirping in the cornfields and squirrels scolding her from high up in the oak trees. Occasionally she looked up at the sound of beating wings to watch a flock of pelicans or a pair of wild geese fly overhead on their fall migrations.

It was on one such day of early autumn, while returning from the field to the house, that she happened to see Angeline gaily visiting with a couple of young men out in the apple orchard. Drawn by the cheery sound of their laughter, she went to see who the two men might be. One of the men standing there was none other than Valentine Williams! Praise the Lord, she exclaimed to herself. He was alive after all! He had not been killed on the battlefield. Indeed, he looked as healthy, fit, and handsome as he had ever been.

Valentine told her that he had been wounded in a battle and left behind in a pine thicket. Picked up by the enemy, he had been hauled to a Federal field hospital. The Confederates had counterattacked the next day, and some Texan troops had overrun the Federal hospital and taken him into their regiment. Moving with the Texans after that, four months had passed before he recovered from his wounds and returned to his original regiment. Even his old comrades had come to presume him dead.

Valentine had long since heard of Mollie's marriage to Henry Cole. Lately he had been informed of Henry's murder. He had also been told of Mollie's drawn-out efforts to find her missing husband. He spoke to Mollie feelingly of her remarkable devotion to her late husband and how faithful she had been to her line of duty to try so hard to bring home his remains for a decent burial.

Valentine allowed that he had never had a crow to pick with Henry over his stealing her away from him. It all came about from the misunderstanding that had developed around his own long absence from his regiment, and that was nobody's fault. Valentine said that all Mollie's misfortunes had resulted from the conditions of war; none of it came of her own making.

As they talked, Mollie felt a resurgence of her former tender feelings for him. He was the same beautiful man, but now he was much more confident and dexterous with his words than before. As for herself, she felt cut off from the merry young lass she had been at the outset of the war. That person had fled. Now she was but a shadow of her former self, robbed of all her youthful grace. She felt awkward standing before him in her black dress and bonnet, looking matronly though she was only eighteen years old. She felt a mite ashamed, too. She was so incredulous to see him again in life when she had once mourned him dead. It made her flush with excitement, and she worried that he might see the color in her face as they stood there in the dappled sunlight under the apple tree.

Valentine gave her no sign of a renewal of their previous engagement. Still, there was so much warmth in his words and manner that it gave her hope. Indeed, in a strange way it took her back to that far off time before the war when she was first smitten by him, when she had hung on his every word and glance. Now the memory of their betrothal, on that day on the mustering ground when the band played "Dixie," seemed almost dreamlike to her, as if it had never really happened except in her youthful imagination. But she knew their engagement had been real; he had written her a letter quilled with his own blood! And she remembered reading that cherished letter aloud to her cousin Mary Greenhaw, with whom she thought she could discuss the mysterious, luminous matter of love. And she recalled how Mary Greenhaw, who was just twelve years old then, had proven incapable of understanding a young woman's heart at her age, and had set her adrift to wonder all on her own.

Mollie wanted to love Valentine all over again. But there remained the problem of the mourning period for her departed husband, Henry Cole. A while after their meeting she asked herself soberly, "Might I not aspire to the hand of my former lover without shame?" And she told herself that she could, in her hard circumstances, but only with appropriate discretion. She would not trifle with this. If Valentine Williams did not come back to her readily, she would look upon the whole episode of his coming back to Richland as an enchanting dream and leave it at that. In the brush arbor long ago, he had sung like an angel. On the mustering ground, he had slipped from her embrace like an angel. Then lately in the apple orchard he had *appeared* like an angel. She reasoned with herself, if he was so angelic to her, then maybe this soldier's return was no more than an enchanting dream, and she might have to leave it at that.

As the autumn advanced, Mollie finished cribbing the corn, preparing the apples, and digging and binning the potatoes to last them through the next winter. At last, they had plenty of food again. A feeling of peace and security returned to the valley. The menace of marauding guerrillas receded into the past, and the simple pleasures of life returned. With a little leisure time in front of her, Mollie decided to pay a visit to the Greenhaw family with whom she had lived at the opening of the war. Dressing in her black attire but wearing a much brighter countenance than she had worn all summer, Mollie hiked down the road to her aunt and uncle's place with the intention to visit for a few days.

Someone in the Greenhaw family saw Mollie approaching and summoned the whole family into the yard to give her a hearty welcome. There in front of the cabin were Aunt Usley and Uncle Jim and all their sons except Calvin and all their daughters including the widow Elizabeth. Despite the family's good intentions, the scene presented Mollie with a rude surprise. There in the Greenhaw lineup was Valentine Williams. It was immediately and painfully clear to her that he was at the Greenhaw place for the purpose of courting her own cousin Mary.

She concealed her disappointment and tried to be as joyous at the sight of all her cousins as she could be. But it hurt—no, it seared—to see her cousin Mary behaving so coquettishly. For the first time in her experience, the bilious taste of jealousy welled up inside her. Mary, or "Mollie"—the name her cousin now used most often, a further painful irony—looked radiant in the presence of her own former lover. Her younger cousin did not seem the least bit solicitous of her feelings in the circumstances. Indeed, despite the fact that Mollie Cole was now the widow of Henry Cole and was cloaked from head to foot in widow's weeds, she could not help but see an issue of trespass in her cousin's conduct. But she kept the indictment to herself, maintained her composure, and soon filched an excuse to cut short her visit. Valentine treated her kindly yet persisted in directing most of his attention to Mollie's cousin Mollie Greenhaw.

~

Valentine Williams now lived about fifteen miles from Richland with his mother, Susan, and one of his brothers. His father, Ambrose, had died of natural causes during the war. The new Williams place was a prosperous little farm occupying rich bottomland in a bend of the Buffalo River.

The Coles, meanwhile, had relocated to another abandoned farm in Richland. It was an improvement over the ramshackle place they had shared with a second homeless family in the last months of the war. The house they now occupied had no floor, however. By and by, Saba asked Mollie if she would go to Mr. Valentine Williams and ask permission to use the floor boards in the Williams's former house in Richland—more of the same sturdy planks they had used for making a coffin for Henry. They would pull up the boards to make a temporary floor in their new house, Saba suggested. As soon as the sawmill was running again, they would acquire their own floorboards and return the Williams's boards to the house. Mollie was reluctant to go on this errand so soon after seeing Valentine courting her cousin. But Saba had an ulterior motive, of course. She could sense that Mollie was in love with him again. She had a notion that the situation surrounding her daughter-in-law and Mr. Williams and Miss Greenhaw needed a little nudge. She insisted that those floor boards in the old Williams house would be a big help to them with winter coming on. So, Mollie relented and agreed to pay a visit to Mr. Williams.

Mollie rode to the Williams's new place along the Buffalo and was greeted at the door by Valentine's mother. Mrs. Williams invited Mollie to have a noon meal with her and her oldest son and await Valentine's return in the late afternoon. Mrs. Williams was cordial, but the ensuing conversation was a bit strained. To Mollie, Mrs. Williams seemed protective of her son and a little ill-disposed toward her. By Mollie's doleful reckoning, Mrs. Williams knew that her son was courting Miss Greenhaw and she wanted her son to marry the rosy-cheeked, laughing-eyed, sweet little girl of sixteen rather than herself, the poor and unfortunate widow of Henry Cole, notwithstanding the fact that the widow Cole was once upon a time betrothed to Valentine.

Valentine finally arrived home many hours later as Mrs. Williams was putting dinner on the table. Mollie hastily brought up the reason for her visit: the floorboards. Valentine cheerfully told her the floorboards were hers for the taking. She should go right ahead. He would offer to help her with her project but the old Williams place was a long way away and she would perhaps not want to wait until he was free to make that trip. Following the meal, Mollie prepared to leave the Williams residence without further ado. However, it was getting dark and everywhere the brush was so overgrown that she felt unsure of finding her way back to the road. She asked Valentine to get her started on the right path. He said he surely would. He saddled up his horse and accompanied her for the first six miles of her homeward journey, seeing her as far as the junction with the main road. Along the way they talked about the ruined condition of the country. As both of them felt sensitive to Mollie's condition of being in her mourning period, they did not raise the matter of their previous engagement. But as they bid each other goodnight, Valentine asked if it would be all right if he visited her at her home. She answered him "yes" with all the enthusiasm and warmth she dared.

After some weeks went by Valentine came to the house. Mollie showed him the new floor and other improvements she and Saba had made, and then she led Valentine on a stroll around the farm. It was a lovely afternoon in early November. The autumn-colored oaks were dropping their leaves in the golden rays of the sun. As the oak leaves rained down, it looked as if the big, old trees were weeping over the two of them—tears of sorrow and gladness both. Their conversation was not as sentimental as Mollie wished, but the easy way they had with one another while circumambulating the place made up for it. Their relationship still held promise, she thought.

After that, Valentine began to visit both Mollie Greenhaw and Mollie Cole fairly regularly, alternating between them, trying to make up his mind which one he would ask to marry him. When the pattern of courtship became manifest to all, Mollie and her cousin pledged to one another that whoever should receive a proposal, the other would handle it with equanimity so they would remain friends. They even discussed their respective chances of success. Pushing their bond even further, they mutually pledged that whoever bested the other in this contest, the bride-to-be would ask the other to be bridesmaid at the wedding.

Sadly, for Mollie Cole, a letter came to her from Valentine one day informing her of his engagement to Mollie Greenhaw. The message was brief and formal, announcing the date of their wedding. Mollie had steeled herself for this disappointment. Now she stood determined to honor her part of the pledge, to hold her feelings of jealousy in check, and to push through the ordeal with every stitch of grace she could muster.

But for all of Valentine's coolheaded deliberation, he had blundered into the wrong marriage choice. Fortunately, it did not take long for him to find this out. Discussing the wedding arrangements with his fiancée, he asked her who she wanted to be her bridesmaid. Mollie Greenhaw answered him with pique, "Your little, loving widow, Mollie E. Cole." Her choice took him by surprise, and combined with the offensive pique in her voice, it stung him to the quick. He responded as calmly as he could that her choice would not do at all; he could not stand at the altar and wed another woman in the presence of Mrs. Cole. At this hurtful rejoinder, Mollie Greenhaw flew into a jealous rage. They quarreled. Valentine stood his ground, insisting she must choose someone else or have no bridesmaid at all. In a fit, Mollie Greenhaw ordered him to leave her house and come back in a few days, and she would have an answer for him then. He left the house as she directed, but he never went back.

Mollie first learned of the broken engagement by way of her cousin. From the unfeeling way in which her cousin told the story, Mollie concluded that the marriage was never meant to happen and that good fortune had smiled on all three of them. Clearly, her cousin did not love this man the way she did. Now it should be plain to all three who Valentine truly belonged with, and she was confident he would soon come back to her. After a few days passed, she received a letter.

Dear Mollie: **Buffalo, Jan. 16, 1866**

As you know, I was engaged to marry Miss Mollie Greenhaw, but for reasons I will explain later on the engagement has been canceled. If agreeable to you, will be pleased to pay you a visit.

Yours truly,
V. H. Williams

Mollie found this message most promising, and she carefully crafted her reply.

My Dear Mr. Williams: **At Home, Jan. 18, 1866**

Your kind favor received, and your request is cheerfully and cordially granted. Have heard of your unfortunate misunderstanding with your fiancée, and deeply regret the same, as I seemed to be innocently involved in it. I look upon it as a case of honest differences wherein no one is particularly to blame. With kindest wishes and fond regards,

Affectionately,
Mollie E. Cole

A few days later, Valentine visited Mollie at her home again. He explained his reason for breaking off the engagement. She said she felt satisfied by his explanation. They renewed their courtship, their meetings becoming more and more frequent as spring came on. In July of 1866 they were engaged to be married. On February 17, 1867, they celebrated their wedding.

Chapter 21

The Song of the Whippoorwill

Over the years, Mollie and Valentine Williams prospered. At first, they raised cows, hogs, and a corn crop just as the older generation did before the war. Soon they began producing a small cash crop of cotton as well, trundling the cotton to the cotton gin and taking a little more cash to the bank each year. A few years into the marriage, Valentine built a two-story frame house in place of the original homestead cabin. More than a decade into the marriage, in 1878, they rented out their farm on the Buffalo and moved to Marshall, the former Burrowsville, to enroll their children in school. In town, Valentine worked as the county surveyor while Mollie ran a small hotel. Mollie bore eight children in the years from 1868 to 1881, six of whom survived to adulthood. In 1887, they moved across the Buffalo River to a new hamlet then known as Monkey Run. With the coming of the railroad, Monkey Run would receive the more dignified name of St. Joe. Valentine bought a share in a nearby zinc mine. Some years later, when the railroad eventually came to Searcy County, Valentine and his partners sold the mine to the railroad for an impressive $25,000. The windfall from the sale of the mine property at last placed the family in "easy circumstances." The year was 1901, and that was when Mollie chose to write her autobiography.

Mollie published *A Thrilling Romance of the Civil War* in 1902. Her slim book joined an immense literature of Civil War memoirs, stories, and commentary. In that torrent of writing about the Civil War, one could distinguish numerous currents and eddies. In the immediate postwar period Americans did not show a great appetite for reading about the war, and publishers mostly waited. Then some fictional stories and reminiscences began to appear in the Northern magazines, and interest began to grow. Memoirs by the great generals began to appear, followed by a more systematic solicitation and production of military accounts by former generals and colonels who had been in the second and third tiers of command. As veterans' organizations formed, regimental histories and soldiers' memoirs abounded as well.

The geographic coverage of the war in this postwar literature was uneven. The eastern theater of war dominated. All the great battles and campaigns had been fought in Virginia, it seemed. The entire western theater of war from the Appalachians to the Mississippi River was remembered as a sideshow, while military operations in the Trans-Mississippi West were barely acknowledged at all.

What was more, a prevailing bias toward the Southern point of view soon emerged in the postwar literature. It was not because Southerners did more writing and publishing, for exactly the opposite was true. Northern veterans outnumbered Southern veterans by more than two to one, and publishing outlets were heavily skewed toward the Northeast. Rather, the emphasis on the Southern point of view developed because writers and readers in all part of the United States displayed a fascination with the Southern experience of defeat. Moreover, the South was the setting for most of the war's activity and for Northern readers the region held an element of exoticism.

But there was something much more significant than mere curiosity about the Old South going on in the production of this literature. The nation was trying to bind up its wounds. In this national project of reconciliation, there was a natural impulse to give sympathetic treatment to the side that was vanquished. White Southerners conditioned their support of national reconciliation on Northerners' acceptance of an interpretation of the causes and conduct of the war that would salvage white Southerners' pride and position in Southern society. Northerners accepted the Southerners' terms with surprising alacrity. The myth of the Lost Cause took shape. The Lost Cause mythology permeated the postwar literature about the Civil War in everything from fiction and poetry to generals' accounts of battles to politicians' speeches.

In essence, the myth of the Lost Cause maintained that the war had come about from a tragic misunderstanding. The North had fought to preserve the Union; the South had fought for independence. Yankee soldiers had sacrificed their lives and spilled their blood to ensure the survival and renewal of the republic; the South's soldiers had fought gallantly against great odds; they had finally laid down their arms when the North's overwhelming resources made further struggle pointless. The myth of the Lost Cause sidestepped the central issue of slavery as the war's fundamental issue and simply ignored the fact that the emancipation of blacks from slavery was the war's principal outcome. It focused on the equal valor of Northern and Southern combatants, and it projected a moral equivalency between the war aims of both sides.

To appreciate Mollie's true story of the Civil War fully, we need to reckon with how the myth of the Lost Cause affected her storytelling in *A Thrilling Romance of the Civil War*. One feature of the myth of the Lost Cause is its indulgence in Southern Romanticism, with its antiquated notions of chivalry and patriarchy. In Mollie's rustic story from the Ozarks we find no great Southern plantations, no cavaliers and cottonfields, no flowering magnolias or Spanish moss. Her story, however, is infused with the sentimentality of the Victorian age. We accept Mollie's sentimentality because it was a reflection of the culture in which she lived. Moreover, we can appreciate that her sentimentality made her open herself up to her readers in a way that allows her story to feel intimate to a twenty-first century audience, now six or seven generations removed from the Civil War era.

Notably, Mollie made just one reference to slavery in her book. Concerning the rising tensions around the secession crisis, she wrote, "The two great sections of our nation—North and South—had grown bitter in their hatred of each other over the question of slavery, and were straining their energies and resources in preparing to engage in a fratricidal war." She went on from there to "earnestly wonder" how the two sides had blundered so helplessly and pointlessly into so terrible a war of brother against brother. This was precisely the script of the Lost Cause. It cast aside the issue of slavery and lamented that a rift had occurred.

Mollie added her story to the mass of Civil War memoirs and reminiscences because she had something unique to offer. She wanted to bring attention to the guerrilla war. While it was bad enough that brother fought brother, she needed her readers to understand that America's fratricidal war carried an even more disturbing strain of evil in it: the guerrilla assault on civilians. She was right that the guerrilla war had been largely overlooked. But the myth of the Lost Cause influenced her storytelling in ways that led to some distortions in her account of the guerrilla war.

Mollie insisted that there was no real difference between Union and Confederate guerrillas. It was her contention that pro-Union jayhawkers and pro-Confederate bushwhackers were equally loathsome characters; they stood with one another on the same low, disgusting moral plain. She consigned them all to a fraternity of shame. Here she inverted the myth of the Lost Cause, suggesting there was a moral equivalency in each side's degeneracy rather than each side's valor. Her evaluation of the guerrilla fighters on the Union and Confederate sides was fair enough in a narrow sense of individual responsibility, perhaps. But she glossed over the fact that it was the Confederate government that sanctioned guerrilla units in the first place and that it was the Confederate army, far more than the Union army, that increasingly blurred the line between regular and irregular fighting units as the war went on. She did not hold the Confederacy to account for these things, even though the main theme of her book was to expose the perils of guerrilla warfare.

Forty years on from the war, Mollie would not own the fact that her first husband Henry Cole was a guerrilla fighter. Even as she used her personal story to shine a light on the guerrilla war, she dissembled to her readers about her own husband's involvement in it. Perhaps one might excuse her for dissembling if she had notions about propriety that made her want to protect her late husband's reputation as a Confederate veteran. But there was more to it than that. Her dissembling about Henry Cole's unit went along with her effort to draw a false moral equivalency between the two sides' conduct in the war.

Mollie might also be taken to task for dissembling when she wrote about Henry Cole's decision to desert from the Confederate army in September 1864. Modern historians, in their effort to understand why the Confederacy collapsed so quickly in 1864–65, have looked hard at Confederate desertion rates and individual deserters for clues about the true character of Southern nationalism. If the myth of the Lost Cause romanticized how the nascent Confederate nation waged a war of independence or liberation against overwhelming odds, modern historians take rather the opposite view and wonder why the South's war of liberation became so enfeebled by 1864. They ask what caused the Confederate army to melt away on the battlefield while defeatism ran rampant through the civilian population (including, it should be noted, among women who had supported the Confederate cause at the beginning). We can speculate on the factors that led Henry Cole to desert from regular service and to resume guerrilla fighting in 1864, but we cannot quite know what was on his mind because Mollie pulled a veil over it. Here again one suspects that when Mollie wrote her book she was not just protecting her first husband's memory but that she was doing her bit to protect Southern memory as well.

Apart from dissembling over the facts of Henry Cole's guerrilla activity and his desertion from the regular army, Mollie's book can be taken as a forthright account of her experiences. Even with all the hundreds of Civil War memoirs and reminiscences published at the end of the nineteenth century, her account filled a gap. There were relatively few memoirs written by Confederate women of Arkansas, and even fewer by female denizens of the Ozarks. Her perspective is valuable because it is so rare. As one historian wrote of this region in the Civil War, "The faraway Trans-Mississippi affords a look at warfare at its worst, perhaps even at its most pointless." Mollie would not have disagreed.

There remains the question of who murdered Henry Cole. Mollie provided clues that point to Lewis Meek, but she did not name the man. According to Erd W. Cole, a grandson of Saba Cole who was interviewed about 1970, he remembered his Grandmother Saba telling him when he was a child that another man, Newt Cooper, murdered her son. This appears to be false information, perhaps a confusion of names by Erd after many decades. We know something about Newt Cooper, and he is in some ways a plausible suspect in Henry Cole's murder. Cooper came from Tennessee and settled in Bear Creek in 1853. He served in both the Confederate and Union armies; in fact, his service record closely parallels the "dual enlistment" pattern of the Bratton brothers. First, he served as a corporal in the Forty-fifth Regiment Arkansas Militia, Company G, in November and December 1861, participating in the suppression of the Arkansas Peace Society. Next, he was drafted into the Thirty-second Arkansas Infantry Regiment (Confederate) in June 1862. The regiment's muster roll listed him as "joined from desertion" on May 1, 1863—meaning that he deserted, got caught, and was forced back in—at which point he was detailed to a saltpeter works in Searcy County (probably the same one above Big Creek where the Bratton brothers were stationed). On January 1, 1864, he enlisted in the Third Arkansas Cavalry (Union), Company M. Family records say he was mustered out on May 22, 1865. He was then twenty-eight years of age. According to Searcy County lore:

> It was said that Newt "turned mean" during the Civil War, in response to the way bushwhackers treated (robbed and murdered) his family and neighbors while he was away on military duty. His wife and surviving neighbors identified the bushwhackers involved and he is credited with carrying out a personal vendetta by chasing perhaps as many as a dozen of them one at a time and killing them, in some cases single handedly. While he was never formally indicted (possibly because the acts were committed during the time of war) it seems evident that he was indeed guilty of some of the killings attributed to him.

Cooper made his home in Bear Creek after the war, becoming a successful miller and for a time the local postmaster. He died in 1888 from injuries sustained when his horse fell on him.

A great-great grandson of Cooper recently wrote a novel about his ancestor. In the novel, *Call Me Newt*, Cooper's wife Sarah is able to identify a gang of eight bushwhackers who victimized her, and Cooper stalks and kills each one. Henry Cole was not among them.

If Newt Cooper of Bear Creek killed Henry Cole, then it is a mystery why Mollie did not state his name in her book, especially as he had been dead for several years when she wrote about it. What she did state in her book was that the man who murdered Henry was "one of the guerrillas who had plundered and burned our home." Thus, by Mollie's account Henry's killer was part of a gang, not a lone gunslinger, and he was motivated to murder Henry so that Henry would not hunt him down in retribution for what he had done to the Coles. What we know about Newt Cooper's vigilante activity does not fit that description. Rather, Mollie's description of the killer points to Lewis Meek, since it was his gang that killed Henry's brother John and later returned to burn the Coles out of their home.

Mollie may have had her own private reasons for withholding the name of Henry's killer in her book. But in pulling that punch she missed her opportunity to make a key point about the guerrilla war. The often-personal nature of guerrilla fighting sowed seeds of revenge in the local population that took years to work their way out. Tragically, Mollie's own late husband's unit, Captain Love's Company, which the Confederate government sanctioned and supported for its nominal defense of the Confederacy, played a role in the revenge cycle that led to Henry's murder at the conclusion of the war.

For her own part, Mollie wanted to forgive and forget. Valentine did, too, apparently. In a modest way the couple took part in the movement toward national reconciliation. Around the year 1875, an old man named James Scott Smith called at their farm home and asked for a meal. After this old man finished eating, he told them he was a Union soldier from Wisconsin and a Republican, and if they were agreeable, then he would like to stay for a few days and rest up. Valentine allowed as how he was a Confederate soldier and a Democrat, but as their guest did not appear to have any mean or inebriate habits then they would gladly accommodate him. The next day the old man went to work on mending their farm tools and making other repairs around the place. And instead of staying with the Williamses for a few days, this Union veteran lived with them for seven years. Never an angry word passed between this man and Valentine about bygone days. "Strange things now and then occur in the line of human experience," Mollie marveled, with a touch of self-congratulation. "Instances like these prove the existence of an internal kinship, and that if we were not victimized and prejudiced by political parties and religious creeds, we might be united into one universal brother and sisterhood, which seers and prophets have long since foretold."

Valentine lived to the age of seventy-five. In 1915, a year before his death, he published a letter in the Marshall newspaper. "As I see a request from the *Mountain Wave*, asking letters from old settlers of Searcy County, I feel welcome to make a few remarks," he began. "I never saw a college and all the education I ever received was sitting on a split-log bench three months of the year, or by a grease lamp, or by a pine knot fire." He reminisced about those weeks in the fall of 1847 when his family first settled in Richland. He closed his letter with a favorite hunting story.

> I have been in several bear scrapes, and have had scrapes with numerous other wild animals, but the most dangerous combat I ever had was with two wounded bucks with large heads of horns. I had shot both of them, and they started at me though one got so sick he had to stop and lie down. The other one got to me before I could reload my gun, and all the show I had was to fight him with my knife. I caught him by the horns, and pushing his head to one side, I struck him behind the shoulder one lick with a long knife and he sank to the ground dead. I then loaded my gun and killed the other buck. I have killed almost all kinds of wild animals.

Mollie survived her husband by eighteen years and died at the age of eighty-six on February 25, 1934. She was laid to rest beside her husband in Woodland Cemetery in Cleveland, Oklahoma.

Saba Cole, Mollie's mother-in-law and close companion through two years of war, stayed in Richland and lived vibrantly into old age, dying in 1905. She rests beside her husband Jack and son John in the tiny Nars Cemetery on a knoll overlooking the Buffalo River.

The gravestones of Usley and Jim Greenhaw and some of the Greenhaw children may be found in the town cemetery in Marshall. The gravestones of Mollie's sister-in-law Angeline and her husband Hanable Love sit in the Love Cemetery near St. Joe. Most of the Robertson boys—Americus, Irvin, Christopher Columbus, Carleton Lafayette—are buried in the Hall Cemetery in Richland.

Today, Richland shows little sign of the 388 souls who inhabited the valley in 1860. The people's log homes, corn patches, and fallow fields studded with skeleton trees have all but vanished without a trace. The beautiful Richland Valley today presents a scene of broad hayfields with a scattering of shade oaks—a lovely and serene setting nothing like how it appeared in 1860. The dense farm population melted away long ago, scattering to towns and cities and new farmlands out west. The one-room schoolhouse at Point Peter is no more. The two-story frame house that Valentine built after the war now teeters on the edge of collapse in overgrown fields at Cash Bend.

Along the Buffalo one still hears the trill of the whippoorwill. If Mollie could hear that bird's mournful song she would think of all those graves and all those people who once filled her life in Richland. And she would think of the dark eddies in the Arkansas River that took the body of her first husband, Henry Cole, and spun it away to its last home in the mud of ages at a point downriver only God knew where. There is a time to search and a time to rest, a time to be silent and a time to speak, a time for love and a time for hate, a time for war and a time for peace. Nowadays along the Buffalo, most old-timers will tell you this: when you hear the whippoorwill's call in the springtime, it means it is corn planting time.

Chapter 22

The Freewoman of Richland

After Parthenia and her boy Newt Wyatt were emancipated, Parthenia chose not to go anywhere but to hold onto what she had in Richland. And what she had was her home with the Wyatts.

Not long after she was emancipated, Parthenia gave birth to her second and last child, a girl. This time, the child was freeborn, not someone's property at birth. She named the girl Lucinda Wyatt. It is not recorded who fathered Parthenia's second child. According to today's conventions, the girl's last name of Wyatt would appear to indicate that the father was Billy Wyatt again. But today's conventions do not necessarily apply in this case. The child's christening came at a moment in history when many freed people were choosing surnames, for they had never had surnames till then, and many took their former master's surname because they regarded it as a significant part of their personal background, sometimes signifying place as much as family. So, Parthenia could have named her daughter Lucinda Wyatt simply because she lived in the Wyatt household or at the Wyatt place. There is no record that Billy Wyatt claimed paternity this time as he did after Newt was born.

The ambiguity of Parthenia's relations with Billy Wyatt does not end with her second child. Parthenia stayed with the Wyatt family all her life. She never married, unless one counts as a kind of marriage the indistinct and enduring relationship she had with Billy Wyatt. One modern genealogy of Billy Wyatt does in fact list Parthenia as another spouse beside Louisa. Of course, legal marriage between Billy Wyatt and Parthenia was out of the question because both polygamy and interracial marriage were unlawful in Arkansas. So far as is known, no contemporary relative of either of them said that they were a couple in a conjugal sense. On this point, facts dissolve into clues and clues shade into innuendo. Perhaps the best we can do at this distant point in time is to note there were various possibilities and withhold judgment.

In the US census of 1870, Parthenia and her children were listed as residing in the same household with Billy and Louisa Wyatt. Parthenia's occupation was recorded as housekeeper. In the 1880 census, she is still found living with Billy and Louisa in Marshall. Goodspeed's *Biographical and Historical Memoirs of Arkansas* states that Wyatt sold goods in Marshall for about ten years, then returned with his family to Richland. There is no 1890 census record as it was destroyed in a fire, but presumably the family was back in Richland by then.

In 1900, Parthenia, Louisa, and Billy Wyatt were still living together in Richland. This time, the census recorded Parthenia's occupation as servant—seemingly casting her as a barely emancipated house slave. Again, one should not infer too much from this fact in the record. The title of servant could have been pronounced to the census taker by Parthenia herself, or it could have been supplied prejudicially by Billy or Louisa, or it could have simply come from the census taker observing the racial makeup of the household.

By then they were all getting old. Billy and Louisa gave their ages as seventy-one and sixty-nine; Parthenia's age was recorded as fifty-five. All of their children were grown up and out of the home. Two grandchildren of Billy and Louisa—a grandnephew and grandniece to Parthenia—now lived with them. Parthenia's grandniece, who was thirteen in 1900, would take her great aunt "Thene" into her home two decades hence when Parthenia was in her final years.

What we should take from Parthenia's remaining with the Wyatts all those years is that she cherished home and family, and as a freewoman she chose to continue with what she knew. Her choice was not one of inertia, but rather one of grit and fortitude. It was hardly an easy road.

~

Some 200,000 blacks moved from other Southern states to Arkansas in the post-Civil War era. Most of the black migration to Arkansas went to the lowland counties in the eastern and southern sections of the state where large black populations already existed and the newcomers could feel greater safety in numbers. A few trickled into the Ozarks, looking for cheap land in that remote hill country. Besides the draw of cheap land, freedmen and women were attracted to the state by the relatively high wages and the promise of equality. Although the promise of equality in Arkansas faded by the end of the nineteenth century, it was strong in the Reconstruction era, for Arkansas Republicans defended black voting rights and promoted black migration, and the power of blacks grew during the 1870s and 1880s. Even as repression of the black vote increased across the South in the 1880s, the number of black state legislators in Arkansas grew from four in 1880 to twelve in 1890. For a period, Arkansas held promise as "the great Negro state of the country," a land of opportunity for blacks.

Race relations in Arkansas in the 1870s and 1880s were somewhat better than in much of the South. Nevertheless, racial segregation took root early in the state after the Civil War. The state was hard-pressed after the war to provide public schools for all its citizens, so it soon backpedaled on its early commitment to black education, excluding black children from the public school system. As black families coped with school segregation, their communities willingly established their own churches, eager to create their own social spaces away from white racial prejudice and to develop their own leaders through the church ministry. But if the African American church offered a refuge from white supremacy, blacks still had to integrate with the white majority in the labor force and share other public spaces such as hotels, theaters, and saloons. During Reconstruction, with the Civil Rights Act of 1866, blacks secured a law that purported to protect their equal access to public accommodations and transportation. Yet the law ultimately failed to protect them from growing instances of segregation and the gradual imposition of a racial caste system known as Jim Crow.

Following a period of relative fluidity and experimentation in race relations in the 1870s and 1880s, white oppression of African Americans worsened in the 1890s and 1900s. Whites grew more racist and insistent about drawing a "color line." State and local laws and ordinances instituted racial segregation in many public spaces, while the US Supreme Court legitimated the "separate but equal" doctrine in *Plessy v. Ferguson* (1896). A wave of white mob lynchings of blacks occurred across the United States, primarily in the South, with the largest number of incidents occurring in Texas, Mississippi, and Georgia. Lynchings often revolved around accusations of sexual assaults or transgressions by black men against white women. The wave of lynchings terrorized blacks and served to enforce separation between the races. Lynchings sometimes erupted into violent pogroms aimed at driving away whole black communities.

Wherever black populations were small, they were vulnerable to expulsion because they were not essential workers for the local economy. Whereas the agricultural interests in the lowland counties of Arkansas needed and wanted blacks for their labor supply, the mostly white farm communities in the northwest section of the state did not have that concern. As new high-wage jobs arose around railroad construction and mining, whites aimed to restrict those good paying jobs to white labor only. Sometimes black transient labor moved into an area only to be driven out in a practice known as "white-capping." Sometimes the instigators of white-capping used trumped-up charges of sexual misconduct by a black man to incite mob action. The charges could lead to a lynching or the torching of black homes. These actions were generally perpetrated by lower class whites. The modern term for white-capping would be racial cleansing.

White resentment of black labor competition became strongest in rural areas of the South as poor whites sensed they were losing ground relative to other regions of the country and other sectors in the industrializing economy. The Democratic Party in Arkansas and elsewhere in the South faced defections from farmer and labor groups that were attracted to third party movements such as the Agricultural Wheel and Union Labor organizations. In the 1890s, the Democratic Party in Arkansas began to advocate racial segregation as a way to bolster support among its base in rural white counties. It found a fighting cause in a law to segregate streetcars. Ironically, the law found little support among the urban population in Little Rock where most of the streetcars were. The law was offensive to urban blacks and it did not please most urban whites either. Yet its real aim was to rally rural whites to the cause of white supremacy and bring them back into the Democratic Party fold. The streetcar law succeeded in its purpose, with blacks reporting from all over the state that they experienced an upswing in racial prejudice about the time the law was passed.

Race prejudice in and around Searcy County reached a fever pitch at the turn of the twentieth century. White women wrote letters to the *Mountain Wave* trying to outdo one another with their vitriol. One Searcy County woman insisted that the "African contingent of the Republican party" was responsible for an alleged crime wave of rape, murder, and arson. Another provided an oblique defense of Southern lynchings of black men, saying "the Southern people are just as much concerned as those of the North in guarding against disorder and mob violence. But they do not place, as some female Bostonians seem to do, the life of a brute above the honor of an innocent and virtuous woman." This writer went on: "The greatest crime ever committed was in turning negroes loose on the South. As the times are now, one cannot pick up a paper that one does not read of some horrible outrage by one of the black devils."

About thirty miles northwest of Richland, the town of Harrison was founded in 1870 and grew to have a population of 1,500 by 1900, including 115 blacks. The blacks living in Harrison at the turn of the century were by and large hardworking, religious, and family-oriented. In 1905, mob violence against the whole black community suddenly erupted after one black man broke into a white home apparently seeking shelter from cold. Two days after this individual was incarcerated, a mob stormed the jail and seized the prisoner together with another black man in the jail, tied them to trees, and whipped them. The mob then rampaged through the section of Harrison where the black people lived, whipping others and warning everyone that they must leave town. All but three black families left. Four years later there was a second occurrence of racial violence after a white woman accused a black man of raping her. Again a mob gathered outside the jail, and this time the prisoner was transferred to the jail in Marshall. Fearful of more mob violence, the three remaining families made a hasty departure from Harrison. The accused man was later hanged although the case against him was dubious.

The expulsion of the black population in Harrison in 1905 and 1909 followed similar mob actions in Springfield and Joplin, Missouri. These events had a chilling effect on the black population scattered across the Ozark region. Most black communities broke up and disappeared.

In the early 1970s, sociologist Gordon Daniel Morgan with anthropologist Peter H. Kunkel conducted a study of this all but extinct population of "mountain blacks" in the Ozarks. Dr. Morgan was the first African American faculty member at the University of Arkansas Fayetteville. The two professors made numerous trips to the hill counties looking for subjects to interview. They did not find a single black person, but they documented twenty "extinct" black communities using evidence of burial grounds. They found very few whites living who remembered when blacks were present. Morgan and Kunkel wrote that "records on them are inaccessible or non-existent, and evidence of black presence in some counties has been purposely destroyed."

In Richland, after emancipation, a small black community formed around the Wyatt place and hung on longer than most, though it too eventually disappeared. Parthenia stayed in Richland with her children. Anthony Hensley stayed, too, and another black family settled there. As the years passed, a second and third generation emerged, so that by 1899, there were sixteen black residents in the valley. As white racial prejudice intensified in and around Searcy County, one resident, writing anonymously to the *Mountain Wave*, defended the tiny black community in Richland, saying "they are all well thought of by the whites, which is proof that they are good people."

~

Parthenia praised God that her children did not grow up in slavery like she did. Her son Newt left home of his own free choice when he entered his teens. The 1880 census found him working and boarding with several other young farmhands at a place over in Bear Creek. He was then about eighteen years old. Year by year, Newt Wyatt carefully saved up a part of his wages. By the end of the decade, he was back in Richland working on his own farm. On November 12, 1894, he obtained a patent for 160 acres under the Homestead Act of 1862. As Parthenia probably appreciated, when Newt acquired ownership of his own farm he achieved something vital to him that few young black men of his generation succeeded in doing.

Parthenia's daughter Lucinda married a black man named Ed Crenshaw in 1887. There was no legal marriage between slaves in slavery times, so this, too, was an act of freedom that Parthenia would have rejoiced over for her child's sake. The couple settled on a farm along the Buffalo within Searcy County. According to county tax records, Ed Crenshaw owned two horses, one mule, one cow, two sheep, and two hogs in 1888. The couple had one child, Dottie.

A story was passed down that a few years after Lucinda married, Billy Wyatt advised his son Newt to go to Springfield to find himself a wife. There was still at that time a prospering African American community in Springfield. Moreover, Billy Wyatt had a half cousin on the Tutt side of his family who belonged to the African American community in Springfield. Lewis Tutt, a mulatto and former slave in the Tutt family, had done very well for himself since emancipation and now owned a grocery store and several investment properties. Newt apparently took his father's advice, went to Springfield, and met a nineteen-year-old woman by the name of Lucy Byers. They married in 1891.

Newt and Lucy had two daughters and one son. When the two girls got to be school age, they enrolled in the little country school at Point

Peter in Richland. Newt donated some of his own land for the school, which was named the Wyatt School. There is a surviving photograph from 1909 that shows the two Wyatt girls, Bess and Francis, standing with all their white classmates and the white teacher in front of the school. Today, some Searcy Countians claim that this racially integrated country school is proof that the white majority in the area treated the black community in Richland better than what generally passed for race relations in that era.

Newt and Lucy supported the single Christian church in Richland. Occasionally, when the right preacher came along, their church put on an African American religious service. Then the clapping, dancing, and shouting all became livelier, much to the amusement and glee of the whites.

Louisa Wyatt died in 1902. After her half-sister's death, Parthenia moved in with her son. She finally chose to live apart from Billy Wyatt with whom she had shared a residence for more than fifty years. Billy Wyatt remarried a younger woman from Georgia, and they moved to the nearby town of St. Joe. Billy died in 1916.

Newt Wyatt died suddenly in 1914 while plowing his field. His white half-brother and neighbor, Perry Wyatt, saw him collapse, and ran across his field to render him aid, but Newt was already dead. After Newt died, his wife Lucy moved back to Springfield with the three children, and Richland's black community began to wane. However, their youngest child, a boy named Fon, when he got older would ride the bus to Richland to visit his grannie, Parthenia.

Parthenia lived with her half-sister's offspring—two nieces and a grandniece—after her son died. First she lived with Louisa's daughter Lillie. Then she moved in with Louisa's youngest daughter Alice. In the end, she lived with a grandniece Maude Short, the daughter of Mary Powhatton Wyatt, one of the twins Parthenia had closely tended before the Civil War. This grandniece of Parthenia's was the same one who had lived in the Wyatt household in 1900.

Being so fondly integrated into this large extended family, Parthenia often stayed with one family or another when there was a childbirth, an illness, a crisis in the family, or the loss of a loved one. She was a healer. One imagines that at these clutch times she brought her strong religious faith to bear in performing her healing, moved by the spirit and perhaps influenced in one way or another by her African roots. She still made a strong impression at funerals, "shouting and praising the name of the Lord" while she twirled around the grave on her old but steady legs.

Near the end of her life, she moved with Maude Short's family to nearby St. Joe (the same village, coincidentally, where Mollie and Valentine Williams had taken up residence for a time before they moved to Oklahoma). There, still making herself useful, she accompanied her white family's children to and from school each day.

A story is told that every Friday afternoon Parthenia carried a dishpan of freshly baked molasses cookies to the school when she went to pick up her little charges. Of course, the other school children loved these tasty treats and looked forward to the sight of the old woman coming up the road. But children absorb their parents' prejudices, so these St. Joe school children saw in the dark-skinned Parthenia a person whom they thought they must abuse. A ritual "game" developed between Parthenia and all the white school kids. As she approached up the road, she would call out to the kids a playful warning, "School butter! School butter!"—an old Southern expression that signaled a child was about to receive a flogging. The kids would scream in mock fear and throw rocks at her to keep her at a distance. Parthenia would set her cookie tray down and retreat back down the road a little. Then the kids would come forward and help themselves to the cookies.

~

Parthenia Hensley died in 1929 at the age of eighty-five or eighty-six. She was buried with most of the Wyatt family in the Hall Cemetery in Richland. Though she was integrated into the family in life, she was laid to rest in an unmarked grave well down the sloping graveyard from the graves of Billy and Louisa Wyatt. Parthenia's grave was placed in a row with two other unmarked graves belonging to her son and Anthony Hensley.

In the winter of 2008–09, the Hall Cemetery received historic preservation work. As part of that effort, the three unmarked graves were identified by a local man as the graves of Thene Hensley, Newt Wyatt, and Anthony Hensley, and each one was given a grave marker engraved with their name, life span, and the label "free slave."

This curious term "free slave" referred to a person who lived both free and unfree. Ostensibly, the term "free slave" simply recognized that a person's lived experience spanned the time before and after emancipation. But there were darker historical undercurrents in the term. In slavery times, "free slave" was commonly used to describe a runaway slave living in a free state. Sometimes the term "free slave" referred to a hired-out slave living in relatively liberal circumstances. More rarely, the hybrid form "free-slave" was applied to a "quasi-free" slave who was on an agreed path to manumission by the owner. Occasionally, the term was used synonymously with another racial epithet, "coolie," which described a Chinese or South Asian laborer who worked in America (and in other places around the globe) under a harsh labor contract that was regarded by whites as being barely a step above enslavement. The racialized thinking behind the term "free slave" in that era was this: slave status attached to a person at birth because of the person's race, and since a person's race was immutable, their slave status was immutable too. The "free" part of the "free slave" identity was a condition, maybe even an aberration.

Before the Civil War, Southern defenders of slavery came to view the small population of "free slaves" as a threat to the system, and so they sought to rid their states of them. Most Southern states banned manumission in the late antebellum period. Some Southern states, including Arkansas, passed laws to expel their tiny populations of free blacks. An Arkansas law enacted in 1859, required all free blacks to leave the state by January 1, 1860, or face re-enslavement. The racist thinking behind the move against free blacks prefigured the racial caste system that arose in Arkansas and other former slave states after the institution of slavery was destroyed.

In the decades following the Civil War—in the long shadow of the Lost Cause—the racist thinking that was embedded in American slavery continued to infect all the white people around Parthenia in Richland, even her closest white family members. The tragedy of Parthenia Hensley's story is that she gave her entire self to her blended family of whites and blacks, and yet, to all those white relations, she always remained a "free slave"—their racial inferior.

The tragedy of Mollie Brumley's story is that she gave so much of herself to a cause that was not truly her own. She never recognized the Confederate cause for what it was, a war to defend slavery. Unwittingly, she fought and bled to keep her sister unfree.

Notes to Chapters

Chapter 1: Mollie Brumley

For Mollie's memories of early childhood, I relied on her autobiography: Mollie E. Williams, *A Thrilling Romance of the Civil War; forty-two days in search of a missing husband—a lesson of woman's fidelity, fortitude, and affection* (Chicago: Reprint [1902], 1992). The May Day parade was reported in *Memphis Daily Appeal*, April 29, 1858. My primary source on Richland in 1860 was the US Census, which lists residents by household, name, age, sex, and state of birth, and gives the occupation and household worth for most heads of household. I used the census schedule in conjunction with Arkansas General Land Office records and plat maps, cemetery records, oral history records, and topographic maps as well as ground truthing to make an educated guess as to where specific families lived within Richland. Most families did not obtain legal title to their homesteads until years after the Civil War, so the land title records offered only imperfect, piecemeal evidence as to who lived where in 1860. In forming a picture of what the Richland farms looked like then, I relied principally on the following scholarly articles and local history sources: John Solomon Otto and Augustus Marion Burns III, "Traditional Agricultural Practices in the Arkansas Highlands," *Journal of American Folklore* 94 (1981); J. S. Otto and N. E. Anderson, "Slash-and-Burn Cultivation in the Highlands South: A Problem in Comparative Agricultural History," *Comparative Studies in Society and History* 24, no. 1 (1982); Beth Herrington, *Tomahawk Tales* (Tahlequah, OK: East Central Baptist Press, 1981); *Mountain Wave* (Marshall, AR), April 30, 1915; and Wesley Dozier interview by Works Progress Administration, February 24, 1939, WPA No. 150, University of Arkansas Special Collections, Fayetteville, AR. See also James J. Johnston, "Searcy County, Arkansas during the Civil War," (1963), typescript in Searcy County Library, Marshall, AR. On schooling and social life, I used Tom A. Tate, interview by James J. Johnston, October 22, 1970, Historical Files, Buffalo National River, Arkansas; Walter F. Lackey, *History of Newton County, Arkansas* (Point Lookout, MO: S of O Press, 1950); Clara B. Kennan, "The Birth of Public Schools," in *Arkansas: Colony and State*, edited by Leland

DuVall (Little Rock, AR: Rose Publishing, 1970); Fred Arthur Bailey, "Tennessee's Antebellum Common Folk," *Tennessee Historical Quarterly* 55, no. 1 (Spring 1996); and Maris A. Vinovskis and Richard M. Bernard, "Beyond Catherine Beecher: Female Education in the Antebellum Period," *Signs* 3 (1978). On Mollie's farm chores, I augmented her own account by consulting "Pulling Fodder," *Delmar Historical and Art Society* (blog), October 25, 2016, delmarhistoricalandartsociety.blogspot.com/2016/10/pulling-fodder.html, and Elliott West, *Growing Up with the Country: Childhood on the Far Western Frontier* (Albuquerque: University of New Mexico Press, 1989). I speculated on the games Mollie played based on Orville J. McInturff, *Searcy County, My Dear: A History of Searcy County, Arkansas* (Marshall, AR: Marshall Mountain Wave, 1963); and West, *Growing Up with the Country*. The detail about the "Nars" is a thing I imagined young people in Richland would have done back then, having scrambled up on that curious rock formation myself.

Chapter 2: Free and Enslaved

For context on Mollie's coming of age, I read, among other works, Anya Jabour, *Scarlett's Sisters: Young Women in the Old South* (Chapel Hill: University of North Carolina Press, 2007); Victoria E. Ott, *Confederate Daughters: Coming of Age during the Civil War* (Carbondale: Southern Illinois University Press, 2008); and Drew Gilpin Faust, *Mothers of Invention: Women of the Slaveholding South in the American Civil War* (Chapel Hill: University of North Carolina Press, 1996). For the geographic setting I consulted the very detailed National Register of Historic Places Multiple Property Documentation Form for "Historic and Architectural Resources of Searcy County, Arkansas" by William D. Baker (1993) as well as my book-length study for the National Park Service, *Life, Leisure, and Hardship Along the Buffalo: Historic Resource Study, Buffalo National River* (2008). My information about the Cole family derives from the US Census; cemetery records; genealogy websites; "Aunt Sabe" Cole obituary in the *Mountain Wave* (Marshall, AR), January 21, 1905; and Erd W. Cole interview by James J. Johnston, 1970, in Waldo E. Fowler, "History of the Wyatt Family and Richland Creek," bound undated typescript at Boone County Library, Harrison, AR. Since the Coles did have a pet bear cub, as did many other Richland families, I took the liberty of inserting Valentine Williams's story here of how *he* obtained *his* pet bear cub. See Valentine Williams, "A Remarkable Dream of St. Joe," *Mountain Wave* (Marshall, AR), June 27, 1919. The information on Hiram Brumley's slave Nance is in an untitled, undated report held in the Memphis/Shelby County Archives. On the slave trade scene in Memphis, see Steven Deyle, *Carry Me Back: The Domestic Slave Trade in American Life* (New York: Oxford University Press, 2005).

Chapter 3: Parthenia Hensley

Reference to the slave law simplifies the legal framework of American slavery, which derived from "a complicated mixture of customs, statutes, and court decisions." Each slave state had its own slave laws, while the federal government passed legislation for slavery in the District of Columbia, federal territories, and on interstate matters such as the African slave trade and the return of fugitive slaves. See Paul Finkelman, "United States Slave Law," in *The Oxford Handbook of Slavery in the Americas*, edited by Robert L. Paquette and Mark M. Smith (New York: Oxford University Press, 2010). For information about the Wyatt and Hensley families I used the same primary sources as I did for other Searcy County families cited above. Hensley family records are at the Searcy County Library, Marshall, AR. The 1841 Hensley estate document is reproduced in *Searcy County Ancestor Information Exchange* 12, no. 5 (February 2003), 7–8. Other sources on families and local history include Mary Frances Harrell, ed., *History and Folklore of Searcy County, Arkansas* (Harrison, AR: New Leaf Press, Inc., 1977); and Jim Liles, *Old Folks Talking: Historical Sketches of Boxley Valley on Buffalo River, A Place of Special Value in the Ozarks of Arkansas* (Washington, DC: Government Printing Office, 1998). All the facts about Parthenia, including her rape, come from the Wyatt and Hensley family histories. For context on slavery in the Ozarks, I turned to John Solomon Otto, "Slavery in the Mountains: Yell County, Arkansas, 1840–1860," *Arkansas Historical Quarterly* 39, no. 1 (Spring 1980): 35–52; Brooks Blevins, *A History of the Ozarks, Vol. 2, The Conflicted Ozarks* (Urbana: University of Illinois Press, 2019); Orville W. Taylor, *Negro Slavery in Arkansas* (Durham, NC: Duke University Press, 1958); Carl H. Moneyhon, "The Slave Family in Arkansas," *Arkansas Historical Quarterly* 58, no. 1 (Spring 1999); Dwight Pitcaithley, "Settlement of the Arkansas Ozarks: The Buffalo River Valley," *Arkansas Historical Quarterly* 37, no. 3 (1978); Billy D. Higgins, "The Origins and Fate of the Marion County Free Black Community," *Arkansas Historical Quarterly*, 54, no. 4 (Winter 1995); Clyde W. Cathey, "Slavery in Arkansas," *Arkansas Historical Quarterly* 3 (Spring 1944); Robert B. Walz, "Arkansas Slaveholdings and Slaveholders in 1850," *Arkansas Historical Quarterly* 12 (Spring 1953); William J. Harris, "The Organization of Work on a Yeoman Slaveholder's Farm," *Agricultural History* 64 (Winter 1990): 39–52; Philip V. Scarpino, "Slavery in Callaway County, Missouri, 1845–1855, Part II," *Missouri Historical Review* 71 (April 1977); Diane Mutti Burke, *On Slavery's Border: Missouri's Small-Slaveholding Households, 1815–1865* (Athens: University of Georgia Press, 2010); H. C. Bruce, *The New Man: Twenty-Nine Years a Slave. Twenty-Nine Years a Free Man* (York, PA: F. Anstadt & Sons, 1895); and my multichapter report for the National Park Service, *"When the War Come Up": Historic Resource Study, Pea Ridge National Military Park, Arkansas* (2024). On horse racing, I consulted Katherine C. Mooney, *Race Horse Men: How Slavery and Freedom Were Made at the Racetrack* (Cambridge, MA: Harvard

University Press, 2014). Hensley's lost bet and court case were reported in *Times-Picayune* (New Orleans), March 9, 1859. The description of Hensley as a "slave driver" is in James J. Johnston's interview with Garland Robertson, 1976, at the Searcy County Library, Marshall, AR. On the slave trade, I read Deyle, *Carry Me Back*; Taylor, *Negro Slavery in Arkansas*; and Walter Johnson, *Soul by Soul: Life Inside the Antebellum Slave Market* (Cambridge, MA: Harvard University Press, 1999). For a look into Hensley's slaveholding, I used the US Census, *Slave Schedules—Arkansas, 1850 Census*, M 432, Roll 32, and US Census, *Slave Schedules—Arkansas, 1860*, M 653, Roll 54, at the Arkansas Historical Commission. See also James J. Johnston, "Slaves in Searcy and Newton Counties," *Searcy County Ancestor Information Exchange* 7, no. 1 (June 1997); *Newton County Historical Society Newsletter* 14, no. 3 (Fall 1998); and *Newton County Historical Society Newsletter* 14, no. 2 (Summer 1998). Anthony Hensley's interview was quoted in "Those Richland Negroes," newspaper clipping posted at "Anteny Hensley" on the Find a Grave website. For context on Parthenia's girlhood experience and her situation in becoming pregnant by her enslaver, I consulted Wilma King, *Stolen Childhood: Slave Youth in Nineteenth-Century America* (Bloomington: Indiana University Press, 1995); Deborah Gray White, *Ar'n't I a Woman?: Female Slaves in the Plantation South* (New York: W. W. Norton, 1985); Harriet Jacobs, *Incidents in the Life of a Slave Girl, Written by Herself, with Related Documents*, edited by Jennifer Fleischner (Boston: Bedford/St. Martin's, 2010); Peter Bardaglio, "The Children of Jubilee: African American Childhood in Wartime," in *Divided Houses: Gender and the Civil War*, edited by Catherine Clinton and Nina Silber (New York: Oxford University Press, 1992); Marie Jenkins Schwartz, *Birthing a Slave: Motherhood and Medicine in the Antebellum South* (Cambridge, MA: Harvard University Press, 2006); Gregory D. Smithers, *Slave Breeding: Sex, Violence, and Memory in African American History* (Gainesville: University Press of Florida, 2012); and Melton A. McLaurin, *Celia: A Slave* (Athens: University of Georgia Press, 1991). I also returned to a few classic works on slavery, Kenneth Stampp, *The Peculiar Institution: Slavery in the Ante-Bellum South* (New York: Vantage Books, 1956); John W. Blassingame, *The Slave Community: Plantation Life in the Ante-Bellum South* (New York: Oxford University Press, 1972); Eugene Genovese, *Roll, Jordan, Roll: The World the Slaves Made* (New York: Pantheon Books, 1974); and Herbert G. Gutman, *The Black Family in Slavery and Freedom, 1750–1925* (New York: Pantheon Books, 1976). A helpful bridge from the older to the newer literature is Peter Kolchin, *American Slavery 1619–1877* (New York: Hill and Wang, 1993).

Chapter 4: Under the Brush Arbor

On brush arbors, I found Samuel J. Touchstone, "The Brush Arbor," *North Louisiana Historical Association Journal* 14, no. 4 (Fall 1983); and Daniel J. Pezzoni, "Brush Arbors in the American South," *Pioneer America Society*

Transactions 20 (1997). The quotation that Parthenia was "filled with the spirit" comes from Liles, *Old Folks Talking*. See also Tina Lewis Johnson, "The Life of Parthena Hensley (1843–1929)," *Searcy County Ancestor Information Exchange* 7, no. 1 (June 1997). On the "Frenzy," see W. E. B. DuBois, *The Souls of Black Folk: Essays and Sketches* (New York: Fawcett Publications, Reprint [1903], 1961); and Albert J. Raboteau, *Canaan Land: A Religious History of African Americans* (New York: Oxford University Press, 1999). My sources on the secession crisis in Arkansas were as follows: James M. Woods, *Rebellion and Realignment: Arkansas's Road to Secession* (Fayetteville: University of Arkansas Press, 1987); Thomas A. DeBlack, *With Fire and Sword: Arkansas, 1861–1874* (Fayetteville: University of Arkansas, 2003); Ralph Wooster, "The Arkansas Secession Convention," *Arkansas Historical Quarterly* 13, no. 2 (Summer 1954); Jack B. Scroggs, "Arkansas in the Secession Crisis," *Arkansas Historical Quarterly* 12, no. 3 (Autumn 1953); James J. Johnston, ed., "Letter of John Campbell, Unionist," *Arkansas Historical Quarterly* 29, no. 2 (Summer 1970); Brian G. Walton, "How Many Voted in Arkansas Elections before the Civil War?" *Arkansas Historical Quarterly* 39, no. 1 (Spring 1980); Charles B. Dew, *Apostles of Disunion: Southern Secession Commissioners and the Causes of the Civil War* (Charlottesville: University of Virginia Press, 2001); and Fred W. Allsop, *History of the Arkansas Press for a Hundred Years and More* (Little Rock, AR: Parke-Harper, 1922). Information about the Greenhaw boys' enlistments comes from "Arkansas Edward G. Gerdes Civil War Home Page," couchgenweb.com/civilwar/ (hereafter Gerdes website). This award-winning website, compiled by the late genealogist and amateur historian Edward G. Gerdes, was an invaluable source of military records for all the individual soldiers who are mentioned in these pages. Unfortunately, it was recently discontinued. See also James J. Johnston, *Searcy County Men in the Civil War, Union and Confederate: A Compilation of Muster Rolls* (Fayetteville, AR: James J. Johnston, 2001). Other information about the Greenhaw family comes from Mollie's account, the US Census, cemetery records, and genealogy websites. To round out what Mollie wrote about her response to the advent of war, I used Drew Gilpin Faust, "Altars of Sacrifice: Confederate Women and the Narratives of War," *Journal of American History* 76, no. 4 (March 1990). All of the details about the Greenhaw-Robertson wedding are factual with the exception of the wedding celebration itself, which is imagined from general sources.

Chapter 5: To Arms! To Arms!

The governor's pronouncement was printed in the *Arkansas True Democrat*, July 25, 1861. Richland's first enlistments are documented in Gerdes website. Information on James H. Love is from the US Census, genealogy websites, and James J. Johnston, "J. C. Love recalls hearing of his father and of Civil War times," undated typescript, Historical Files, Buffalo National River, AR.

My sources on the Arkansas Peace Society are as follows: James J. Johnston, *Mountain Feds: Arkansas Unionists and the Peace Society* (Little Rock, AR: Butler Center Books, 2018); Johnston, "Reminiscences of James H. Campbell's Experiences During the Civil War," *Arkansas Historical Quarterly* 74, no. 2 (Summer 2015); Ted R. Worley, ed., "Documents Relating to the Arkansas Peace Society of 1861," *Arkansas Historical Quarterly* 17 (Spring 1958); Worley, "The Arkansas Peace Society of 1861: A Study in Mountain Unionism," *Journal of Southern History* 24 (November 1958); Luther E. Warren, *Yellar Rag Boys: The Arkansas Peace Society of 1861 and other Events in Northern Arkansas—1861 to 1865*, edited by Sandra L. Weaver, Amy M. Cranford, and Bernard L. Cranford Jr. (Marshall, AR: Sandra L. Weaver, 1993); McInturff, *Searcy County, My Dear: A History of Searcy County, Arkansas*; A. W. Bishop, *Loyalty on the Frontier* (St. Louis: A. P. Studley, 1863); and James K. Tyler, "Peter Adams Tyler," 1990, typescript, Historical Files, Buffalo National River, AR. The story about Wyatt helping John Morris is in Bishop, *Loyalty on the Frontier*, reproduced in *Searcy County Ancestor Information Exchange* 12, no. 5 (February 2003): 14–16. The story about George Wells is in Ava Work, interview, in Harrell, ed., *History and Folklore of Searcy County Arkansas*.

Chapter 6: Arkansas Invaded

On the military history of the Civil War in Arkansas I relied principally on the following: DeBlack, *With Fire and Sword*; Thomas W. Cutrer, *Theater of a Separate War: The Civil War West of the Mississippi* (Chapel Hill: University of North Carolina Press, 2017); Mark K. Christ, ed., *Rugged and Sublime: The Civil War in Arkansas* (Fayetteville: University of Arkansas Press, 1994); Elmo Ingenthron, *Borderland Rebellion: A History of the Civil War on the Missouri-Arkansas Border* (Branson, MO: Ozarks Mountaineer, 1980); William L. Shea and Earl J. Hess, *Pea Ridge: Civil War Campaign in the West* (Chapel Hill: University of North Carolina Press, 1992); James M. McPherson, *Battle Cry of Freedom: The Civil War Era* (New York: Oxford University Press, 1988); Wiley Britton, *The Civil War on the Border: A Narrative of Operations in Missouri, Kansas, Arkansas and the Indian Territory during the Years 1861–1862 Based Upon the Official Reports of the Federal Commanders Lyon, Sigel, Sturgis, Fremont, Halleck, Curtis, Schofield, Blunt, Herron, and Totten, and of the Confederate Commanders McCulloch, Price, Van Dorn, Hindman, Marmaduke, and Shelby.* (New York: G. P. Putnam's Sons, 1890); and John M. Harrell, "Arkansas," in *Confederate Military History: Vol. 11*, edited by Clement A. Evans (Atlanta, GA: Confederate Publishing Company, 1899). On the dearth of information reaching Richland after the war started, I formed my impressions from Michael B. Dougan, "Life in Confederate Arkansas," *Arkansas Historical Quarterly* 31, no. 1 (Spring 1972); H. L. Hanna, *The Press Covers the Invasion of Arkansas, 1862* (2 vols.; Widener, AR: Southern Heritage Press, 2011); Michael Fuhlhage, Jade Metzger-Riftkin, Sarah Walker, and

Nicholas Prephan, "The News Ecosystem During the Birth of the Confederacy: South Carolina Secession in Southern Newspapers," *American Journalism* 37, no. 2 (2020); Sidney Kobre, *Foundations of American Journalism* (Tallahassee: Florida State University, 1958); Frank Luther Mott, *American Journalism: A History of Newspapers in the United States through 260 Years: 1690 to 1950* (New York: MacMillan, 1950); John Nathan Anderson, "Money or Nothing: Confederate Postal System Collapse during the Civil War," *American Journalism* 30, no. 1 (2013): 65–86; and Edward C. Newton, "Arkansas Telegraph History," *Arkansas Gazette*, November 20, 1919. On the poor news coverage of major battles in Arkansas see Hanna, *The Press Covers the Invasion of Arkansas*; William Baxter, *Pea Ridge and Prairie Grove; Or, Scenes and Incidents of the War in Arkansas* (Cincinnati: Poe & Hitchcock, 1867); and David Bosse, "'The Enemy Were Falling Like Autumn Leaves': Fraudulent Newspaper Reports of the Battle of Pea Ridge," *Arkansas Historical Quarterly* 54, no. 3 (Autumn 1995). John Cole's experience is from Gerdes website.

Chapter 7: On the Mustering Ground

Besides following Mollie's account, I based the scene at the mustering ground on Bell Irvin Wiley, *The Life of Johnny Reb: The Common Soldier of the Confederacy* (Indianapolis, IN: Bobbs-Merrill, 1943); Anya Jabour, "'Days of lightly-won and lightly-held hearts': Courtship and Coquetry in the Southern Confederacy," in *Weirding the War: Stories from the Civil War's Ragged Edges*, edited by Stephen Berry (Athens: University of Georgia Press, 2011); Dorothy Denneen Volo and James M. Volo. *Daily Life in Civil War America* (Westport, CT: Greenwood Press, 1998); as well as Gerdes website. On women's war work, see Hanna, *The Press Covers the Invasion of Arkansas*; United Confederate Veterans of Arkansas, comp., *Confederate Women of Arkansas in the Civil War 1861–'65, Memorial Reminiscences* (Little Rock, AR: H. G. Pugh, 1907; Mary P. Fletcher and Susan Fletcher, "An Arkansas Lady in the Civil War: Reminiscences of Susan Fletcher," *Arkansas Historical Quarterly* 2, no. 4 (December 1943); and Clara B. Eno, "Activities of the Women of Arkansas During the War Between the States," *Arkansas Historical Quarterly* 3, no. 1 (Spring 1944). On the Confederate army's foraging, see Volo and Volo, *Daily Life in Civil War America.*

Chapter 8: A Letter from Valentine

The incident around the delivery of the letter is from Williams, *A Thrilling Romance of the Civil War.* Soldiers' letter writing is described in Wiley, *The Life of Johnny Reb.* Information about Valentine's regiment is found in Silas C. Turnbo, *History of the 27th Arkansas Confederate Infantry*, edited by Desmond Walls Allen (Conway, AR: Arkansas Research, 1988); and Johnston, "Reminiscences of James H. Campbell's Experiences During the Civil War." Calvin and Green Berry Greenhaw enlistments are in Gerdes website. Some details on camp life come from Volo and Volo, *Daily Life in Civil War America*. On the writing career of Silas Turnbo, see "Silas C. Turnbo (1844–1925)" at https://missouriencyclopedia.org/people/turnbo-silas-c. Valentine's story of his dream is in *Mountain Wave* (Marshall, AR), June 27, 1919, while his reasons for going to war and his story of the prayer may be found in *Mountain Wave* (Marshall, AR), April 9, 1915, reproduced in *Searcy County Ancestor Information Exchange* 13, no. 2 (August 2003): 44.

Chapter 9: The War Closes In

There is a burgeoning scholarly literature on the guerrilla war. My principal sources were as follows: Daniel E. Sutherland, "Guerillas: The Real War in Arkansas," in *Civil War Arkansas: Beyond Battles and Leaders*, edited by Anne J. Bailey and Daniel E. Sutherland (Fayetteville: University of Arkansas Press, 2000); Sutherland, *Guerillas, Unionists, and Violence on the Confederate Home Front* (Fayetteville: University of Arkansas Press, 1999); Sutherland, *A Savage Conflict: The Decisive Role of Guerrillas in the American Civil War* (Chapel Hill: University of North Carolina Press, 2009); Michael Fellman, *Inside War: The Guerrilla Conflict in Missouri during the American Civil War* (New York: Oxford University Press, 1989); Stephen V. Ash, *When the Yankees Came: Conflict and Chaos in the Occupied South, 1861–1865* (Chapel Hill: University of North Carolina Press, 1995); Rebecca A. Howard, "No Country for Old Men: Patriarchs, Slaves, and Guerrilla War in Northwest Arkansas," *Arkansas Historical Quarterly* 75, no. 4 (Winter 2016); Matthew M. Stith, "Guerrilla Warfare and the Environment in the Trans-Mississippi Theater," in *The Guerrilla Hunters: Irregular Conflicts During the Civil War*, edited by Brian D. McKnight and Barton A. Myers (Baton Rouge: Louisiana State University Press, 2017); Leo E. Huff, "Guerrillas, Jayhawkers and Bushwhackers in Northern Arkansas During the Civil War," *Arkansas Historical Quarterly* 24, no. 2 (Summer 1965); James J. Johnston, "Jayhawker Stories: Historical Lore in the Arkansas Ozarks," *Midsouth Folklore* 4, no. 1 (Spring 1976); Blevins, *A History of the Ozarks*; and Albert Castel, *William Clarke Quantrill: His Life and Times* (New York: Frederick Fell, 1962). Newer scholarship tends toward a more sympathetic treatment of guerrillas in the Civil War running somewhat counter to Mollie's perspective. See especially Joseph M. Beilein Jr. and Matthew C. Hulbert, *The Civil War Guerrilla: Unfolding the Black Flag in History, Memory, and Myth* (Lexington: University Press of Kentucky, 2015), including the important chapters by Andrew William Fialka and Christopher Phillips. See also Aaron Sheehan-Dean, *The Calculus of Violence: How Americans Fought the Civil War* (Cambridge, MA: Harvard University Press, 2018). I found these more localized studies helpful for comparison with the situation around Richland: Michael A. Davis, "The Legend of Bill Dark: Guerrilla Warfare, Oral History, and the Unmaking of an Arkansas Bushwhacker," *Arkansas Historical Quarterly* 58, no.4 (Winter 1999); Kenneth C. Barnes,

"The Williams Clan: Mountain Farmers and Union Fighters in North Central Arkansas," *Arkansas Historical Quarterly* 52, no. 3 (Autumn 1993); James F. Keefe and Lynn Morrow, eds., *The White River Chronicles of S. C. Turnbo: Man and Wildlife on the Ozark Frontier* (Fayetteville: University of Arkansas Press, 1994). On Standridge, see Evelyn Flood, "Kinfolks Stories," posted on Rootsweb.com. On Wyatt, see Fowler, "History of the Wyatt Family and Richland Creek." While Mollie's tormented state of mind about Valentine's death on the battlefield come from her own account, for context I drew on Mark S. Schantz, *Awaiting the Heavenly Country: The Civil War and America's Culture of Death* (Ithaca, NY: Cornell University Press, 2008); and Drew Gilpin Faust, *The Republic of Suffering: Death and the American Civil War* (NY: Alfred A. Knopf, 2008). The two paragraphs around the report that Valentine was missing and presumed dead are inferred from Mollie's account: "From the army came the sad tidings that my soldier lover had failed to answer at the roll call of his company, and that he was numbered with the dead on the field of a recent battle." The loose chronology of Mollie's account points to the Battle of Prairie Grove, in which Valentine's regiment fought and did lose many men at the next roll call. The song "Weeping, Sad and Lonely" was written by Charles Carroll Sawyer, put to music by Henry Tucker, and published in 1863. Information about Henry Cole's desertion from the regular army and his joining Captain Love's guerrilla company is derived from Gerdes website. Local historian James J. Johnston has done considerable research on James H. Love, and I benefitted from his work here and in many other instances. Note that Love's guerrilla company did not have an official muster role, but it is mentioned often in other sources. The quotation by the regimental officer is from Gerdes, also reproduced in Johnston, *Searcy County Men in the Civil War.* I corrected the highly irregular spelling in the original.

Chapter 10: Skirmish on Christmas Day

For facts and description around the small-scale military operations in the Arkansas Ozarks that intersected with Mollie's story, I consulted relevant volumes and pages in the multivolume US Department of War, *War of the Rebellion: A Compilation of the Official Records of the Union and Confederate Armies* (Washington, DC: Government Printing Office, 1880–1901) (hereafter *O.R.*) Captain Worthington's report on his scout is in *O.R.*, Series I, Vol. 22, 779–81, 913–14. I relied solely on Mollie's account to describe Henry's part in the skirmish and Mollie and Henry's subsequent time in a cave.

Chapter 11: The Hensley Sisters

The capture of John M. Hensley is recorded in *O.R.*, Series I, Vol. 22, 780. Hensley's military record is from Gerdes website. Other accounts of the events of December 26 are found in Warren, *Yellar Rag Boys,* 37; Harrell, ed., *History and Folklore of Searcy County, Arkansas,* 306; and in the Hensley family records in the Searcy County Library at Marshall, AR. On Christmas traditions, see Robert E. May, *Yuletide in Dixie: Slavery, Christmas, and Southern Memory* (Charlottesville: University of Virginia Press, 2019); and Jenny Fillmer, "Traditions Run Deep in Ozarks Christmas," *Springfield News-Leader*, December 25, 2003. The key firsthand account concerning Wright was written by Mary Pell Ledbetter and is reprinted in Harrell, ed., *History and Folklore of Searcy County, Arkansas*, 306, and in its entirety in *Arkansas Family Historian* 54, no. 1 (Spring 2016). The detail about the Wyatts taking the Coles' cattle is in Erd W. Cole, interview, in Harrell, ed., *History and Folklore of Searcy County, Arkansas.* My speculations about Louisa's and Parthenia's relationship on the Wyatt farm were sharply influenced by Thavolia Glymph, *Out of the House of Bondage: The Transformation of the Plantation Household* (Cambridge: Cambridge University Press, 2008).

Chapter 12: The Murder of John Cole

The increasing savagery of the guerrilla war was documented by the Union side in reports published in *O.R.*, Series I, Vol. 34, 86–96, 518, 640, 939. My sources on the Confederate side are James J. Johnston, "Reminiscences of James H. Campbell's Experiences during the Civil War"; George T. Maddox, *Hard Trials and Tribulations of an Old Confederate Soldier* (Van Buren, AR: Argus, 1897); and General Shelby's report in *O.R.*, Series I, Vol. 34, 925. On the contested subject of rape in the Civil War, I landed on the side of Michael Fellman, "Women and Guerrilla Warfare," in *Divided Houses: Gender and the Civil War*, edited by Catherine Clinton and Nina Silber (New York: Oxford University Press, 1992) and James J. Johnston, "Jayhawker Stories: Historical Lore in the Arkansas Ozarks," *Midsouth Folklore* 4, no. 1 (Spring 1976), whose studies center on the Ozarks and whose findings conform best with Mollie's narrative. However, for a darker view, see Kim Murphy, *I Had Rather Die: Rape in the Civil War* (Batesville, VA: Coachlight Press, 2014); Lisa Tendrich Frank, "The Union War on Women," in *The Guerrilla Hunters: Irregular Conflicts During the Civil War*, edited by Brian D. McKnight and Barton A. Myers (Baton Rouge: Louisiana State University Press, 2017); Lisa Tendrick Frank, "Bedrooms in Battlefields: The Role of Gender Politics in Sherman's March," in *Occupied Women: Gender, Military Occupation, and the American Civil War*, edited by LeeAnn Whites and Alecia P. Long (Baton Rouge: Louisiana State University Press, 2009); and E. Susan Barber and Charles F. Ritter, "'Physical Abuse . . . and Rough Handling': Race, Gender, and Sexual Justice in the Occupied South," also in *Occupied Women*. The murder of John Cole is recorded in Harrell, ed., *History and Folklore of Searcy County, Arkansas*, 26; and James J. Johnston, "J. C. Love recalls hearing of his father, and of Civil War times," undated typescript, Historical Files, Buffalo National River, AR. The identification of John's executioners as the Meek gang comes from Maddox, *Hard Trials and Tribulations of an Old Confederate Soldier*, 49, while information about the Meek clan was gleaned from Christopher A. Meek, "The Meek/Meeks Family of Tennessee and Arkansas," 2008, at meeksgeneology.com; family history recorded in Betty Powell Renfroe, "The Wagon Train Story," March 4, 2019, 3sistershistory.blogspot.com/2019/03/the-wagon-train-story.html; and from my own research in the US Census and in genealogy records at the Newton County Library in Jasper, Arkansas. Note that these sources are inconsistent and none is totally satisfactory or reliable. The contemporary descriptions of Lewis Meek and the Meek gang are found in *Searcy County Ancestor Information Exchange* 23, no. 2 (September 2012), 37; and the Ledbetter account in *Arkansas Family Historian* 54, no. 1 (Spring 2016).

Chapter 13: Battle Lines in Richland

Actions involving Love's Company in the first quarter of 1864 are recorded in *O.R.*, Series I, Vol. 34, 88–89, 93, 96. My principal sources on the skirmishes at Richland in May 1864 are: *O.R.*, Series I, Vol. 34, 908–9, 939; Maddox, *Hard Trials and Tribulations of an Old Confederate Soldier*; James J. Johnston, "A Skirmish on Richland, Searcy County," undated typescript in Historical Files, Buffalo National River, AR.; and Tom A. Tate, interview by James J. Johnston, October 22, 1970, Historical Files, Buffalo National River, AR. My information about Jackman comes from Maddox as well as Sidney Drake Jackman, *Behind Enemy's Lines: The Memoirs and Writings of Brigadier General Sidney Drake Jackman*, edited by Richard L. Norton (Springfield, MO: Oak Hills Publishing, 1997). Mollie's role is drawn from her own account. The identity of the Robertson farm comes from Maddox. The identity of Private Bishop comes from *O.R.*, Gerdes website, and *Report of the adjutant general of Arkansas for the period of the late rebellion, and to November 1, 1866* (Washington, DC: Government Printing Office, 1867). These sources all provided valuable corroboration of Mollie's recollection of events. The song "For the Dear Old Flag, I Die" was composed by Stephen Foster using a poem written by George Cooper.

Chapter 14: Hunting Down the Meek Gang

The episode of hunting down the Meek gang is drawn entirely from Maddox, *Hard Trials and Tribulations of an Old Confederate Soldier*. Not surprisingly, Jackman made no mention of it in his autobiography. I tried various avenues to find corroborating sources on this episode without success. At least two other historians have reported Jackman's hunting down the Meek gang as fact, relying solely on Maddox as I did. On Jackman's recruiting efforts and his junction with General Shelby at Dover, I used Jackman, *Behind Enemy's Lines*; and John N. Edwards, *Shelby and His Men: The War in the West* (Cincinnati: Miami Printing and Publishing, 1867). See also Mark K. Christ, "'Sun stroke & tired out': Chasing J. O. Shelby, June 1864," *Arkansas Historical Quarterly* 68, no. 2 (Summer 2009).

Chapter 15: Army Laundress

My narrative of Mollie's trip to Batesville and her experience as an army laundress is taken principally from her book. I consulted several works for context including Edwards, *Shelby and His Men*; Nola A. James, "The Civil War Years in Independence County," *Arkansas Historical Quarterly* 28, no. 3 (Autumn 1969); Jennifer J. Lawrence, *Soap Suds Row: The Bold Lives of Army Laundresses 1802–1876* (Glendo, WY: High Plains Press, 2016); and Scott A. Porter, "Thunder Across the Arkansas Prairie: Shelby's Opening Salvo in the 1864 Invasion of Missouri," *Arkansas Historical Quarterly* 66, no. 1 (Spring 2007). For the war's effects on the countryside, see Megan Kate Nelson, *Ruin Nation: Destruction and the American Civil War* (Athens: University of Georgia Press, 2012). Henry's second desertion from the Confederate army is undocumented and must be inferred from Mollie's incomplete account. Here and elsewhere, I was interested in Confederate morale and why and how Confederate soldiers deserted. I was strongly influenced by Armstead L. Robinson, *Bitter Fruits of Bondage: The Demise of Slavery and the Collapse of the Confederacy, 1861–1865* (Charlottesville: University of Virginia Press, 2005). Among other works that I consulted on the subject were: David Williams, *Georgia's Civil War: Conflict on the Home Front* (Macon, GA: Mercer University Press, 2017); Bessie Martin, *Desertion of Alabama Troops from the Confederate Army: A Study in Sectionalism* (New York: Columbia University Press, 1932); Ella Lonn, *Desertion during the Civil War* (New York: Century Company, 1928); and James McPherson, *For Cause and Comrades: Why Men Fought in the Civil War* (New York: Oxford University Press, 1997). One cannot be certain about Henry Cole's reasons for deserting the Confederate Army in September 1864, but of all the sources I consulted the one that resonated most keenly with Henry's circumstances was Peter S. Bearman, "Desertion as Localism: Army Unit Solidarity and Group Norms in the US Civil War," *Social Forces* 70, no. 2 (December 1991).

Chapter 16: The Last Hideout

This brief chapter is drawn primarily from Mollie's book. In trying to imagine Henry's motivations and mindset, besides sources cited above for the previous chapter, I was influenced by Chandra Manning, *What This Cruel War Was Over: Soldiers, Slavery, and the Civil War* (New York: Alfred A. Knopf, 2007); and Gregory J. W. Urwin, "'We Cannot Treat Negroes as Prisoners of War': Racial Atrocities and Reprisals in Civil War Arkansas," *Civil War History* 42, no. 3 (1996).

Chapter 17: Collapse

The desperate plight of civilians at the end of the war is described in several sources that I have cited above, especially Dougan, "Life in Confederate Arkansas," and the local history sources. Sarah Baker's story came from James J.

Johnston, "Noah Barnett recalls hearing of Civil War times on Tomahawk Creek," undated typescript, Historical Files, Buffalo National River, AR. The digging up of smoke house floors was recorded in Wesley Dozier, interview by Works Progress Administration, February 24, 1939, WPA No. 150, University of Arkansas Special Collections, Fayetteville, AR. Saba's dialogue with the drifter is from Erd W. Cole, interview by James J. Johnston, 1970, in Fowler, "History of the Wyatt Family and Richland Creek." Torturing of women is reported in numerous sources, for example, *Confederate Women of Arkansas in the Civil War 1861–'65, Memorial Reminiscences.* On the Bratton family: genealogy websites; Gerdes website; *Mountain Wave*, May 28, 1915; Georgena Duncan, "Uncertain Loyalties: Dual Enlistment in the Third and Fourth Arkansas Cavalry, USV," *Arkansas Historical Quarterly* 72, no. 4 (Winter 2013); Kenneth Radley, *Rebel Watchdog: The Confederate States Army Provost Guard* (Baton Rouge: Louisiana State University Press, 1989); Lorien Foote, "Aid and Comfort to the Enemy: Escaped Prisoners and the Home as Site of War," in *Household War: How Americans Lived and Fought the Civil War* (Athens: University of Georgia Press, 2020); James J. Johnston, "Bullets for Johnny Reb: Confederate Nitre and Mining Bureau in Arkansas," *Arkansas Historical Quarterly* 49, no. 2 (Summer 1990); and Brian K. Robertson, "Men Who Would Die for the Stars and Stripes: A Socio-Economic Examination of the 2nd Arkansas Cavalry (US)," *Arkansas Historical Quarterly* 69 (Summer 2010). On refugees, see Michael A. Hughes, "Wartime Gristmill Destruction in Northwest Arkansas and Military-Farm Colonies," *Arkansas Historical Quarterly* 46, no. 2 (Summer 1987); John F. Bradbury Jr., "'Buckwheat Cake Philanthropy': Refugees and the Union Army in the Ozarks," *Arkansas Historical Quarterly* 57, no. 3 (Autumn 1998); Mary Elizabeth Massey, *Refugee Life in the Confederacy* (1964, reprint, Baton Rouge: Louisiana State University Press, 2001); and my own *"When the War Come Up": Historic Resource Study, Pea Ridge National Military Park, Arkansas*, which summarizes many first-hand accounts of the plight of civilians in nearby Benton County, Arkansas.

Chapter 18: Jubilee

On the slave community's religion I relied on Blassingame, *The Slave Community*; DuBois, *The Souls of Black Folk*; Raboteau, *Canaan Land*, Anthony B. Pinn, *The African American Religious Experience in America* (Gainesville: University Press of Florida, 2008); and Matthew Harper, *The End of Days: African American Religion and Politics in the Age of Emancipation* (Chapel Hill: University of North Carolina Press, 2016). The slave spiritual is quoted in Leon Litwack, *Been in the Storm So Long: The Aftermath of Slavery* (New York: Alfred A. Knopf, 1979). On enslaved persons' information about the war, I consulted Herbert C. Covey and Dwight Eisnach, *How the Slaves Saw the Civil War: Recollections of the War through the WPA Slave Narratives* (Santa Barbara, CA: Praeger, 2014). The fact that Parthenia remained in the Wyatt household after her emancipation is recorded in several sources, including Erd W. Cole, interview by James J. Johnston, 1970, in Fowler, "History of the Wyatt Family and Richland Creek"; *Newton County Historical Society Newsletter* 14, no. 3 (Fall 1998); and *Newton County Historical Society Newsletter* 14, no. 2 (Summer 1998). For additional perspective on Parthenia's choice to stay put after emancipation, see Ryan M. Poe, "The Contours of Emancipation: Freedom Comes to Southwest Arkansas," *Arkansas Historical Quarterly* 70, no. 2 (Summer 2011); Bobby L. Lovett, "African Americans, Civil War, and Aftermath in Arkansas," *Arkansas Historical Quarterly* 54, no 3 (Autumn 1995); and my own *"When the War Come Up": Historic Resource Study, Pea Ridge National Military Park, Arkansas*, in which I collected and synthesized sources on blacks' transition from slavery to freedom in the Arkansas Ozarks in particular. The quotations of enslaved women on their imminent freedom are taken from Litwack, *Been in the Storm So Long.* See also the five WPA interviews pertinent to the black experience in the Arkansas Ozarks as distilled in *"When the War Come Up."*

Chapter 19: Requiem

On guerrilla activity along the Arkansas River in 1865 and Confederate surrender, *O.R.*, Series I, Vol. 48; *Arkansas State Gazette* (Little Rock), May 23, 1865; Jerry Ponder and Victor Ponder, *Confederate Surrender and Parole: Jacksonport and Wittsburg, Arkansas, May and June 1865* (Doniphan, MO: Ponder Books, 1995). J. C. Love's remarkable 1962 letter about his father and Civil War times is quoted and abstracted by J. J. Johnston at several places in the *Searcy County Ancestor Information Exchange.* The quotation is *Searcy County Ancestor Information Exchange* 12, no. 4 (December 2002): 19. The historian quoted is Daniel E. Sutherland as quoted in Sheehan-Dean, *The Calculus of Violence.* On the parole system, see Sheehan-Dean. Mollie's travails are detailed in her book with corroboration here and there from genealogical sources on the Coles and Brattons cited above.

Chapter 20: In the Apple Orchard

All of this chapter comes from Mollie's book except for the details on Valentine's disappearance on the battlefield, which is from Turnbo, *History of the 27th Arkansas Confederate Infantry.* I was unable to reconcile Mollie's version of Valentine's disappearance with Turnbo's version, which describes the episode in convincing detail but places it late in the war, well after the period when Mollie was courted by and married Henry Cole. I concluded that most likely both accounts are accurate—that is, Valentine was probably reported missing twice, the first time after the Battle of Prairie Grove when a great many soldiers in his company, including another man named Williams, were missed in the first roll call after the battle, and the second time after the battle that Turnbo discusses.

Chapter 21: The Song of the Whippoorwill

On the myth of the Lost Cause, I turned mainly to David W. Blight, *Race and Reunion: The Civil War in American Memory* (Cambridge, MA: Belknap Press of Harvard University Press, 2001); Rollin G. Osterweis, *The Myth of the Lost Cause 1865–1900* (Hamden, CT: Shoe String Press, 1973); and David Goldfield, *Still Fighting the Civil War: The American South and Southern History* (Baton Rouge: Louisiana State University Press, 2002). The historian's comment on the Trans-Mississippi West is from William C. Davis, *The Cause Lost: Myths and Realities of the Confederacy* (Lawrence: University Press of Kansas, 1996). Erd W. Cole's interview is in Harrell, ed., *History and Folklore of Searcy County, Arkansas.* Information about Newt Cooper comes from genealogy websites; Gerdes website; Campbell-Cooper family records at the Searcy County Library, Marshall, AR.; and Leon Cooper, *Call Me Newt* (n.p.: Chuck and Lou Stanberry, 2014).

Chapter 22: The Freewoman of Richland

On black surnames in slavery and freedom, see Genovese, *Roll, Jordan, Roll.* Parthenia's residences are recorded in the US Census, and in Tina Lewis Johnson, "The Life of Parthena Hensley (1843–1929)"; and in Erd W. Cole, interview by James J. Johnston, see notes to chapter 1. Goodspeed's *Biographical and Historical Memoirs of Arkansas* got many things wrong about Billy Wyatt, but I trusted its facts on his move to Marshall. Discussion of the African American experience in the Arkansas Ozarks from emancipation to the early twentieth century is drawn from my two studies for the National Park Service, *Life, Leisure, and Hardship Along the Buffalo* and *"When the War Come Up."* In preparing those reports I read the following: Gene W. Boyett, "The Black Experience in the First Decade of Reconstruction in Pope County, Arkansas," *Arkansas Historical Quarterly* 51, no. 2 (Summer 1992); Story Matkin-Rawn, "'The Great Negro State of the Country': Arkansas's Reconstruction and the Other Great Migration," *Arkansas Historical Quarterly* 72, no. 1 (Spring 2013); Louis M. Kyriakoudes, "'Lookin' For Better All the Time': Rural Migration and Urbanization in the South, 1900–1950," in R. Douglas Hirt, *African-American Life in the Rural South 1900–1950* (Columbia: University of Missouri Press, 2003); Randy Finley, *From Slavery to Uncertain Freedom: The Freedmen's Bureau in Arkansas, 1865–1869* (Fayetteville: University of Arkansas Press, 1996); Brooks Blevins, "Reconstruction in the Ozarks: Simpson Mason, William Monks, and the War that Refused to End," *Arkansas Historical Quarterly* 77, no. 3 (Autumn 2018); John William Graves, "Jim Crow in Arkansas: A Reconsideration of Race Relations in the Post-Reconstruction South," *Journal of Southern History* 55, no. 3 (August 1989); Story Matkin-Rawn, "'Send Forth More Laborers into the Vineyard': Understanding the African American Exodus to Arkansas," in *Race and Ethnicity in Arkansas: New Perspectives,* edited by John A. Kirk (Fayetteville: University of Arkansas Press, 2014); Guy

Lancaster, "Sundown Towns: Racial Cleansing in the Arkansas Delta," also in *Race and Ethnicity in Arkansas*; Jacqueline Froelich and David Zimmermann, "Total Eclipse: The Destruction of the African American Community of Harrison, Arkansas, in 1905 and 1909," *Arkansas Historical Quarterly* 58, no. 2 (Summer 1999); Kimberly Harper, *White Man's Heaven: The Lynching and Expulsion of Blacks in the Southern Ozarks, 1894–1909* (Fayetteville: University of Arkansas Press, 2010); James Loewen, *Sundown Towns: A Hidden Dimension of American Racism* (New York: Simon and Schuster, 2006); and Gordon D. Morgan and Peter Kunkel, "Arkansas's Ozark Mountain Blacks: An Introduction," *Phylon* 34, no. 3 (1973). Letters to the *Mountain Wave* around the black community in Richland are from James J. Johnston, *Shootin's, Obituaries, Politcs; Emigratin', Socializin', Commercializin', and the Press: News Items from about Searcy County, Arkansas 1866–1901* (Fayetteville: James J. Johnston, 1991). Facts about Parthenia's later life and the lives of her children come from posts about Parthenia Hensley, Newton Wyatt, and Lucinda Wyatt found at the Find a Grave, Family Search, and other genealogy websites; marriage and tax assessor records at the Searcy County Library, Marshall, AR; James J. Johnston's interview with Garland Robertson, 1976, also at the Searcy County Library; Liles, *Old Folks Talking*; Fowler, "History of the Wyatt Family and Richland Creek"; US Census data; the Bureau of Land Management's GLO records website; Ava Work, interview, in Harrell, ed., *History and Folklore of Searcy County, Arkansas*; and James J. Johnston, *Shootin's, Obituaries, Politcs; Emigratin', Socializin', Commercializin', and the Press*. The circumstances of Newt's death are from his obituary, *Mountain Wave* (Marshall, AR), May 30, 1914. I was intrigued by Billy Wyatt's family connection to Lewis Tutt of Springfield. Wyatt's mother's brother was Hansford Tutt of Tutt-Everett War fame. Hansford Tutt fathered Lewis Tutt by his slave Millie. Lewis was born in 1844. Hansford Tutt's widow Nancy Tutt fled to Springfield with her enslaved grown stepson Lewis when Federal troops pulled out of Yellville in 1863. At the end of the war, Nancy Tutt returned to Yellville while her stepson, now emancipated, stayed in Springfield. With Billy Wyatt's family connection to Lewis Tutt, I wondered if Wyatt lived with Tutt when he was a refugee in Springfield. I could not find proof that they lived together, but the family connection, the extreme shortage of housing in wartime Springfield, and Wyatt's later advice to his son to go to Springfield to find a wife all point to it. On the Wyatt-Tutt connection, see Mysty McPherson and Vicki Roberts, eds., *Genealogies of Marion County Families 1811–1900 Vol. II* (Yellville, AR: Marion County Arkansas Heritage Society, 2012). On Lewis Tutt, see *History of Greene County, Missouri* (Chicago: Goodspeed Brothers, 1893). On wartime Springfield, see Larry Wood, *Civil War Springfield* (Charleston, SC: History Press, 2011). Billy Wyatt's first cousin Davis Tutt died in a gunfight with William ("Wild Bill") Hickock on Springfield's public square on July 21, 1865. Interestingly, years later Lewis Tutt paid to have his half-brother reburied in a better spot. See Larry Wood, *Ozarks Gunfights and other Notorious Incidents* (Gretna, LA: Pelican Publishing, 2010). Separate from this, I was intrigued that Billy Wyatt took part in Arkansas's constitutional conventions in 1868 and 1874, advocating for black voting rights. See Eugene G. Feistman, "Radical Disfranchisement in Arkansas, 1867–1868," *Arkansas Historical Quarterly* 12, no. 2 (Summer 1953): 142; and Richard L. Hume, "The Arkansas Constitutional Convention of 1868: A Case Study of the Politics of Reconstruction," *Journal of Southern History* 39, no. 2 (May 1973). The story of the molasses cookies was shared with me by a Hensley descendant and also stated in a post on the Find a Grave website. Information about the Hall Cemetery comes from personal inspection as well as research in the following sources: "Hall Cemetery, Searcy County AR," submitted by Lina Boyd, October 26, 2008, at US Gen Web Archives website; grave marker photographs posted on Find a Grave website in April and May 2009; and Tammie Trippe-Dillon, *Grave Concerns: A Preservation Manual for Historic Cemeteries in Arkansas* (Little Rock: Arkansas Historic Preservation Program, n.d.). Use of the term "free slave" before the Civil War was identified through a word search in Nineteenth Century US Newspapers database. See also Loren Schweninger, "The Free-Slave Phenomenon: James P. Thomas and the Black Community in Ante-Bellum Nashville," *Civil War History* 22, no. 4 (December 1, 1976); John J. Zaborney, *Slaves for Hire: Renting Enslaved Laborers in Antebellum Virginia* (Baton Rouge: Louisiana State University Press, 2012); and William McKee Evans, *Open Wound: The Long View of Race in America* (Urbana: University of Illinois Press, 2009).

Index

www.ingramcontent.com/pod-product-compliance
Lightning Source LLC
Chambersburg PA
CBHW032041200326
41610CB00011B/89/J

* 9 7 8 0 8 0 6 1 9 6 5 0 3 *